RESURRECTION

The story *of* Christ
after the Passion

GENE MORRISON

FREILING
PUBLISHING

Published by Freiling Publishing, a division of Freiling Agency, LLC.

P.O. Box 1264,
Warrenton, VA 20188

www.FreilingPublishing.com

ISBN 978-1-950948-57-4

Printed in the United States of America

To Nancy, the dearest woman I know.

You have always given me hope and inspiration, always encouraging and praying for me when I was down and about to give up.

DEDICATION

I dedicate this book to my two daughters and son (Christina, Aaron, and Alyssa) along with my grandchildren (Eli, Isabella, Ayla, Lillian, Jayce, and Gianna). I also dedicate this book to my mother, who was a prayer warrior and encourager. She read the manuscript and loved it but never got to see the publication here in this world. She certainly knows about it now in Heaven with our Lord and Savior Jesus Christ.

TABLE OF CONTENTS

ACKNOWLEDGMENTS

I want to thank Bob Griner for the encouragement and foresight to write this creative non-fiction novel from the screenplay of the same name, *Resurrection After the Passion*. I had never intended to write the book, but after Bob read the screenplay, he continuously impressed upon me to write a book from the script. Many thanks to the prayer team for their encouragement and prayers: Nancy, Jeff Morrison, Donna Kafer, Donna Cagann, Dan and Cherie Malberg, Dennis Malberg, Mague Perez, Christina Race, June and Don Harris, Dr. Corkie Haan, Dan Dickerson, Uriah Morris, Linda Wright, Pastor Scott and his wife Debbie Thurber, Maxine Davis, Ray Antocicco, Vera Riggs, Kathy and Steve Schlegal, and many others who have prayed this project through.

To Nancy, whose never-ending encouragement and belief in me are beyond my words. Much love to you. I want to thank my parents, June and Don Harris, for their reassurance that I was doing the Lord's will; and for Dan and Cheri Malberg and Donna Cagann for their continuous cheer and support that I was doing the work of the Lord. To Maxine Davis for your powerful prayers, inspiration, and prophecies the Holy Spirit gave you concerning His will and direction in my life over both the screenplay and this manuscript. Not to be forgotten, Pastor Scott Thurber and the congregation of North Valley Assembly of God church: for your prayers and prophecies; for Pastor Scott's bringing to the congregation's awareness the script and book; and for calling me up to the front to have the whole church pray for me, the book, and the script. For those who proofread the manuscript and those who were my test audience readers, my thanks and acknowledgment to you: Daniel Malberg, Dennis Malberg, Scott Thurber, Donna Cagann, and Nancy.

And **most important**, to my Lord and Savior Jesus Christ, for giving me the inspiration, the knowledge, the ability, and His anointing to put the greatest historical event ever known to man into a creative non-fiction novel to get the word out about His most marvelous gift to humankind, the gift of salvation.

FOREWORD

A book can never be divorced from the author. I know the author. I know his heart, a heart that runs after God. The heart of Gene Morrison shows through *Resurrection After the Passion*. As a pastor, I am often frustrated when I read Christian books, especially those with biblical themes. Often the author takes so much liberty that you hardly recognize the story. Gene has kept his story historically correct, and most importantly, biblically correct. Reading this book, you are going to learn some things that are worth knowing. The descriptive language is excellent, and most of all, I hope you get to know the central character—Jesus Christ. He really did suffer, He really did die on a cross outside of Jerusalem, and He really did come back from the dead to live forevermore and to save you and me from our sin. I pray, dear reader, that you will have a similar experience as I did while reading this book. My desire is to know Christ and to follow Him as my own! I commend Gene for such a great work. May the Lord receive all the praise!

Pastor Scott Thurber
North Valley A/G
Phoenix, Arizona

PREFACE

As a child of about the age of nine, I would be sitting in church with my parents and getting bored. I would flick through my Bible and read passages about the resurrected saints coming back to life in Matthew 27:52–53. I would read about the whole land spiraling into darkness during the Crucifixion and the pictographic details of God and His throne room in Ezekiel and Revelation. The stories would leave me spellbound with vivid imageries in my creative mind. The stories seemed to leap off the pages, causing me to always ponder and wonder with a curiosity of what befell the inhabitants of Jerusalem including Pilate, Caiaphas, Annas, the Sanhedrin, the Pharisees, and the Sadducees during the supernatural events of the Crucifixion and the Resurrection. Questions populated my mind as to what their reactions were when they saw loved ones and friends come back to life and of the unnatural happenings taking place right before their eyes. They had to be frightened and horrified. I ruminated on what Pilate must have thought upon hearing the intelligence reports of the resurrected dead and of Jesus' resurrection. Pilate, being of a superstitious mind and believing in the gods of Rome, must have been shocked and alarmed; or at best, tried to reason things out.

Movies always depict the darkness, during the Crucifixion, falling upon the land by way of dark clouds and a thunderstorm. However, it says in the Bible that it was dark all over the land. I saw a total eclipse of the sun once, and I was amazed by how dark it became—just like night, except the horizon was light, similar to twilight. I could see the stars. I have read various histories and antiquities from Roman historians and letters from Pilate to Tiberius and to Herod, which declared that there was a reddish fog or mist, and that the moon was full and looked as though it were dipped in blood. I have also heard that during a volcanic eruption, the ash is so thick that it blocks out the sun, it looks as dark as night, and there is a reddish fog or haze. If this is so, my question then becomes this: Was there a volcanic eruption somewhere in the world that caused the earthquakes and the strange reddish fog, or was it an eclipse, or was there some unexplained supernatural phenomenon such as when God held the sun in place for a day when Joshua prayed for the sun to stand still?

I have contemplated these events my entire life. The fascination has never left me. I can see now that the Holy Spirit put these captivations into my heart and mind so that I would write a screenplay and a book about the subject. For such a time as this, I believe I was born.

Upon researching, I have studied various writings, letters, lost books of the Bible, and other sources. There is disagreement among theologians and scholars about whether these writings are accurate, real, or just storytelling. The letters of Pilate, for example—some think they were written during the Middle Ages. I personally tend to believe that they are factual; Pilate had to make reports to Tiberius during his term as procurator of Judea. If these are not actual letters from Pilate, I am sure they are pretty close to what he must have transcribed and sent out. The book of Nicodemus and the lost book of Peter go along pretty near to the Scriptures. Whether the visions of St. Catherine Emmerick are true or not, they do well in filling in the blanks and not distracting from God's Word. With the Archko Volumes, it gives a good illustration of what Caiaphas must have been going through, wrestling with his conscience and duties as the high priest.

While in the process of writing another screenplay called *Charioteer*, the Holy Spirit began to nudge me about writing *Resurrection After the Passion*. I ignored the calling at first because I was really into *Charioteer*. It was shortly after *The Passion of the Christ* came out and Mel Gibson had said he had no intention of making a sequel. That was when the prompting of the Holy Spirit became clearer in my spirit until I could no longer ignore it. I put away *Charioteer*, began researching the Resurrection, and started writing the screenplay. I could not stop writing! The things that were in my mind since childhood came flooding to the surface. I finished the script, and Bob Griner, who was my area operations manager when I worked at the newspaper, read it and was fascinated by it. For about a year, he kept pressing me to write a book based on the screenplay, but I was reluctant. Writing a book and a screenplay are two different ways of writing. I was not sure I was up to it. Finally, after his continual insistence, I acquiesced and started writing the book you now have in your hands. Again, same as before, when I was writing the screenplay of the same name, I could not stop writing. I am glad that my good friend Bob was persistent.

Many times during the writing of this book, I have felt and experienced the anointing of the Holy Spirit. At times, it seemed as though I were actually there with the disciples and others, either listening to Jesus or observing as a bystander. I hope you, as the reader, are blessed and come to know the Lord as your personal Savior, and if you are a Christian, that it will strengthen and deepen your faith.

A word of advice to the reader: Some may find segments of the book to be slow or too graphic. With a purpose, I vividly detailed the Crucifixion, scenes in hell, and the scourging of the Christ. My intent is to reveal how Christ suffered for you and me. I do not mean to be revolting and disgusting. If you find that some portions are too hard to read, then gloss over and continue on, but do not give up on the book. Many passages will encourage, illuminate, and give you hope and restoration.

~ Gene Morrison

INTRODUCTION

The main objective of this book is to reach as many people as possible, throughout the earth, with the Gospel and the way of salvation. The main intent is for every person reading this book who has not asked for forgiveness of their sins will come to know the Lord Jesus Christ as their personal Lord and Savior and repent of their sins; and those who are Christians will be strengthened and encouraged in their faith.

Many may wonder about differing accounts in the Bible such as the resurrected saints of old, Jesus' descent into hell, angelic warfare, and various supernatural events. Let me assure you that I did a massive amount of research, prayed, continually sought the Holy Spirit's guidance, and consulted with various clergy. The Bible is not specific on certain events that happened in the Scriptures, nor does it go into much detail about incidents. So in some of the events, happenings, and miracles, I have taken artistic license to fill in what may or could have possibly happened. I am always careful not to undertake in my writing anything that would distract from the scriptures or be inflammatory in doctrine, and I always avoid heresy. Though the reader may not agree on all or certain things, I understand. Many of the happenings in the Bible are open to interpretation, and my hope is that some theological questions will be open to discussion and studying the Scriptures.

Cast of Characters

Abaddon (ab–a–don): A herculean creature of great strength. He is known as the Keeper of Hell. Some theologians say Abaddon is actually Satan himself rather than an individual personality.

Abenadar (a-ben-a-dar): Roman centurion in charge of the Crucifixion Detail. He was a rough man of Arab descent whose duties were to oversee the Crucifixion with the responsibility of maintaining order.

Ada: Rabbinical teacher.

Ageus (A-gee-us): A Levite and priest.

Andrew: The one who brought his brother Peter to Jesus after saying to him, "We have found the Messiah." He was later crucified on a diagonal or X-shaped cross.

Annas ben Seth (an-uhs): An unofficial high priest removed for offenses against the Roman government. His son-in-law was Joseph ben Caiaphas, a puppet high priest through which Annas exercised his authority and power.

Archelaus (ahr-kee-LAY-uhs): A Pharisee who was a member of the Sanhedrin.

Charinus: Among the crowd amassed in protest against Pilate's use of the Temple treasury. He was one of two brothers who were the proud sons of the same High Priest Simeon who had declared in the Temple while holding the baby Jesus: "Mine eyes have seen Thy salvation."

Cleophas (KLEE-oh-pas): A companion of Luke who was also a follower of Christ. Some theological scholars think this may be Peter the apostle.

Dismas (dis-mus): The good thief on the cross who defended Jesus, and whom Jesus said would be with Him that day in Paradise.

Gaius Cassius Longinus (lon-jin-uhs): A young centurion duly in second command of the Crucifixion Unit to execute the criminals.

Gamaliel (gam-uh-lay-el): A Pharisee and a member of the Sanhedrin.

Gesmas: The thief on the cross who challenged Jesus to save Himself.

Herod the Tetrarch: Puppet leader of Israel, put in place by Caesar Tiberius.

Herodias (he-rod-e-uhs): The wife of Herod the Tetrarch, the previous wife of Herod's brother, and who had been Herod's adulterous lover.

James the Greater: Was ambitious and short-tempered, a favored companion of Peter and John. James would be the first of the apostles to seal his faith with his own blood, being put to the sword by King Herod Agrippa.

James the Lesser: The son of Alphaeus, later be called the Pillar of the Church. He would die by being thrown off the pinnacle of the Temple and then stoned and clubbed to death.

James: The half-brother of Jesus who was later to become a disciple and would write the book of James.

John: The son of Zebedee who was ambitious and judgmental. He was the beloved disciple whose head had lain upon the Lord's breast during the Last Supper. At one time, he wished to "call down fire from heaven on a village of Samaritans," but he would live on to write three epistles and the book of Revelation.

Joseph ben Caiaphas: A puppet high priest through which his father-in-law, Annas ben Seth, exercised his authority and power.

Joseph of Arimathea (erh-uh-muh-THEE-uh): A wealthy merchant and aged member of the Sanhedrin. Some scholars and theologians believe that Joseph was the brother of Mary, the mother of Jesus, and that he had lived in Egypt and gained his wealth as a miner of metals. He would have been the uncle of Jesus. Later, he was imprisoned for his role in taking the body of Jesus for burial.

Judas of Gaulon: A big black-bearded burly zealot killed in riot ten years before Crucifixion by the Centurion Longinus.

Judas, the brother of James: Called also Lebbaeus or <u>Thaddius,</u> who would eventually be the author of the last epistle Jude in the New Testament. He was one who followed Jesus because he believed in Him, not always understanding the details of God's plan. He was later to be crucified at Edessa.

Lazarus: The poor beggar in Jesus' parable of the rich man and the beggar. Not to be confused with Lazarus whom Jesus raised from the dead.

Lazarus: The one whom Jesus raised up from the dead.

Lenthius (len-thee-uhs): Among the crowd amassed in protest against Pilate's use of the Temple treasury. He was one of the two brothers who were the proud sons of the same High Priest Simeon who had declared in the Temple while holding the baby Jesus, "Mine eyes have seen Thy salvation."

Lucifer: Known as Satan, the name gave him by his Creator, the God Almighty, when cast out of heaven.

Luke: A meticulous and fastidious doctor who wrote the book of Luke and the book of Acts.

Malchus: Captain of the temple guard.

Marcus: The six-year-old boy whose mother, Rebecca, had perished while shielding him from the maddening crowd ten years earlier in the massacre of the Market Square, and who became a fledgling young soldier in the Roman army.

Martha: Sister of Mary and Lazarus.

Mary Magdalene: Woman whom Jesus delivered from seven demons.

Matthew: A tax collector who would, in time, write the first gospel called Matthew. He would meet death by a halberd (a pike fitted with an ax head) in Nadabah.

Michael the Archangel: The head of the armies of God.

Nathaniel: Also known as Bartholomew, who initially rejected Jesus by saying, "Can any good thing come out of Nazareth?" but then upon meeting Jesus, he exclaimed, "Thou art the Son of God, thou art the King of Israel." Yet, he is the same of whom the Lord said, "An Israelite without guile," because Jesus respected honesty, even when challenged. Nathaniel (Bartholomew) was honest with straightforwardness. He would encounter death by first being skinned alive and then beheaded at Derbend on the Caspian Sea.

Nicodemus: Member of the Sanhedrin and friend of Joseph of Arimathea, a follower of Jesus who believed in His teachings.

Peter: Impulsive Simon bar Jonah, also known as Simon bar Jochanan or Cephas in the Aramaic, of whom Jesus had renamed Peter, which means the "Rock." Peter had repented with bitter tears for denying the Lord.

Philip of Bethsaida: The first disciple to whom Jesus had said, "Follow Me," and the one who told Nathaniel to "come and see" the promised Messiah. He had a questioning attitude and had wondered aloud how Jesus could feed five thousand. He suffered martyrdom at the Heliopolis in Phrygia where he would be flogged, imprisoned, and later crucified.

Phinees (fi-nus) the priest: He had acknowledged Charinus and Lenthius at the Temple.

Pilate: Procurator of the Roman government, the one who ordered the crucifixion of Jesus. He was in his mid-thirties, but because of the severity of his temperament and the pressures of his occupation, he appeared to be somewhat older. It was said by some that he was insensitive, belonging to an obstinate nature, both cruel and merciless with a vindictive and furious temper, which included a blend of self-will and relentlessness. He maintained peace throughout the region by brutal force and subtle negotiation.

Rebecca: The woman had perished while shielding her son Marcus from the maddening crowd ten years before the Crucifixion in the massacre of the Market Square Riot.

Rich Man: Recalled with dread and sorrow his happenings upon the earth with the poor beggar called Lazarus, which is not to be confused with Lazarus who had been dead four days and was raised back to life by Jesus.

Simon: Called "The Canaanite." He had once been a member of the famous Zealot party, a fierce advocate of Jewish home-rule and an enemy of Roman supremacy. He had become zealous for the kingdom of Christ and believed Jesus to be the Messiah.

Tiberius (ti-beer-e-uhs): The Great and Awful Emperor Caesar who reigned over Rome when Jesus was crucified.

Flames from several oil lamps shiver like the tongues of serpents, throwing fluttering shadows alongside a wall, and across a piece of parchment. The glow of the oil lamps illuminates one who sits in dim outline, a first-century Roman-Jewish scholar, and recorder of Roman and Jewish history: Flavius Josephus. His ancient hand scribes these words:

> *About this time, there lived Jesus, a wise man, if indeed one ought to call him a man, for he was one who wrought surprising feats and was a teacher of such people as accepts the truth gladly. He won over many of the Jews and many of the Greeks. He was the Messiah. And when Pilate, upon the accusation of the principal men among us, had condemned him to a cross, those who had first come to love him did not cease. He appeared unto them spending a third day restored to life, for the prophets of God had foretold these things and a thousand other marvels about him, and the tribe of the Christians, so called after him, has still to this day not disappeared.* (Flavius Josephus)

Josephus signs his name with his hand scrawling out of view.

The parchment fades to desert sand with the words affixed. The words and sand swirl about in a centrifugal turbulence that grows into a furious and raging hot wind, whipping the sand, words, and topsoil high into the air to become a whirling spire and funnel that hurries along the desert floor.

PROLOGUE

Jerusalem 26 A.D.
Ten Years Before the Crucifixion

HEAT WAVES DANCED off the desert floor as the city of Jerusalem wavered in the distance like a mirage. Out of the expanse came a long shout, then a cacophony of complaints and reproaches that rose like heat waves to a voluminous pitch of ten thousand.

Trumpets blew.

A dust devil roared by with a violent up-blast of wind, thrashing the topsoil into a fury as it rushed across the desert floor toward the Temple Mount, clouding the distance and obscuring the horizon. The swirling vertical column of dirt and sand broke against the formidable wall of the Temple Mount, dissipating into billows of dust that dashed across the large outer court of the Temple Mount like paranormal horsemen to an area called the Market Square, where a temporary Judgment Seat rested.

Occasionally a flapping red cape obscured the Judgment Seat, with every flap of the red cloak unveiling a hand resting on the hilt of a sword. Sparks of light flashed diagonally across the hand from sunlight glistening off a gold ornamental breastplate worn by a solitary man named Pontius Pilate. He stood adjacent to the Judgment Seat, his flame-red cape fluttering in the slight breeze as he gazed steadily before him.

Never wincing; never moving; his attention never straying.

In front of him—PANDEMONIUM.

Roman soldiers camouflaged in common garments of the populace and armed with staves and daggers pounced upon the crowd of ten thousand with fierce abandonment, the clubbing malicious, causing many to perish.

Charinus and Lenthius stood amongst the crowd amassed in protest against Pilate's use of the Temple treasury, from which Pilate had financed the building of an aqueduct to carry off the refuse of the Temple sacrifices on the southeast side of the mountain on which the Temple stood. The brothers, in their prime of life, happened to be the proud sons of the High Priest Simeon who had declared in the Temple while holding the baby Jesus, "Mine eyes have seen Thy salvation."

The two stared in silence at the scene before them, aghast with disbelief and shock as they caught sight of their fellow citizens trampled to death while falling under the feet of those fleeing the Roman soldiers in panic-terror. Nearby, someone cried out! With a sudden upheaval and a rush, the brothers found themselves hemmed in from all sides by the upsurge of the runaway throng. Soon they were in the midst of a great struggle of swarming humanity.

A young centurion of about the age of thirty-and-five, Gaius Cassius Longinus, unmercifully bludgeoned his way through the crowd: striking and hunting, bashing and thrashing without prejudice. Laying down a civilian with a stave, Longinus stepped over the body and put two more civilians out of action before coming upon the two brothers. Before the brothers could react, Longinus was on them like the specter of death, coming face-to-face with Charinus first. Longinus felled him without warning, spilling his blood upon the ground while the great crush of the crowd drove Lenthius further away.

Close by, a big burly zealot known as Judas of Gaulon, in a rage, tore away a stave from a Roman soldier's grasp and neatly put his opponent to sleep. Reeling about, Judas' black-bearded jaws and pockmarked cheeks formed a menacing scowl. His lips wrinkled like that of a dog about to bite, his coarse wide mouth spreading to an aggressive snarl as he growled.

Glancing about wildly from side to side, his bullish head swiveled on a bulky neck, his owlish eyes observing men and women fighting for their lives, running to and fro throughout the Market Square. He caught the brief glimpse of a woman draped in a shawl, running through the surreal patches of combat while holding onto the hand of her six-year-old son. Whirling about, he encountered Longinus.

Judas struck with ferocity!

Longinus countered the downswing. Immediately the two were engaged in combat. Like gladiators, they fought through the ever-increasing riot, furiously spinning and flailing. Judas struck Longinus on the side of the head, propelling him sideways in a stumbling daze.

Without hesitation, Judas leaped upon Longinus' back, wrestling away the stave, which clattered to the pavement as Judas wrapped a huge forearm under Longinus' chin in a stranglehold. Longinus grabbed Judas' arm with his one hand and stabbed at Judas' eye with his thumb. With a howl, Judas fell back, allowing Longinus to rotate out of the grip—off balance and waving his arms in a frantic effort to regain his equilibrium.

The woman named Rebecca blindly ran wild, dropping her shawl with no idea of direction. She lost the fierce grip on her six-year-old son Marcus as Longinus slammed into the boy, knocking him to the ground. Rebecca spun around with her hands raised to her head, tearing at her hair in grief and horror. Before she could react, Judas smashed into Rebecca as he came hurtling through the crowd with great savagery, sending her sprawling over the corpse of Charinus while he landed on top of Longinus.

Bringing a knee up hard and fast, Judas drove it into Longinus' chest with an effort to hold him down. He wrapped his beefy hands under Longinus' jaw and pressed his fingers tightly around Longinus' throat. He dug his thumbs into the neck with an iron-hold of strength.

Lenthius swept past them, carried along in the current of the crowd. With crazed eyes, he tried desperately in vain to reach his fallen brother Charinus, while being pushed and swayed further away by the mass. He wrestled through the press of the horde, elbowing and shoving against the escaping mass of humanity. Suffering a push from behind, followed by a shove, the swarm of panicked protesters pummeled Lenthius violently, hurtling him hard to the ground, his face hitting the pavement with a bone-crushing smack. Spitting out teeth and blood, Lenthius fought with all his strength to get to his knees. Tossed back and forth, he once again was sent sprawling as the multitude trod on his helpless body in desperate attempts to save their own lives. Trepidation overcame Lenthius with the realization that he was not getting out of this alive! In a natural reaction, he covered his head as his own compatriots stumbled and fell over him in mass panic.

Rebecca lunged past Lenthius in an effort to get to her son. She gathered Marcus into her arms, hugging the ground on her knees to shield him as the crowd surged about to topple and tumble over her. Struggling to breathe, with crushed ribs piercing her lungs, she looked up, her eyes taking in her surroundings. Seeing Longinus in his death throes, her eyes dropped to her son, panting heavily beneath her body. She leaned over him to provide more protection. The deafening noise grew quieter.

Soon, there befell nothing more than silence.

Her expression flattened as she withdrew from this reality and into a deep, dark hollow in her mind. At that moment, there was nothing more as she gave her last breath in saving her son. Her expressionless eyes drooped to a lifeless stare upon Longinus as he thrashed about violently, trying free himself from the zealot's death grip. His eyes welled up from the sockets and his tongue protruded from his mouth. With growing dizziness, Longinus' vision blurred to black spots before his eyes. An ensuing throb of pressure built within his head, the blood rushing in his ears. He grew faint, his strength vanishing as he tried to fend off the ever-increasing blackness. His body convulsed with his eyes rolling upward, showing the whites that were quickly growing red. Darkness enveloped him, his brain starved of oxygen. The sound of shouting voices invaded his consciousness. His eyes fluttered open, barely conscious, only to slip back into unconsciousness—the darkness again encircling.

His head slumped toward Lenthius, who lay stunned on the pavement.

Lenthius, barely aware of the screaming mob as they stepped, climbed, and stumbled over him, lay flat out on his stomach, compressed to the stone pavement under the weight of those who fell on top of him. He raised his head with one eye swelling fast, his eyes dilated with pain and terror. Weakness overcame him as his head lolled to the side to rest on his half-bent arm stretched out before him. He opened his lifeless eyes once more. The eyes shrunk back, losing their stare. The eyelids drooped lower. He became less aware of his surroundings until he was no longer moving under the weight. The last thing he saw was the Roman soldiers hammering away at Judas with staves.

A soldier loosened Judas' hand from Longinus' throat. Another seized the other arm and wrenched it in such a way that Judas yowled. The soldiers together gave one desperate heave, and at last, they managed to drag Judas off Longinus.

Longinus came around for a second time, sputtering in short breaths while trying to recover his breathing. He sat upright with a sense of confusion, as if waking up in the middle of the night. Swallowing with difficulty, he coughed, spitting out blood. He felt the front of his throat that bore red, bearing the imprints of Judas' fingers. In a few seconds, Longinus regained his composure. Turning his head about in a cloudy and sluggish way, he noticed Rebecca lying dead over her son. His gaze fell over to Judas, who staggered back dazed and throttled, blood streaming from his nose.

Judas recovered himself with an insane light in his black eyes. Flexing his biceps, he clenched his enormous fists. With a throaty battle cry, he tossed the soldiers aside and threw a backhanded blow that sent one flying full length to the ground. Another rushed forward, but he hurled him like a sack of salt. He delivered a blow with a fist across the face of one more, sending him sprawling out onto the pavement. For all their strength, the soldiers were not a match for Judas, who was dangerous and difficult to handle; their combined strength was not enough. With more soldiers coming on, Judas broke loose, taking off in a dead run for his life, stumbling over Longinus, who leaned forward, still coughing and spitting up blood.

With much awkwardness and with every bit of strength he could muster, Longinus rolled over to rest on his hands and knees for a moment before dragging himself off the ground, swaying with dizziness. He staggered back a step. With a hand to his throbbing head, he grunted in pain. Regaining his equilibrium, he charged forward into the swirling chaos with a limping shuffle as the populace dropped in tarns of manslaughter, locked in a struggle against the well-organized fighting machine. He saw Judas far up ahead.

Judas rushed past Lenthius, who lay prostrate as another fatality. With a perception of imminent danger, Judas glanced back to discover Longinus in hot pursuit. He ran faster toward the court of priests, next to the holy Temple, for sanctuary. Upon entering the court of priests through the Water Gate, he sprinted up the ascent ramp leading to the uppermost part of the altar of sacrifice, as the sacrifices of immolation were underway.

The Altar, situated in the center of the Court of Priests next to the holy Temple, was a perfect square with dimensions of sixteen feet in height and fifty-two feet in width; the four corners of the altar were each adorned with a horn eighteen inches square by fifteen inches in height. Judas fell upon the nearest horn, hugging it under heavy breath and with the expectation of safe asylum. Anxious and afraid, he closed his eyes in silent prayer, asking the Almighty for protection and to pardon him of his sins.

Judas' eyes suddenly flew wide open. He gasped with a sudden convulsion, the breath knocked out of him by a sharp blow. He slid off the horn as he tried desperately to heave air into his lungs. Pulling himself atop the horn again, he fought to breathe, gulping and swallowing takes of short breaths. He turned his weak and wobbly head, trying to focus on the object of his demise. His eyes blurred and then refocused on Longinus standing over him.

For a frozen minute, Judas' and Longinus' eyes locked; the passion, the horror, the force of the moment etched into each other's expression as Judas' life, little by little, ebbed away.

With both hands, Longinus wrenched free the short sword he had thrust into Judas' side.

Judas kept his focus on Longinus just long enough to utter the words; *"Forgive me,"* as he came to the realization that he was indeed a brutal man with a vicious spirit of revenge. At first, Judas felt no pain, and then suddenly, intolerable pain shot throughout his lower abdomen. A shock wave of agony ripped throughout his entire body, followed by the sickening sensation of vomiting. A dull throbbing at the wound site grew with intensity until, with ferocity, it took over his senses. Grimacing panic acquired his sanity, the pain becoming monumental and excruciating.

At the point of losing consciousness, Judas looked off into the distance, consumed by anguish with nothing more mattering and everything seemingly cloaked in a reddish-white, as though wearing a veil. His face grew pale with drops of sweat sprinkling along his brow and his lips turning blue. He shook, trembling with chills, panting in dreadful spasms. An incredible pressure built around the entry hole of the wound. He held his breath against the pain, and then gasped!

The wound was hot, stinging, burning as if someone had poured hot grease into the slash.

Warm tears filled his eyes, his hands grew cold, his teeth chattered, and his flesh crept with tingling sensations as a tremor seized his body, the need for sleep overpowering.

Slouching over the horn, Judas' head dropped. His mouth was dry. He looked up again to find his vision blurring further. He closed his moist eyes to steady himself. Hot tears fell as he opened them a second time to find his vision blurring even more. His head drooped forward. Confusion caught hold. He fought with ever-fading energies to regain control of his faculties. Humming filled his ears. He lay motionless.

An abnormal pattern of rapid breathing and then periods of no breathing ensued, followed by the chilling, unsettling, and disturbing sound of the death rattle. Judas' eyes turned inward. Blinking, his eyes grew cloudy as though underwater. He wrestled to keep them in focus until he stared wide into an eternal night, his blood flowing in rivulets down the sides of the horn.

Sunlight glinted off Longinus' sword, blood trickling off the sharp blade and onto the pavement of the Altar. Judas' words, *"Forgive me—I forgive you,"* was a tortuous haunt to him as he stood gaping at the sight before him. He knew by the words spoken to him that Judas was indeed sorrowful of his actions. Suddenly, Longinus felt a sharp lump in his throat. His breathing fell into short gasps followed by an abrupt juddering of small gulps with a quick urge to belch.

Feeling an involuntary spasm of the stomach muscles, as though something were moving within his belly, he experienced an upheaval of the abdomen. Before he could take another breath, he threw up a multicolored mess mingled with spit and stomach juices that splattered all over the pavement.

Faltering, Longinus reeled in nausea, swaggering backward to stumble in a half-turn, falling on one knee to lean on the hilt of the sword. His body shook, his chest vibrating with the heavy pounding of his heart under the metal of the breastplate. His throat burned while his mouth filled with that bitter liquid-sour taste. Longinus' bulk quavered several more times with convulsions of vomiting. Sweat formed in beads across his clammy forehead, his face whitish, his brain lightheaded. He wiped his mouth with a sleeve. Swabbing a shaky hand across his brow, he looked up with a weighty thickness, blinking stinging sweat from his eyes while squinting toward the Market Square, where Pilate stood next to the judgment seat in rapt attention to the massacre before him.

* * *

Pilate, clean-shaven of head and chin, as the normal custom of the Romans, looked much older than his mid-thirties. Along with a nasty disposition of being cruel and merciless, he was vindictive with a furious temper, habitually using brutal force when someone challenged his authority.

Pilate surveyed the mayhem, knowing he was in trouble. He had thought to squelch the uprising by telling the soldiers under his command to surround the protesters and to use staves to hold the people back and to send them home. When the people did not go away at his bidding—and there appeared to be a disturbance of known Jewish rebels in the angry mob—Pilate had signaled the soldiers to use strength. Nevertheless, his soldiers had used brute force with daggers, swords, and staves, slaughtering both the guilty and the innocent. From this moment forward, a bitter rivalry and hatred developed between Pilate and Herod the Tetrarch, the animosity to end in a future event when a god-man named Jesus would be brought before Herod at the request of Pilate. Now, this event was to plague Pilate for the rest of his life and career with a fear of more uprisings.

Annas ben Seth, an unofficial high priest removed for offenses against the Roman government; his son-in-law, Joseph ben Caiaphas, who was a puppet high priest through which Annas exercised his authority and power; and three other members of the Sanhedrin—Archelaus, Gamaliel, and Nicodemus—stood poised before Pilate, staring in surprise at the tragedy before them.

Caiaphas, head and shoulders above everyone, imposing in appearance and suave in manner, held his peace in horror as two thousand lay dead. The mere presence of Caiaphas made a great impression on everyone, including Pilate. In slow motion, Caiaphas' black empty eyes confronted Pilate with a hollow emptiness in them. Pilate, in the same slow motion, showed his eyes in reaction; he and Caiaphas' strong wills and stubborn resolves met stoically as they engaged in eye contact.

In a public stalemate, neither Pilate nor Caiaphas moved. Pilate was the first to give way under the grueling gaze of Caiaphas. He opened his mouth, but no words came forth. Finally, in a beleaguered voice and with as much authority as he could muster, he ordered, "Go away to your homes."

Behind Caiaphas, Annas, Archelaus, Nicodemus, and Gamaliel departed.

Caiaphas held his position in front of Pilate with an irreconcilable gaze, and then in an unforgiving and severe manner, he pivoted on his heels and strolled away. A glimmer of sunlight reflected off Pilate's eyes as he watched Caiaphas march off into the golden glare of the afternoon sun that was now low in the sky.

Wavering, the glimmering refraction of sunlight in Pilate's eyes grew erratic and faint.

The
FIRST
Chapter

IN THE DARK infernal regions of a tomb, a faint light grew with intensity in the black chillness:

"I heard of wonders done by this god-man, greater than by any of the gods whom we worship."

Throughout the stale environment of the tomb, an uttering wind-like voice called forth into the world of eternity: *"Lazarus, come forth!"*

The advancing faint light grew in strength and took on the luminous glow of a spirit. The apparition spun around until it faced upward and floated on its back with outstretched arms. A silver cord extended from its back, between the shoulder blades, and shimmered with an ethereal radiance of vaporous energy.

"There was one—a very mighty deed which is strange to the gods whom we have. He rose up a man who had been four days dead, summoning him by His word alone."

The disembodied spirit floated for a tantalizing moment, with a quickening awareness that was far sharper than perception, and an inner sense of thoughtless inattention as the spirit drifted in what seemed to be a rapid rushing airstream surrounding its spirit form. The spirit hung in this invisible rushing wind for a moment above a swathed corpse laid out on a slab of stone. It rocked with a slight violence as if on the waves of an ocean. The spirit perceived a loud hum, along with a vibration, as the silver cord attached to the corpse like an umbilical cord, providing a life-force from the spirit to the body.

The spirit lowered and dissolved into a misty vapor. With the sound of a mighty rushing wind, the disembodied spirit underwent the sensation of being drawn by a downward pull, as though being sucked into a vacuum, as it merged into the deceased remains.

* * *

A dim light spread crossway into the tomb from an unknown source until it reached the wrapped form. With a sudden jerk, the linen-bound corpse lurched and flinched with an abrupt burst of energy, the hands clenched in spasm. Coughing, the body took in great gulps of air. In rapid, rigid motion, it struggled to breathe, inhaling as much air as its dried-up lungs were able. The diaphragm pulled downward, causing air to be forced into the lungs as they inhaled, and then pushing upward to help force air out of the lungs as they exhaled. Violently, the body drew in air. The breathing became more erratic, and then long and strained, to finally release into a long drawn-out breath.

An eerie moan pierced the chill of the tomb. The hands relaxed.

* * *

Within the brain, twelve to fourteen billion cells were fast becoming active, each cell sending out thousands of connecting tendrils, so that a single cell connected with ten thousand adjoining cells. Each cell exchanged data impulses, giving and receiving the subtlest input in the microcosm of the human mind and body, transmitting and recording everything it experienced.

An electrochemical reaction traveled along the axon of a neuron. Reaching a synapse, it provoked a release of neurotransmitter molecules, which bound to chemical receptor molecules that gave rise to several thousand synapses, allowing neurons to form circuits within the central nervous system, crucial to biological computations underlying perception and thought.

The central nervous system connecting to and controlling other systems within the body gave sensitivity and perception that in a wink increased the mental and physical awareness. As the soul evolved into an emotional state of being, the body rejuvenated with life. The fingers moved with stiffness, the legs twitched, and the feet fidgeted.

Life surged throughout the circulation of veins and tissue, the body twitching with gestures of life and movement. Life continued to flow with restoring new semi-fluid protoplasm and semi-transparent hemoglobin as it traveled through the hollow and limp veins. The heart pulsated with a vigorous vitality and renewed strength of life-force, with the metabolism in rapid reconstruction, the cells receiving nutritive material, its humanity being brought back to life by the power of RESURRECTION.

* * *

In the macabre cavity of light, the wrapped body sat upright with arms outstretched, reaching for life, and to stabilize itself. The feet dropped to the dusty floor of the tomb. The body's ability to discern things with the neurological process of acquiring, mentally accessing, and interpreting information from the five senses were greatly expanding. It gathered within itself the facility to perceive physical sensation in parts of the body. It felt the chill of the tomb as it became aware of the cold, hard, rocky surface of the cave floor. Through the development of its senses, the mummy became acutely aware of its surroundings: the processing of information, the understanding of observation or thought coming into its center of attention.

Gradually and with some difficulty, the resurrected corpse rose. Dizzy, it stood unsteadily for a moment, swaying on its feet trying to gain balance. In slow uneven steps and hindered by the leg bindings, it took an uneasy step, only to stumble and fall on one knee, trembling. After a long moment, it finally stood up again and shuffled in lingering, teetering movements toward the light emanating from the open entryway of the tomb. The renewed being radiated, breathing the glory of God, becoming once again the very apex of God's creation.

Bright sunlight drifted into the interior of the tomb, reaching the resurrected one's eyes in blazing flame through the slits in the facial napkin. It threw up its hands, shielding its eyes from the fiery rays, feeling as though lightning has seared its brain. It clasped its hands over its tortured eyes, seeing nothing but red. Its eyes burned as if scalded. Hands over its eyes, the now living soul peered out through its fingers. Bit by bit, it grew accustomed to the daylight, the full sunlight hitting first through the corneas and then through the focusing lenses where the image struck the retinas, thus stimulating 125 million nerve endings simultaneously that funneled along the optic nerves containing one million separate insulated fibers that sent information back to the energizing brain.

A buzzing reached its ears, fine tuning to the vibrations of sound around him, and Lazarus stepped forth from the grave.

A SCREAM ripped through the stillness.

The
SECOND
Chapter

A RAVEN'S SCREAM filled the malevolent heavens while its circling shadow eclipsed a roughhewn wooden cross. The raven's continuous screech seemed to burn the soul, its squawk calling forth a clarion call of misfortune as if it were blaring out into the world a supernatural prophetic message of ill omen as Jesus hung on the cross motionless, without an appearance of life, His mutilated body beyond that of any man. With a piercing shriek, the raven alighted atop the pinnacle of the wooden cross. Its wings flapped for a moment, causing the cross to jiggle and arousing the One on the cross.

Wrought in pain, loss of blood, dehydration, and lack of sleep, Jesus' mouth hung half open from exhaustion. He licked His dry, parched lips. Raising His pale and disfigured head, His face betrayed a mask of agony. He grimaced in pain, His cheeks raw and red from parts of His beard being pulled out. Contusions marked His countenance. He let out a low moan and pulled Himself up for a gasp of air.

Slouching back down, His head hung low, encircled with that terrible crown of thorns. With each beat of His heart, fresh dark blood spurted from the wounds of the plied thorn spikes, trickling down His forehead and into His eyes.

"I did not wish to crucify Him."

Blood ran in rivulets from Christ's slit veins, coursing from the wrists, down along His elbows, and to His shoulders. His flesh was torn meat of oozing blood from the stripes and wounds of thirty-nine lashes and beatings, while His temples and breast drowned in macerated sweat mixed from the weeping wounds. His legs and thighs, violently distended, seemed to be dislocated; His body a cohesion of black, green, and reeking lacerations and gashes. His whole appearance was that of a corpse ready for interment as He hung upon that hideous mode of tortuous means.

"Since His accusers said, 'He calleth Himself a King,' I crucified Him."

With a screech, the raven took to the ominous sky, its black plumage rising like a shadow of Black Death, the air alive with an evil excitement. Demons masquerading in differing forms rendered the scene more frightful, camouflaged in various appearances such as that of a scorpion making its way through an unorganized mixture of hammers, nails, ropes, and a lone spear lying on the ground near a sharp-clawed dragon lizard that brooded listlessly on a rock neighboring the cross, its forked tongue flickering.

Near to the cross, a horned desert viper slithered through a pile of garments consisting of a belt, a simple short cloak, and a long seamless robe. Creeping and inching its way along, it continued to glide underneath a completely blood-saturated undergarment, exiting without a sound through a group of vile, half-drunk, swearing, blaspheming executioners who gambled for the robe.

The spear lay undisturbed near the Roman Centurion Longinus, who found himself in second command of the Crucifixion Unit, which executed the criminals. Having finished the work, he settled down to gamble. Shaking a leather dice cup, he negligently tossed out the dice, with one cube rolling out from among the group of gamblers and under the hoof of a prancing steed, whose rider was the Roman centurion in charge of the Crucifixion Detail, known by the name of Abenadar. He was a rough man of Arab descent whose duties were to oversee the crucifixion. His responsibility was to maintain order and to see that no one interfered with the execution to free the prisoners or to torment them physically. The chestnut stallion pranced gracefully under him, its mane flowing like flames. Abenadar touched a flank with a spritely kick. The animal leaped forward, pounding the dice into the dirt.

Astride the stallion, Abenadar rode majestically back and forth among the crowd of spectators who appeared exhausted, some by grief and others by the efforts made in bringing about their wicked intent: jockeying past Pharisees, Sadducees, priests, elders, and citizens. In their bloodthirstiness, they were like a wolf having its first taste of blood from a fresh kill. The stallion neighed, tossing its head nervously, the nostrils flaring. Abenadar brought the mount to a slow walk around the rueful crowd, many falling away as he approached. Some cursed the centurion as his proud eyes arrogantly announced another triumphant delivery of a Roman crucifixion under his command. Having no emotional stake in the crucifixion, it did not matter to Abenadar who was being crucified.

The big chestnut came to a halt, prancing and snorting in distrust, its lungs loudly forcing air in and out, the nostrils dilated with enough transparency to show the red blood vessels through the cartilage. The chaotic hard-breathing horseflesh turned its head on an outstretched neck toward the group of bystanders and spectators, the veins popping out of the quivering muscular shank, the wild eyes rolling back until the whites looked bloodshot.

Abenadar let the stallion have its way, watching its eyes, seeing a little of the wildness leave, its nostrils no longer trembling. Shaking its head, the stallion looked away and drew a loud breath, snorting out through its taut nostrils. It started and then pricked up its sharp ear. Shaking its head once more, the high-spirited chestnut restlessly stamped one hoof after the other. It drew in a deep breath and turned its head once again toward whatever had first caught its attention. Its trembling body relaxed. Intrigued as to what the stallion was eyeing, Abenadar turned in the saddle to see one in the crowd who stood alone, her eyes fixed upon the cross before her.

Mary, the mother of Jesus, was entranced, her grief-stricken heart ready to burst with the motherly ardent desire to comfort her son.

Drawing up the slack, Abenadar gently pulled the chestnut's head toward him to square up in front of the cross. The odor of sweating horseflesh and dust reached Abenadar's nostrils. The sweet-sickening stench of death and blood lingered in the air. Hesitating a moment, Abenadar twisted once more in the saddle, the leather creaking, to gawk at Mary before gazing scornfully, with an opprobrious expression, into the face of the One who was to bear the sins of mankind.

Jesus was near the point of fainting.

> *Although their accusations appeared to be groundless, I, Pilate, the administrator of the eastern provinces, have done so, for fear of their alleging to the emperor that I encourage insurrections, and cause dissatisfaction among the Jews by denying them the rights of justice.*

The
THIRD
Chapter

A GOLDEN EAGLE, the symbol of sovereignty and of Rome, overlooked an opulent apartment of Antonia, which served as the headquarters for Pilate and his officers. Armor adorned the walls, along with some standards bearing the image of Caesar Tiberius. Many expensive marble statues adorned the apartment in company of a bust of the previous Emperor Augustus.

Expensive Persian rugs covered marble floors while lamps and torches softly lit the quarters.

> *I have been compelled, for fear of an insurrection, to yield to the wishes of the high priests, the Sanhedrin, and the people who tumultuously demanded the death of Jesus of Nazareth, whom they accused of having disturbed the public peace, and also of having blasphemed and broken their laws.*

An expensive, hand-carved onyx table, inlaid with ivory and gold, stood adjacent to a decorated, plush red chair—the judgment seat. An ornamental bronze bowl rested on the onyx table, the bowl Pilate had symbolically used for the ceremonial washing of his hands. Lifeless over the armrest of the judgment seat, a hand barely clasped a decorative ivy-wreathed silver chalice. Red wine dribbled from the lip of the goblet to splash onto the marble floor, giving the appearance of spilled blood. Fingertips clutched the goblet and took a firm hold, moving upward to reach the lips of the one called Pilate. Upon taking another sip, he remained seated and motionless. Moody shadows from the soft glow of oil lamps and torches encircled Pilate.

In a disparaged tone of voice, Pilate declared, "For this, I have given Him up to be crucified." His words seemed to echo in the cavernous apartment. His arm fell back over the armrest with the silver chalice slipping from his grasp and falling with a clang on the marble floor. The red wine spilled out and spread across the floor toward three clerks who sat around and in front of the judgment seat, each clerk writing on papyrus with silver ornate styluses as Pilate finished his dictation. These reports were going out to the distant areas of the country and to the Caesar Tiberius himself.

The rise and fall of flame from an adjacent torch cast diabolical shadows across Pilate's dreadfully agitated face, playing diagonally across and over his countenance. He was lost in deep thought—even perplexed.

His lips moved barely as he murmured to himself, "What is truth?"

The
FOURTH
Chapter

SQUINTING AT THE SUN, Archelaus frowned in puzzlement and then gawked at the eerie, foreboding phenomenon taking place. The world was transforming into twilight, growing dark with a peculiar quality. Archelaus' eyes drifted away to the horizon where the whole landscape, sky, and atmosphere were growing dusky.

He gazed upward for the second time. The heavens were an appalling spectacle. The moon was full with a lurid red glow, as though dipped in blood. On the outer edge of the sun, a faint lip of shade grew into a shadow as the disc of the moon slid in a slow, smooth, and continuous motion across the luminescent surface of the sun. A deep gasp of fear slipped out of the mouth of Archelaus and fellow onlookers as the sun continued to extinguish its light and grow darker.

The blood-red moon positioned itself to obscure the sun in bloody darkness with a ring of fire encircling the moon in scarlet flame, an aureole in yellow and deep purple. Then the stars made their appearance in the celestial drama, the twinkling luminosities performing in the theatrical atmosphere.

Pharisees, Sadducees, priests, elders, scribes, soldiers, and spectators alike stood with eyes fixed upon the sky, frightened by the sudden, unearthly twilight. They groaned in terror until a hush fell amongst all and ominous quiet filled the place with stillness as silent as death. Every sound ceased. Remorse and wretched panic struck at petrified hearts—both men and beasts—stricken to the very core of their inner beings in terror. An unnatural slight chill of wind seemed to blow amongst all, lifting the hair on one's arms, bristling the hairs on the back of the neck, and causing chills to slide down the spine.

Within the span of several moments, many were languishing and troubled lest the sun had set while the crucified were still alive. Others, stricken with remorse, beat their breasts in anguish. Reverberating throughout the thick air was a haunting voice crying forth a proclamation, *"May His blood be upon His murderers!"* Upon hearing this, many fell upon their knees, entreating Jesus for forgiveness. Slowly raising His head in great agony, Jesus' blood-filled eyes compassionately surveyed those crying out to Him.

Some of the more fearful of the bystanders began to distance themselves away from the cross, while the faithful bowed their heads in awe and worship. An old white-bearded man took to heckling the accusers of Jesus by saying with a loud voice, *"I challenge you to acknowledge whether or not Jesus is indeed the Son of God!"*

Longinus, growing aware of the reactions around him, noticed the dim light. Looking up from the game of dice, he rose in consternation. By degrees, the day was darkening like that of a twilight winter. Thoroughly bewildered, Longinus staggered back a few paces, tripping over the hammer he had used in nailing the Savior to the cross. With flailing arms, he grasped hold of anything that might break his fall. One hand caught hold of the roughhewn cross. A white flash exploded in his brain as jaw-packed energy of an unforeseen Force knocked him to the ground.

Sitting upright, Longinus shook uncontrollably, grasping one trembling hand with the other in an effort to stop the tremors. Utter weakness surged throughout his whole being. Becoming aware of something warm and viscous on the palm of his hand, he held it up to see a red gelatinous, gooey substance. Looking up at the roughhewn side of the cross, he noticed a tributary of blood streaming down its surface. Nausea overcame him along with light-headedness, the earth swimming under him as his senses rapidly departed.

And the darkness continued to ever increase.

Dismas, the good thief, if there ever was such a one, having turned his soul over to the Savior earlier, raised his head in quiet concern. Jesus acknowledged Dismas with a look of reassurance, and then His eyes fell upon Archelaus, provoking a long and dramatic exchange between the two that troubled Archelaus.

Archelaus beheld something in the Savior's eyes, like that of a divine nature that expressed forgiveness and a deep love for him and humankind, which sprung a deep awareness of the sins in his life. The Lord's head drooped again, reminding Archelaus, *"Truly, He is suffering."*

Almost in a daze, Archelaus turned away, a softer look in his eyes. What had awakened in his heart? In a few minutes, he recollected himself, almost resentful in spirit and mind, becoming aware of the wickedness of his heart. On compulsion, he gathered his senses to capture one more look at the Messiah. Frightened by a nearly overwhelming depth of apprehension and hard-pressed conviction, Archelaus started down the hill, his mind swathed with uncertainty.

Darkness prevailed by the time Archelaus hit the streets of Jerusalem, the sun altogether hidden and the sky appearing dark as unto night while it was yet day. The stars' luster, obscured, cast a garish light. Birds flew low among the dark and gloomy streets. The raven swooped low overhead, flying over Archelaus, who watched in disbelief to see it dropped to the ground—dead! *"What kind of strange omen is this?"*

Archelaus glanced about. Suddenly, all motion seemed to freeze into a temporary state of interruption where tempo and rhythm halted in the present. Flickering candlelight in windows locked in place. Pedestrians carrying torches and lanterns froze in position, flames from their torches held in suspension. It was as though Archelaus were caught in a temporary flux, a time-warp where only *he* had freedom of movement.

Archelaus continued past dogs frozen in their steps, where moments before they had been skittering back and forth, trying to find a place to hide. He hastened past others who sat on the ground with heads veiled, suspended in the midst of striking their breasts in lamentation. He overtook those feeling their way about in the dark unlighted recesses, but not moving.

Time commenced to catch up in varying degrees and movements, with seconds seeming to last forever. The resonance of animals, caught in a slow reel, brought forth mournful cries. A tied donkey brayed as it slunk farther into the deep shadows with its head cast downward.

Pedestrians moved about at a snail's pace with torches and lanterns illuminating the way before them. Frightened voices called out to one another.

With a sudden abruptness, this envelope of time distortion was interrupted, with everything blurring into normal real time, catching Archelaus frozen and helpless of any movement, as though he were standing still with everything moving about him. Two anxious dwellers clambered around a corner and past Archelaus, lanterns held high as time rushed forward. He could not make out what they were saying, but he knew their attitude was apprehensive, perfectly overcome with fear and terror as they hurried headlong into an alley.

Suddenly, as though nothing had ever happened, Archelaus plunged back into reality.

The
FIFTH
Chapter

IN THE SANCTUARY of the Temple, ominous darkness crept along the walls and floors, as if a black infestation of ill omen sought to ravage. On the Temple Mount plaza, Jews crowded together, intent on the immolation of the Paschal Lamb. The darkness continued to increase. Trepidation, shock, and dread grew into mournful cries and howling while the priests endeavored to maintain quiet and order.

In the women's court of the Temple Mount, the priests lighted the four large golden candelabras, the light emanating from these large lamps being so strong that a woman could sift wheat by the light. Mystification and confusion continued with every passing moment.

* * *

Antonia stood stark against the otherworldly dusk.

Standing on the terrace of Antonia, Pilate and Herod the Tetrarch studied the eerie twilight, trying to comprehend its meaning. Both were disturbed. The two stood next to each other, unable to move. Herod gazed about and asked, "What is the meaning of these things?"

Pilate glanced at Herod and then back up at the dark, gloomy, and ever threatening sky. "It must be the vindication of the gods who are angry at the cruelty bestowed upon this Jesus of Nazareth." Pilate eyes fell to the three crosses in the distance. Stark and disturbingly frightening, the sight caused Pilate's blood to run cold.

* * *

Archelaus ran through the nearly deserted narrow streets and avenues while others scurried about weeping and running for their dwelling places. Upon hearing the distant bellowing of beasts tethered outside the walls of Jerusalem, Archelaus had a look of dread and anxiety.

Finally reaching his home, he tried to force open the door but found it firmly locked. Pounding with his fist, he knocked furiously in panic and anger. Looking about, he noticed many on their rooftops, contemplating the austere sky and bursting forth in lamentations and requiems.

The noise and confusion continued to increase.

Archelaus cocked his head, listening breathlessly to the plaintive bleating of lambs.

Pounding even more furiously upon the door, it opened cautiously as he burst across the threshold.

* * *

All was silent upon Golgotha. Time seemed to have slowed down in a most peculiar and menacing way, the faces of the bystanders looking odd and dead in the shadowy pall. Overhead, the blood-red moon stood locked in front of the sun. Horses and donkeys, Pharisees, soldiers, and onlookers alike crept closer together.

Silence reigned.

Jesus hung alone, forsaken by all. The darkness thickened.

Dancing, spooky, flickering lights glowered in the dusky atmosphere.

Distant sounds like thunder seemed to come from all directions.

Louder and louder.

WHOOSH! A flame flared past, as a roar filled the air with the sound of thundering hoof beats. A ghostly form blurred past, then another and another. Panning about, one could see the ghostly shapes of mounted equestrians riding toward Antonia in the distance, a gloomy silhouette rising up into the angry sky. Their torches cast an eerie glow like an aurora as they rode past Pilate who wore a cloak, masquerading as an ordinary citizen to protect his identity as he made his way down the road leading out to Golgotha.

Pilate observed the living waves of humanity as they strolled away from Golgotha, gloomy and taciturn from what they had witnessed. They were silent and stricken with terror and remorse, recounting in revulsion amongst themselves the day's supernatural events, not realizing that the day of wrath was not yet finished. Every now and then, groups of individuals halted to look back, a few remaining immobile in the expectation of witnessing further happenings. Pilate hastened his way back toward Antonia.

* * *

Footsteps echoed down a long corridor. Feathering shadows and artificial illumination of flickering oil lamps wavered and danced crossways on a tiled surface as sandaled feet strode into view with a purposeful gait. Pilate, with strong will and determination, marched along the hallway of Antonia and out onto the portico of the praetorium. Stopping, he moved to one side to view before him a rabble of terrified citizens, Pharisees, and priests.

Soldiers burst into the praetorium amidst howling screams and shrieks. They surrounded the horrified citizens, priests, and Pharisees on all sides. In one vociferous outburst, the assemblage cried out upon seeing Pilate, "You have brought this down upon us!" Others shouted in defiance, "You are the one to blame for this!"

Pilate looked out over the crowd, sensing they were in a surly mood from panic and fear. "I consider all this," Pilate bellowed forth as he gestured with an outstretched arm toward the shadowy atmosphere, "a terrific proof of the anger of your God!"

The throng reacted with a discordance of protests, objections, curses, and judgments, growing ever more infuriated as they cried out and declared their wrath, "Down with this iniquitous Governor! Let us crucify him! May his veins spurt forth his own blood! May your teeth be washed in vinegar! Pilate is afraid of his own shadow. Look at him!"

"I am no subject of this Jesus whom *you* have put to death unjustly," shouted Pilate in anger. His words echoed along the walls of the praetorium as the crowd grew sullen. Pilate, fiery and fearful as one is when confronted with a hostile mob, burst out, "You alone are guilty! I have nothing of which to reproach myself!" He thrust his open palms outward. "See—I have washed my hands of this whole affair! I am quite innocent!"

As Pilate defended himself, the light reappeared in degrees. Turning slowly, Pilate raised his palms above his head as though feeling the air. The crowd quieted down and then became silent.

The SIXTH *Chapter*

THE BLOOD-RED MOON passed away from the disc of the sun. Shining forth again, its appearance was dim. By degrees, the sun became brighter, the stars vanished, and the sky turned into monochromatic ochre that soon developed into the golden glare of a late afternoon.

Trumpets sounded, announcing the continuation of the immolation of the Paschal Lamb, while thousands of Jewish worshippers proceeded toward the holy Temple Mount, each carrying a lamb for its Passover offering. One such worshipper strolled through the crowd, a lamb draped over his shoulders. As he neared the southern steps of the southern wall leading up to the Temple Mount, a parade of priests and Levites marched down the outer stairs of the Temple Mount wall, blasting on their silver trumpets and greeting the worshippers as they made their pilgrimage to the Temple. In the distance, the worshipper could see the gates of the northern courtyard wall.

The worshipper stopped at the ritual baths, the mikvoth, on the foreground side of the broad steps, where worshippers bathed before entering the Temple Mount to be ceremonially clean before worship. Adjacent to this was a smaller stairway that led to smaller gates, the triple gates, where priests entered the storerooms located under the Temple Mount floor. After performing the ceremonial washing, the worshipper placed the lamb across his shoulders and joined the thousands of others on the large plaza at the foot of the southern stairs.

Marching alongside the assemblage of families and those of various ranks in life—the underprivileged, the affluent, the young and old, along with numerous righteous Jews of diverse tongues and tribes—the worshipper climbed the enormous steps, also called the southern stairs, leading up to the southern wall. The stairs were not less than two hundred feet across, and the staircase was composed of thirty steps. The risers were low—seven to ten inches high—with each tread twelve to thirty-five inches deep, which made the ascent slow and respectful by way of a dignified and deliberate stride.

On this side of the double gates, the exterior was austere. Passing through the massive double gates and under the magnificent passageways, the worshipper admired the extravagantly carved columns and ornamented domes of the Herodian archways with its carved vines, rosettes, flowers, and geometric patterns covering every inch of the impressive entryway leading into the Court of the Gentiles on the Temple Mount.

Before the Hulda Gate, the worshipper stooped to take off his sandals; he could not wear them on the Temple Mount plaza. He continued through the Hulda Gate with thousands of others and into the outer court, called the Court of the Gentiles, where vendors and moneychangers stood or sat behind wooden tables with coins stacked high. The moneychangers exchanged foreign coins for shekels and minas, the only accepted currency by the priests for the Temple taxes and other hallowed requirements. Brawny guards of the Temple Court stood close by, bored with arms crossed, each holding a stout wooden club. The place reeked of dung and piss from animals held in flimsy stalls; caging thousands of sheep, rams, he-goats, and lambs that were to be sold in case someone did not have or bring an animal. Their smells and cries were overpowering.

The worshipper approached the balustrade called the Sorreg, a low wall of about four feet in height that ran along the breadth of the Court of the Gentiles, separating it from the inner courtyard. Only the Jews who were purified by the ashes of a red heifer could go beyond this wall. The worshipper knelt in a gesture of humility and thanks before God on one of the large stones inlaid in the pavement in front of the Sorreg. Words carved into the large stone read:

> LET NO STRANGER ENTER WITHIN THE BALUSTRADE AND THE ENCLOSING WALL SURROUNDING THE SANCTUARY. WHOEVER MAY BE CAUGHT, OF HIMSELF SHALL BE THE BLAME FOR HIS CERTAIN DEATH.

Entering into the inner courtyard, now filling up with other worshippers bringing their lambs to slaughter, the worshipper, with an eager heart, took a place in one of the three long lines.

Everyone's spirits were high with the return of sunlight. The priests led one of the long lines in through one of the gates and into the Court of Israel. Upon entering the Court of Israel, one could now see the Levitical Choir standing on platforms singing Hallel songs of thanksgiving, accompanied by shofars, trumpets, harps, lyres, and cymbals. The devotion of worshippers and their intensity in prayer made this place an expression of awe. There was something mystical and unreal about this area of the Temple, further mystified by an otherworldly aura. The worshipper became aware of a Divine Presence that permeated the very existence of his being. He found this wonderful place profoundly intense with a spiritual hallowedness and an overall sacredness.

The air was thick and alive, heavy with something akin to that of static electricity, which brought about an overwhelming sense of energy. The worshipper, besought with a wide range of emotions, looked about in ascetic wonder. The atmosphere, charged with a ghostly edge of the supernatural, made the energy of this holy place powerful and overwhelming.

Immediately, the worshipper felt a light numinous wind that seemed to blow right on through his inner being rather than on the skin. His hair stood on edge, his flesh prickled and tingled with the sensation of electricity running through his blood, and his knees buckled with ever-increasing weakness. All was ethereal. A distinctive cleanness and holiness of the environment made him aware of God's divine presence, manipulating his senses to an astonishing aspect of awareness that influenced faith, peace, joy, and fullness to such an extent that he felt God's holiness that was beyond thought or reality.

The
SEVENTH
Chapter

THE HIGH PRIEST, splendid in his sacerdotal garments, oversaw the full activity of the white-turbaned priests as they performed their duties. Recommencing from where they had left off, the priests continued the offering of the sacrifices of the Pascal Lamb. Their duties were performed in the slaughter area situated next to the Altar of Sacrifice, sometimes referred to as the Table of the Lord. The altar stood in the Court of Priests between the Temple and the Court of Israel. Smoke rose from the altar in a straight upward fashion, as was always the case when the sacrificing was underway, even when there was a brisk wind or a mild breeze. The sweet smell of cooking meat permeated the space. There were no buzzing of flies; no insects invaded this hallowed site. In this holy place, there existed the conscious understanding of a divine blood relationship to the animal offerings, slaughtered for the sacrificial atonement for the sins of humanity.

The altar, accepted by tradition, resided on the threshing floor of Araunah. To this day, many Jewish scholars believe this to be the identical spot where Abraham bound up his son, Isaac, to be a sacrificial offering. They also consider this same site to be where Noah built the first altar after exiting the ark. It has been a long-established belief that Cain and Abel first brought their offerings to God at this place, where Adam brought his first offering, and where God created Adam.

The worshipper continued on, carrying the lamb to the slaughtering area where everything was in order and ready to perform the ritual slaughter of the lamb. He followed a priest to a section where twenty-four golden rings, affixed to the marble pavement, held sacrificial lambs in place, positioned on their sides in complete rest and submission by way of the gold rings attached over their necks for preparation of the altar.

The priest took the lamb from the worshipper and asked him, "Do you love this lamb?" If the family did not love the lamb, there would be no sacrifice.

The worshipper nodded his head and replied in the affirmative, "Yes, I do." He placed the lamb into the hands of the priest. Today, it is the same for believers. When we give something to God, we place it in His hands.

The priest took the lamb, laid it down on its side, and placed the golden ring around its neck. There, in front of the priest, the worshipper grasped the lamb with both hands and confessed his sins, his guilt being transferred to the lamb as if it were traveling down through his arms and hands and onto the frightened, innocent lamb. The priest and the worshipper prayed together, "Yehuda, receive the blood of the innocent lamb for the sins of the family for this entire year."

With knives flashing all about, the priest stroked the lamb to calm it down while with the other hand he gave a sharp bronze knife to the worshipper. The worshipper slit the lamb's throat. The warm blood flowed through his fingers, inciting him to identify with the lamb that was dying by his own hand and that of his actions as a sinner. The priest, standing before the worshipper and the now lifeless lamb, caught the draining blood in a mizrak, a golden or silver vessel used for gathering the blood to sprinkle on the altar to make atonement for the person's sins.

From this slaughtering area, priests, arranged in rows to the Altar of Sacrifice, passed from hand to hand golden or silver vessels full of the blood of the lambs, with one row handling the golden vessels and the other handling the silver vessels. A priest nearest to the base of the Altar of Sacrifice took the gold or silver vessel and made seven complete trips around the altar, sprinkling the blood from the lamb on each of the four "horns" of the altar. He then handed back the now-empty vessel to the returning line, which had the sole purpose of passing the gold or silver vessel back to the starting point.

Priests and butchers in white garments were full of blood as they stood behind tables. Atop were all the tools necessary for their precision work. They performed with disciplined quickness and order the disembowelment of the lambs, the blood sprinkling each other as well as themselves.

Another special group of priests took the insides, forbidden to eat, and ascended the ramp of the Altar to three separate piles of wood—fig, walnut, or pine—that were in a continuous burn. These priests tossed the offerings onto the flame of the largest fire called the Altar of Burnt Offerings, where roasting meat was as a sweet savoring aroma unto the Lord.

The second fire provided the coals for the Altar of Incense to be used within the sanctuary itself. The third fire was the perpetual fire that always burned, fulfilling the commandment, "Let there be a perpetual fire," as the Torah states: *"And a fire shall burn there on the altar continuously; it shall never be extinguished."* Tradition says this fire was lit directly by the hand of God Himself. It is to NOT to die out! Nothing is placed on it, and no coals are taken directly thereof. If for some reason, all of the lamps of the menorah go out, they are to relight them from the fire on the Altar of Burnt Offerings. A priest removed a portion of ashes from a large pile formed in the center of the Altar from the remnants of these three fires every morning before the sacrifice of the day.

The priest who had taken the lamb from the worshipper took the remains of the lamb and attached it to a special marble post where he began skinning the carcass, the flaying done expeditiously. Since there were not enough of the special marble posts, some of the priests used round wooden sticks or rods to improvise a makeshift post. They loosened a piece of skin, fastened it to the wooden rod, and then proceeded to hang the lamb on the wooden pole that was over their shoulders while at the same time facing each other. Using both hands, they twisted the wooden rod around and around until the whole of the lamb's skin rolled up upon the rod. The process continued repeatedly with a thousand animal sacrifices performed in one day.

The smoke of the three fires rose high and straight from the altar until it mingled into one whole above the Temple area, the Court of Israel, the Nicanor Gate with its circular raised dais, and the Court of the Women. Off into the distance could be seen Golgotha, a reminder of the real sacrifice of atonement taking place at that precise moment.

The
EIGHTH
Chapter

THE LIMP, EXHAUSTED, dehydrated countenance of the Lord Jesus Christ was pale from the loss of blood and pain, the roughhewn wood cross gouging at the lacerated skin and muscles of His shoulders. His face contorted as He pulled Himself up by His nailed wrists, adding more weight on His fastened feet as He gulped in a lungful of air. He sank forward, putting a greater burden on the nailed wrists holding up the weight of His body. Severe pain shot along the fingers and up into the arms, exploding into a blinding white light of pain as the nails in the wrists put more pressure on the median nerve. Immediately He pushed upward off the spike in His feet to avoid the stretching torment. The spike tore through the nerves between the metatarsal bones of His feet, causing a reaction of searing agony. He recoiled, nearly screaming out in pain! Fighting off light headedness and nausea, He eased Himself back into the slouched position.

The first known methods of crucifixion originated with the Egyptians. Their form of crucifixion was to nail a victim onto a single pole with the hands above the head. The Greeks took and redesigned this torturous instrument of slow death by crucifying a victim on an X-shaped cross. The Romans devised it to an exact science of anguished torment, by up-righting the cross to a T shape. The unfortunate person to be crucified usually met death by asphyxiation or heart attack caused by the accumulation of exposure and inexpressible pain. The pain affected one's acute mental faculties and senses with sufferings and agonies beyond human comprehension.

The Lord's arms were giving way to fatigue. Great waves of cramps swept through the muscles, knotting them in deep, relentless, throbbing pain. He found it nearly unbearable to push upward to gather in more air since the lungs were collapsing. Hanging by the arms, the pectoral muscles went into paralysis along with the intercostal muscles that were now unable to act. He grunted in agony as He raised Himself once more, His whole body trembling. A cold sweat broke out on His bloody forehead as He gulped in one short breath. With deep gasps, He tried drawing more air into His lungs. He found He could not exhale as carbon dioxide accumulating within His respiratory system and bloodstream made it impossible. He lowered His body carefully, trying to minimize the pain as much as possible. He sighed as the cramps somewhat subsided.

He hung for a time in a near loss of consciousness.

Thoughts raced through His mind. Within an acute awareness, He could sense God, His Father, abandoning Him. His mind screamed out in terror as the Father deserted Him. Being mentally distraught, He felt the rejection of humankind and the betrayal of some of His followers. Tears streamed down His blood-streaked face from a deep internal hurt, this wounding more agonizing than the physical pain. He shivered with rejection. Crushing from within, He gave way to unrelenting grief. With a sudden convulsive movement, He strained again to push Himself upward to inhale and exhale the life-giving oxygen, gasping for every breath. He fell back into the slouched position. His thoughts flashed back to the last supper:

> *Flickering flames of oil lamps enveloped the room in a saffron glow. He studied the faces around the table, the twelve familiar faces whose reflections were in His pupil, the apple of His eye, the ones who were His friends—His disciples—all but one, who was about to go forth and betray Him. Solomon was right when he said, "Each heart knows its own bitterness." He held no bitterness as He broke the loaves of bread.*

They drank the wine together. It ran down His throat, and it was now icy in His veins.

Blinking, Jesus tried to divert the blood that trickled down His forehead and into His eyes. Closing His eyes, the direct sun penetrated through His closed eyelids to produce a red glare. He opened His eyes, and for an instant, His vision blurred with blood and sweat. He refocused and gazed down at those who were observing Him—some in contempt, some in remorse. He knew that none truly grasped the purpose of why He hung there on the tree, as a curse, for the inhabitants of the earth who were slow and dull in learning and understanding.

He loved them!

Turning His face upward, He grimaced. He became aware of a foreign sensation, a suffocating blackness. It brought fear and restlessness into His thoughts. An unearthly foul odor wafted, not just in His sense of smell, but also within His heart. The pollution awakened within His divine-human nature. The presence of sin waited outside in the darkness. It stole into His very essence, pure evil manifesting itself personally to operate throughout His body, piercing Him with dread. Soon this terrifying blackness of sin would be racing in from the shadows. He felt naked. Dirty. Like Adam and Eve in the garden, He felt and was aware of His physical nakedness in public, becoming embarrassed in front of the rabble before Him. Not just before man was He embarrassed, but also before God, the Creator of the Universe, who could destroy body, mind, and spirit!

Catching a whiff of human excrement, He snorted and turned up His nose. He tossed His head as if to get rid of the lingering odor. The air turned foul with an odiferous stench mixed with brimstone and sulfur. A polluted sweet-sickening reek of decaying flesh reached His nostrils. He recoiled. The horrible smell was both soiled and fetid, and all the while rank and moldy. He could just about taste it! He choked, trying hard not to vomit. His stomach turned. *"What was in the atmosphere causing this disgusting odor?"* He looked from one thief to the other, thinking it came from them. Then He realized—it was Him! The dreadful, disgusting odor of sin and all of its wickedness slithered into His spotless divine being. It was repugnant! Terrible! Suffocating! He had never sinned, but now

He was taking on the iniquity of us all, taking on the sin of humanity. Like the scapegoat, He now became the personification of sin: He was an adulterer, a fornicator, a homosexual, a murderer, a liar, a thief, a hater, a drunkard, a drug addict. He bore all iniquities, depravities, immoralities, and debaucheries of mankind. He was the embodiment of evil.

Now He must face His Father. *"NO! Not like this!"*

The Father in Heaven rises from His great blue sapphire throne, glowing with bright intensity, flashes of light splintering from off His person, arcs of energy erupting from Him. The Father looks down upon the one on the cross who is taking on the sins of mankind: past, present, and future. The universe, multi-dimensions, and unseen worlds shake.

Never had the Son felt the Father's burning rage!

God the Father withdraws His presence from one He called His Son.

The Savior felt a magnetic pull and a sensation of being sucked into a vortex of wickedness as He took upon Himself the vile nature and pleasure of sin. He hung on the cross, wrestling with a sinful nature. The torture, agony, and oppressiveness overtook Him. He looked down from the cross at the vile crowd of persecutors. They shouted at Him, spat at Him. He watched them for a while, their mouths opening and closing, as if in slow motion. He shook His head, His mind sluggish. It felt as though He were in a dream. His body tensed at the abhorrent and revolting thoughts that never ceased.

He continued to take on the sins of humankind.

Jesus sensed the Father's great displeasure. He was beside Himself. "Father! Father!" He cried, "Why have You forsaken me?" He stared up at the one who could not and would not reach down or reply. The Trinity planned this long ago, in the Garden of Eden, when Eve and Adam fell and gave dominion to the serpent called Lucifer, now known as Satan. The Son endured it, the Spirit enabled Him, and the Father rejected Him, the Son whom He loved.

The Father received and acknowledged the sacrifice for sin and was satisfied.

The
NINTH
Chapter

THE SON OF Mary, Jesus, moved up and down against the rough cross, the splinters gouging into His flesh as He strained to inhale enough air to relieve His lungs of the intermittent partial asphyxiation and searing pain. The action caused the tissues to tear from His lacerated back. He gritted His teeth against the sheer agony.

After a while, He twisted around, straining to find some kind of relief from the ever joint-rending cramps. It renewed another terrible crushing throb, deep within the chest, as the pericardium filled with serum:

The heart was compressing.

Hanging in silence for a long time, Jesus occasionally raised Himself to catch a breath.

Another dilemma arose: an overwhelming longing for cool water—thirst!

His lips were dry, the mouth parched, His blood hot, the skin filled with the perception of a running fever. He opened His mouth, the dryness of which produced the necessity of a drop of cool water. *"Cool water, please. Please?"* were the screaming thoughts racing through His mind. He looked down with desire at a bucket full of vinegar-wine. His gaze wandered over to the soldiers drinking from their canteens. He yearned for anything to quench the ever-increasing thirst. He licked His dry, dehydrated lips with a parched tongue. The longing for water was deep; the inside of His mouth was arid. He leaned His head back against the cross. He dreamed of being under a cascading waterfall, drinking from its pool. "I thirst." He half-whispered with a throaty coarse voice.

Marcus, a sixteen-year-old Roman legionnaire, crouched near the cross. Upon hearing the hoarse cry, he looked up into the face of this crucified one that he knew to be Jesus. He had seen this man before and had heard Him teach. Moved with compassion, he wandered over to the bucket full of vinegar and wine and dipped a sponge into the mixture. He stabbed the sponge on the end of his spear and lifted it up to the crucified one, brushing the Savior's lips with the wet sponge. The vinegar/wine mixture was meant to give some relief to the person suffering on the cross. It gave something like a tranquilizing effect, but Jesus wanted to be aware of the pain He was suffering, of why He was doing this. He turned His head.

Marcus shrugged and threw the sponge back into the bucket. He squatted back down and laid the spear next to him. He gazed up at the cross. He had heard of this Jesus for some time.

Some claimed that He was the Son of God. There were times when Marcus was off duty that he went and listened to Jesus teaching. He was taken by His guiding principles, doctrines, standards, and wisdom, as well as His enlightening to a new way of life. *His viewpoints made sense,* Marcus thought. Movement caught the corner of his eye. A woman stood near the cross. He watched her, perceiving her to be the mother of Jesus. His thoughts reverted back to when he was a six-year-old child:

He had been running, holding onto his mother's hand. Tears clouded his eyes as he glanced back-and-forth in fear. They were running for their lives as a riot broke out. He recalled how the Roman soldiers, camouflaged in garments of the common people, were attacking the masses gathered on the Temple Mount. As he grew older, he had found out the reason for the attack. The Procurator Pilate had ordered his soldiers to attack and squelch a protest against his use of the Temple treasury to finance an aqueduct. He and his mother had been caught in the swell of panicking protesters.

Marcus wiped away a tear, hoping no one noticed. He glanced over at Longinus, who at the moment gambled with the other Roman soldiers for the garments of Jesus. Memories once more hurtled through his mind. His eyes dropped. He studied the ground. He remembered:

> *Longinus pummeled into him, knocking him to the pavement, severing the tight clasp of his mother—Rebecca's hand. She had fought back through the crowd to throw herself over his body to keep the crowd from trampling him to death. In the ordeal, she had given up her life to save her own son—himself!*

Tears clouded Marcus' eyes. Once again, he observed Longinus. He was a good man, but rough in nature. The death of Marcus' mother had left him an orphan. Longinus looked after him until he was of an age to join the Roman army. Marcus recalled how he had mixed feelings about becoming a Roman soldier. The cruelties of the Roman army made him hesitate in his decision. Longinus was the one who had enticed him to join the military. He said it was good for someone who had no family, and that the army would take care of him.

Marcus peered over at Mary. *Her heart must be in torment,* he thought. He glanced at the cross and found Jesus looking at him, giving him an expression of gratitude for the kind gesture in trying to give Him the vinegar/wine mixture. Marcus felt moved by the gratefulness. He nodded in return.

The
TENTH
Chapter

JESUS PULLED HIMSELF up to breathe, nearly screaming out in pain and shock. Sagging back down into a slouching position, His heart pounded against His chest like a sledgehammer. His head throbbed with each pulse. A headache erupted. The pain was incredible!

The headache!

Burning, feverish tears filled His eyes from the raw migraine. He squeezed His eyes against the pain. Distantly, through the torment, He became aware of another sensation.

His heart was skipping beats.

The heartbeats progressively grew slower. At times, it seemed there was no heartbeat at all. His swollen eyelids drooped. Suddenly, He bent from a sharp blow deep within the chest, as if someone had struck Him with a mallet. He contorted. A cold, clammy sweat broke out on His forehead. A quick stabbing pain from the middle of the back hit Him with brute force as if something had knifed Him from the inside. His stomach jerked with a reflexive action, which caused violent retching that knotted the muscles in the abdomen. He dry-heaved savagely. The heart jolted back to life and started beating again by the reflexive action of the retching.

It lasted only a moment, but the wrenching renewed the anguish in His physique.

Blinking His eyes, He fought off a blackness that crept over Him. His vision blurred. His head lolled to one side. For a long while, He stayed like that—too weak to move, breathing very shallow. As He came to, He made a great effort to shift His weight to catch a breath. He rose with excruciating pain off His feet, but He could barely move.

Breathing became dreadful.

He opened His mouth trying to suck in air. His head sagged forward. He grew fainter. Sluggishly, He shook His head in an effort to regain consciousness. Eventually, He gave in to a falling swoon from weakness and distress, the entirety of His awareness fading and growing dim.

The pulse of His heartbeat slowed and grew fainter.

He forced open His burning-stinging eyes. His death struggle grew with fierce wrath! He knew His hour stood near. *It's almost over,* He intuitively reasoned. Losses of tissue fluids were reaching a critical level. The compressed heart fought to pump the heavy, thick, sluggish blood into the tissues. The tortured lungs took on a frantic effort to gasp in small quantities of air. The markedly desiccated tissues sent their flood of stimuli to the brain.

His head slumped. He could sense the chill of death creeping through the tissues, the blood beneath His skin turning cold. He lifted His head again, but it felt heavy and fell to the side. Shivering, He longed for warmth and life. His eyes fluttered. A mysterious misty film obscured His vision, a kind of misty vapor that moved stealthily over the dead and sucked the life from them. The realization that the end was near at hand compelled Him to break forth in an exclamation that came out from cracked lips that crimpled like faded old parchment as He shaped the formative, now infamous words: *"It is finished!"* He had undertaken the atonement of sins for humankind. It was completed. Finally, He could allow His body to die!

In one last surge of strength, He pressed His torn feet against the piercing spike. He straightened His legs and took a deeper breath. He uttered in a vocal sound of speech, so strangely pitched, that it seemed to be heard everywhere: *"Father, into Thy Hands I commit My Spirit!"*

The voice that cried out, *"It is finished!"* was heard among those who had departed. It pierced the walls of sepulchers, penetrating burial places and tombs to call forth those who slept in graves. It traveled across the whole earth and the universe and up into Heaven.

Jesus tried to swallow, discovering His throat to be torturous and raw. The loss of the cough reflex and loss of the ability to swallow caused excessive accumulation of saliva in His throat and lungs. The heart was weakening, being overworked. He began hyperventilating, and at times, He stopped breathing at all. No energy was left within Him. The death rattle commenced, the organs getting less and less blood and oxygen. The cells were dying—not enough oxygen to supply them.

He raised His weary head. Trembling, He contracted and opened His hands. His body became stiff and He threw the whole of His weight upon His feet.

The heartbeat faded.

He bowed His head and dismissed His Spirit, His blood-filled eyes half-open and milky. His shriveled lips turned blue, partly forced open by a swollen tongue, the cheeks and temples hollow and sunken.

A moment of time.

The
ELEVENTH
Chapter

THE APEX OF the cross quivered with a slight motion. The Savior's head swayed with the movement. A low muttering rumble growled under the feet of those present along with a heavy vibration and a shudder, then a quiet moment. Suddenly, there came an uplifting and upheaval, like the rolling of waves on an ocean. The rolling continued as the sacred corpse swung senseless on the cross. The powerful earthquake gained momentum and strength, exploding into tumultuous mayhem, the earth igniting with furious anger and violence.

Abenadar tried to keep the chestnut stallion under control as it screamed piercingly, the scream filling the air as it pulled on the reins in confusion and fear, its head held high, its nostrils flaring, its eyes rolling with intensity. It rose, pawing the sky, shrieking even louder and stronger, pulling harder on the reins. Abenadar tried desperately to restrain the mount, but he knew it to be futile, as he could see the horse's wild and instinctive terror rising. The stallion squealed sharply and again rose in the air, its shrill sound mingling with yells and shouts of those who had betrayed Jesus, those who had testified against Him, and those who had cried out into the open, *"Crucify Him! Crucify Him!"* Many of the spineless curs crept a certain distance away while some of the rueful mob flew down the hill past Abenadar, whose steed grew more and more unmanageable.

The stallion reared on its hind legs, its frightening cry chilling, its forelegs pawing madly in the air with bared teeth. The reins jerked free from Abenadar's grip, ripping through his hands as the stallion leaped forward, its thunderous hooves trying to maintain a hold on the shaking earth.

Somersaulting backward off the stallion, Abendar hit the rocky ground with a hard thud, his hand still clutching a rein. Immediately, the stallion tore into a gallop, dragging Abendar along before he let go. Rolling over on his back, he caught sight of the two thieves on the crosses crying out in pain and horror.

The land of Judea continued to buckle and warp, heaving under throes of the great cataclysm. In the city of Jerusalem, houses, buildings, and walls collapsed in one of the greatest earthquakes the region had ever known. In the Temple area, terror reawakened with double force by the shocks of the quake and the terrible noise and confusion caused by falling buildings and walls on all sides.

At first, excess panic rendered the people speechless, but then there arose a burst of cries and lamentations. Individuals near the collapsing buildings and walls ran to and fro like disturbed ants dispersing in all directions from an anthill. Others stood around with nowhere to go.

The holy cadaver, nearly torn from the cross by its own weight, rocked back and forth. The earth quaked with such force and violence that it rendered a deep crack in the rock to the right of the cross where it was anchored, so the site could never be used again for future crucifixions.

In the Kedron Valley, boulders shifted, scraping with grating, grinding, raucous sounds, sending massive chunks of stone tumbling down the precipices and crags with a great rumble that mimicked booming explosions and distant sounds of thunderclaps. In the garden of the tombs, huge stones sealing off sepulchers carved out in the limestone cliffs crumbled into heaps. In the cemetery near the Valley of Hinnom, where the poor and unfortunate had been laid to rest, stone and dirt-covered shallow graves jostled loose and fell away to expose corpses.

In the Court of Israel, there was not so much confusion as the strictest order and decorum were always enforced there as the priests endeavored to calm the people. Inside the Temple, Caiaphas performed the solemn act of burning incense before the veil that separated the Holy of Holies from the rest of the Temple. The veil, which was embroidered with precious silks of blue, purple, and scarlet and blended with finely twined linen, hung between two columns by golden hooks that fastened through sockets made of silver.

As if by an unseen hand, the two-inch-thick veil was suddenly ripped asunder from top to bottom, exposing the Holy of Holies to the public. It augmented the opening of the way into the Holy of Holies by Christ's death. It destined the passing away of the Jewish dispensation and thus gave the revelation that Christ's death on the cross was now the only way of salvation for all mankind.

With the earthquake in full strength, Caiaphas barely made it out alive as the columns to the left and the right fell in opposite directions.

Caiaphas rushed to the entrance of the Temple just before a large stone fell from the wall, causing the arch to be broken. The ground upheaved in front of him, sending him sprawling as many other columns fell in other parts of the Temple.

* * *

The Antonia fortress shook to the core of its foundations. The Praetorium was in mass confusion, with many running to the entrance in an effort to escape falling debris from walls, columns, and buildings. The superstition of Pilate increased his fear, paralyzing him so he became speechless with renewed terror as the earth quaked beneath him.

* * *

The seismic activity subsided to find Longinus lying face down on the ground and the crucifixion throng immobilized with terror and stricken with awe. The Pharisees, Sadducees, and others alike were alarmed by the earthquake, with many lamenting and striking their breasts while contemplating the Christ on the cross. Longinus lay near the cross where the rock had ripped asunder. In curiosity, he dropped a pebble down the deep chasm.

* * *

In the Garden of the Tombs, great stones sealing sepulchers were in broken heaps, some fragmented and shattered, and a number in pieces and rubble. Wrecked tombs were open and graves exposed. In the cemetery, a stone-covered grave quivered. Dirt fell away. A corpse sat upright, brushing off dirt and debris. It unraveled its face cloth as others, in close proximity, disentangled their burial rags. Beyond, more corpses climbed out of burial chambers, sepulchers, and resting places. In the surrounding areas, the righteous deceased wandered about, their bodies the same as when they were active on earth with no signs of decomposition or putrefaction. The death of the Christ on the cross brought forth the resurrection of many holy people, some buried for years and others more recently dead. They came out of the tombs everywhere. This foreshadowed the resurrection of the Christ. After Christ's resurrection, they were going to make their way into Jerusalem and appear as witnesses to the life-giving force of Jesus.

* * *

Shafts of sunlight illuminated floating particles of dust inside a sepulcher. Out of the corners of the darkness and into the shadows, there came a barely distinguishable movement. A shuffling, scraping sound progressed until the dust particles of light exposed two mummies lumbering forth with unsteady steps, encumbered in grave linen. Climbing out of the sepulcher, the two mummies peeled away the stale and musty facial rags to reveal not faces of dead men, but that of Lenthius and Charinus!

The
TWELFTH
Chapter

A LARGE STONE warehouse, primitive but of ample structure and made of rough gray stone, stood in the avenues of the warehouse district. Two immense loading dock doors near the northwest end of the building made communication with loading platforms possible. Along the length of the warehouse near the ceiling line, barred rectangular openings used as windows brought light and air into the spacious storehouse. The late afternoon sun streaked through the transom windows with amber shafts of sunbeams, creating strong linear lines that stretched across the stone floor in rhythmical patterns that highlighted each aisle. The golden haze of sunlight gave the warehouse a somewhat foggy atmosphere.

From the loading dock doors leading into the warehouse, an elongated human shadow spread across the interior stone floor of the warehouse. The shadow stirred. Nicodemus entered the warehouse, his long shadow stretching across the stone floor. Oil lamps and torches lit up the spacious warehouse as he viewed the semi-devastation. The vast interior of the warehouse was murky with a heavy saffron glow, the air somewhat stifling and melancholy. From out of the obscurities of the dim fogginess, Nicodemus could make out wooden beams and rafters, buttressed by granite posts, supporting a high ceiling. Through the haze, he noticed a slightly stooped, timeworn old man ambling down the well-organized spaces with a slight lean to the left, representing the burdens his shoulders carried as he inspected what had once been a careful arrangement of inventory. Though he had endeavored to stack the items uniformly, the inventory was now a jumble of fragmented and cracked granite statues, alabaster boxes, and basalt from Egypt.

The old man weaved in and out among broken jar fragments that lay strewn about bales of wool, fine linen, parchments, tapestries, and carpets from Babylon and Persia. Fruits, figs, and nuts lay scattered around paintings from Rome and Greece. A pungent fruity scent, beginning to turn rancid, together with a whiff of stale peanuts and a musty odor of old clothes permeated the environment. The old man moseyed around slicks and puddles of olive oil beginning to turn bright yellow from being exposed to the air. The oil pooled in low spots amongst broken barrels and pottery shards.

The old man took a sample of olive oil from a cracked barrel. Taking a sip, he artfully rolled it in his mouth, letting it touch all areas of his mouth. It was greasy with a taste of pumpkin. The oil tasted bitter with no fruitiness, mingled with a tang of wine vinegar. He spat it out onto the floor.

Looking about once more, the old man stepped over to a highly polished bronze ornamental mirror near the loading platforms. He inspected it for any damage while it reflected his image, that of Joseph of Arimathea, a wealthy merchant and aged member of the Sanhedrin. His luxuriant full beard and shaggy eyebrows suggested a warm and friendly demeanor. His bluish-grey eyes in a tiresome manner again surveyed the broken, damaged, and otherwise tossed about inventory of the warehouse. Fatigued from overburdened anxiety, he let his gaze fall once more onto the bronze mirror, his head turning a little to one side, his features twisted in thought. From this, he chanced to see his old friend Nicodemus reflected in the mirror near the loading platform. He turned to see Nicodemus approaching.

Nicodemus greeted him. "I wanted to have some talk with you, and to see how you were favoring."

"Not well," answered Joseph, gesturing with his hand toward the stockpile. "The earthquake has ruined much of my inventory, as you can see."

Spent and exhausted, he ambled over to a bale of wool and sat down, his eyebrows twitching and lips moving as he muttered under his breath.

Knowing his friend better than most, Nicodemus could see Joseph struggling with fretful remorse. There was a moment before either spoke. Finally, Nicodemus broke the silence. He spoke in a gentle and kind voice, "Joseph, Jesus is dead."

Joseph remained motionless, sitting on the bale of wool with his head bent low, his face pallid. Tears welled up in his downcast eyes. His lower jaw quivering, he raised his trembling stony face. His eyes had that feverish look of resigning himself to what he knew had to be inevitable. He could barely speak. "I could not bring myself to go, to see Him." His eyes fell to the floor once more.

"They will probably toss the body into a common grave, as is the custom for those who have been crucified; or else they will toss His body into the burning trash heap of Gahanna," Nicodemus asserted.

Joseph, aroused out of his state of despondency, groaned, clasping his head with both hands. The blue veins in his neck seemed to pop out through his transparent old skin, his face turning red. He raised his hands together in clenched fists with face upraised and lashed out with veritable agitation. His eyes shone fiercely and his lips shook, "Never! I will *never* allow them to do such a thing!" he growled in anger. He lowered his head upon his chest after expending so much energy and then suddenly scowled, annoyed at himself. Joseph raised his head, embarrassed by his sudden outburst. "I'm sorry for you to have been the object of my anger. It was not directed at you, my friend. It's just that I will not allow them to do such a thing!"

Nicodemus, never saying a word, acknowledged Joseph with a nod of his head, full of compassion and understanding. "Aye," Nicodemus finally said tender-heartedly, "say what you must, for I have the same motivation, but how will you stop them?"

Joseph shrugged his shoulders and shook his head. He looked away in thought. "I have a freshly hewn sepulcher in the garden of the tombs that I am reserving for myself. It is near Golgotha. I will beseech Pilate of a favor he owes me. I will ask him of the body of Jesus and lay him away in my own tomb." Turning to face Nicodemus with a gleam in his eyes, his face was full of composure. "Yea, that is what I will do." Glancing back at the inventory, he continued, "I'll gather together spices and the finest linen for burial. It is the last thing I can do for Him."

The
THIRTEENTH
Chapter

SMALL HANGING OIL lamps lighted the passageway leading to Pilate's quarters, creating a forbidding and shadowy ambiance. Multicolored standards, rusting shields, and swords of various lengths and shapes hung on cracked walls in the funereal light. Marcus, who had just came back from his duties at the crucifixion, led Joseph of Arimathea to the end of the corridor where an elaborately carved wooden door hung on loose hinges. A helmeted sentry stood by with a javelin in hand. Marcus knocked four times on the unsteady door, which was answered by an unintelligible bellow from inside the quarters. Marcus pushed on the door, which creaked loudly in protest upon its damaged hinges, and entered with Joseph of Arimathea on his heels.

In the midst of rubble and devastation, Pilate stood clutching the familiar silver goblet. He was in the halfway point of giving instructions to an orderly, "...And tell the executioners to end the lives of the criminals before the Sabbath cometh."

Pilate was unnerved, barely hanging on to his sanity. As the orderly left, Pilate cast a weary eye on a crack in the marble floor, studying it with an absent mind, full of anxiety.

Following the crack to the onyx table, he poured himself another drink. He drank deeply and heavily. Swallowing, he closed his eyes, savoring the rough and sour taste of the young wine as it ran across the palate and down his throat. Opening his eyes, he discovered Joseph standing before him with bold humility. With a slight annoyance, he took another sip, using the goblet as a shield in front of his eyes to block the view of Joseph, wanting to be left alone.

With indulgence, he motioned with the goblet. "The red fruit of the vine is from the regions of my country." He waved the chalice soberly before him. "It wields a well-balanced finesse and breed, as the winemakers say." His face suddenly became dour. "Yet its finish leaves me," he smacked his lips, "with a sour taste of bitterness in my mouth." He raised the goblet as if he were giving a toast and was about to bring it to his mouth again when he hesitated, the goblet poised at his lips. Eyeing Joseph, he lowered it. "I hear that Jesus had wine with his disciples afore night, during their Passover meal, saying something about, 'This is my blood, drink.'" There was a momentary pause as Pilate gave Joseph a look of dark scrutiny, "Have you ever had the taste of blood, Joseph of Arimathea?"

Joseph gave no reaction, nor did he answer, but he wondered secretly how Pilate had gathered such information: *There always exists with him an awareness of doings and hearsays,* he surmised silently, *probably through his many spies.*

"It's warm and deep, like licking a copper pot." Pilate frowned. "The gods know I've had my taste."

"I would think it to be more like the taste of freedom and life," replied Joseph.

Pilate belched. "What matter brings you here?"

"I call upon you to pray that I may take the body of Jesus for burial, especially as the Sabbath draws nigh, for it is written in the law that 'The sun not set upon one that hath been put to death.'"

"The Galilean is dead, before now?"

Joseph nodded affirmatively. "Verily, I heard this from one who bore witness."

Pilate being astounded, disquieted in mind, and filled with anxiety, sluggishly rubbed the back of his neck. He glanced at Marcus. "Send for Abenadar, the centurion in charge of the crucifixion detail. I need confirming."

Being somewhat intoxicated, Pilate swayed a little on his feet and then caught hold of the onyx table to steady himself. His attention fell to the bronze bowl that was still full of the ceremonial water he had used in washing his hands of guilt. Pondering, he poured the red wine into the bronze bowl, giving it the effect of blood being mixed with water. Lights and shadows played across Pilate's features from the surface ripples. Intrigued and beguiled, he dipped a hand into the blood-red water and watched it trickle through his fingers. "I am surprised that the death of this Jesus should have taken place so readily," he said to Joseph. A dark malignancy spread across his countenance upon hearing the sound of his voice echoing up from the basin. He cuffed the water mix with a quick and sharp slap of the hand. The blood-red water dribbled from the table and out onto the marble floor, where it continued in a stream toward the crack in the marble flooring.

The
FOURTEENTH
Chapter

DROPS OF BLOOD splashed into a pool of the life-giving substance, as if in slow-motion. A tear fell into the scarlet puddle with a slight ripple, obscuring the reflection of Mary, the mother of Jesus, as she wept, her tears mingling with His blood. All was silent. The crowd had dispersed, leaving John, Lazarus, Mary Magdalene, Mary of Cleophas, and Salome alone, either standing or sitting before the cross, weeping in silence.

Six Roman soldiers made their way along a path that led up the crucifixion site as the sun lowered in the distant horizon. They brought with them ladders, ropes, and large iron staves for the purpose of breaking the legs of the criminals to hasten their deaths through severe traumatic shock and blood clotting. Marcus, armed with orders from Pilate, broke from the group and approached Abenadar to relay the message. As soon as the soldiers came near, the friends of Jesus retired back a few paces to make way for the soldiers to place their ladders against the crosses.

The ladders thumped against the wooden crosses. The two thieves moaned like wounded animals as their crosses vibrated. With the iron staves, the soldiers broke the thieves' arms above and below the elbows with a loud, sickening snap, while another broke the legs above and below the knees. The loud crack of bones mingled with the horrific cries of the two thieves was more than Mary and the others could bear.

Gesmas, the ungrateful thief who had berated Jesus while on the cross, defecated and continued to wail. For that reason, one of the soldiers finished him off with three heavy blows of a cudgel to the chest. Dimas, the thief who had repented and said, "Remember me when you come into your kingdom," and Jesus replied, "This day you shall be with me in paradise," gave out a deep groan as his last breath expired. The cords were loosened and the bodies fell heavily to the ground with a thump.

The soldiers then turned their attention to our Lord and Savior. They were approaching the cross when Mary, the mother of Jesus, seeing what they had done to the other two, and that the same would be done with her son, leaped forward to stop them, but the others grappled with Mary to hold her back.

A soldier threw a ladder up against the roughhewn wood of the Lord's blood-stained cross, causing the body to sway from the juddering of the impact and from the soldier climbing the ladder. Jesus hung there, unmoving, eyes wide open. As the soldier hauled up his iron stave, he laughed. "This one pretends to be dead already."

Longinus ran over to stop him. "This one *is* dead already."

The soldier snarled and looked over at Abenadar to see what he wanted him to do.

Abenadar, overcome with the sight of the cruelty displayed by the soldiers and the deep sorrow of Mary, seized the lance Marcus had laid near the cross. With both hands, Abenadar gripped the lance and thrust it violently upward into the right side of Jesus. It struck against the raw flesh with a sound similar to that of a lance striking sand. The lance drove through the fifth interspace between the ribs, upward into and through the pericardium, and into the heart. Immediately, there oozed out a great amount of blood and water. An escape of water-fluid from a sac surrounding the heart gave postmortem evidence that Jesus was indeed dead, not by the usual death of suffocation, but due to the failure of a broken heart, owing to the shock and constriction of the heart by fluid in the pericardium.

Mary vicariously felt the wounding of the lance as though she herself had been pierced. Then she remembered the prophecy of Simeon, *"And a sword shall pierce thy soul,"* when she had taken the baby Jesus to the Temple to complete her ritual purification after childbirth and to complete the dedication of her firstborn son.

Startled, she rushed forward as Abenadar yanked the lance out with some difficulty, the flesh tearing outward as the lance left the wound. Along with it came a quantity of the blood serum, gushing out in a small geyser all over Abenadar's face.

Abenadar leaped back, not expecting the spewing spring of postmortem water and blood. He fell to his knees disoriented, trying to wipe off the blood and water from his eyes and face. After what seemed a long minute, he paused, something catching hold of his spirit. He gazed up into the face of Jesus, enlightened that he was indeed born a sinner, and he still was a pathetic sinner.

"Truly, this was the Son of God!" he exclaimed.

Burying his head in his hands, he let out a terrible wail, alarming everyone. His body shook, his shoulders bent over in anguish of soul and spirit, quaking with sobs.

Mary looked on with great compassion. She reached out and laid hands on Abenadar's shoulder, "May the Lord graciously forgive you."

Rocking back and forth, Abenadar cried out, "Have mercy. Lord, have mercy. Have mercy on me! Forgive me for such a sinner as I."

Longinus looked on with astonishment. He had never seen the centurion act this way. He glanced around to see everyone else overcome by the display of blood and water and that of Abenadar. His eyes followed the frothy stream of blood and water to where it fell to foam and bubble in a hollow of rock before spilling over into the fracture cleaved by the earthquake next to the cross where he had earlier dropped the pebble.

The blood and water coursed like a river of forgiveness into the crevice. Deep down, directly below the cross, the blood and water flowed.

The crevice in the limestone rock ran for a depth of about twenty feet underneath and directly below the cross of Christ. The blood and water mixture continued its course through the crack and into darkness where a golden light spawned. This light grew with intensity until something of a shiny luster was visible and took on the appearance of two pairs of wings. The wings blazed as the light increased to a flashing brilliance to reveal wings made of pure gold. The light continued to increase, unveiling the golden wings attached to a twin pair of golden cherubim, which in full light revealed to be a part of an even greater whole: the ark of the covenant!

Between the cherubim, the blood and water trickled onto the mercy seat of this sacred and holy relic. Vaporous smoke rose from the mercy seat where the blood and water dribbled with the life-giving substance. With a *whoosh* of wind and flame, a reddish-orange glow emanated and grew with ferocious power. A blue electrical flare of energy arced between the golden wings, scintillating and dazzling with a glow of immense energy and force until it appeared as molten fire!

The
FIFTEENTH
Chapter

FLAMES OF A torch seemed to fill the room with crackling and hissing. Through the flame could be seen Pilate, pacing back and forth, disturbed in mind and spirit. Abenadar entered.

Pilate stopped mid-pace and asked, "Is it true that this Jesus of Nazareth is already dead?"

With a suggestion of sadness, Abenadar answered, "It is as you say. The Galilean is dead."

Pilate characteristically rubbed his bald pallet, sorrowful and yet a little fearful after witnessing and experiencing the supernatural events of the day. With a grave face, he gave permission for Joseph of Arimathea to take the body of Christ for burial: "I grant thee leave." To Abenadar he ordered, "See the orders executed!"

* * *

Hammering in the distance amplified throughout the deathlike stillness as soldiers stood nearby like black ghosts tethered to the ground, silhouetted against the lowering sun. More hammer blows rang throughout the countryside as a nail fell to the ground and danced before Mary. The other women behind Mary shed tears before the cross, including that of Mary Magdalene, Mary of Heli (Mary's sister), and Mary the mother of James, Veronica, Johanna, Chusa, Mary Salome, Salome of Jerusalem, Susanna, and Anne.

Another nail fell past Abenadar, who with great difficulty, drew out the spike that transfixed Jesus' feet to the cross.

In a gentle and respectful manner, Nicodemus and Joseph of Arimathea separated the body of Jesus from the cross. Tears fell as they looked upon His bruised and lacerated form. It brought to remembrance the words the Lord had spoken: *"As Moses lifted up the serpent in the wilderness; even so must the Son of Man be lifted up."*

The body of the Lord slunk down to its knees. Nicodemus and Joseph climbed down the ladders while supporting the upper part of the body. Longinus mounted a stool to grab a hold of the legs around the knees. Abenadar helped them lower the body to the ground.

Mary, already on her knees, outstretched her arms to receive the dead body of her son. Reaching out to assist, John supported the head while Mary Magdalene took the feet. Reverently and with tear-filled eyes, they placed His upper torso into the arms of His sweetest mother with John bearing the weight of the head until Mary could take hold of it. In mixed sorrow and consolation in seeing Him thus wounded and disfigured beyond recognition, the sorrows of Mary's heart renewed with incomparable mourning. With the head supported on her lap and overwhelmed in sorrow, she bathed the body with tears from a mother's heart, permitting the sharp thorns to wound her as she pressed His face to hers.

She drew off the crown of thorns, not caring whether it ripped her flesh. She laid aside the crown next to the nails. She then proceeded to draw out the thorns that had remained in the head. One last time she held her son in her arms, gazing at the mangled, blood-caked form and then at the face. Even in death, it had not lost the deep, haggard furrows of agonizing struggle and suffering. She embraced His bloodstained cheeks.

Mary Magdalene pressed her face upon His feet while Mary, the mother of Jesus, closed the eyes and mouth. Mother Mary pressed her face upon His face, rocking back and forth in lamentation. John, Joseph of Arimathea, and Nicodemus stood at the foot of the cross before Mary without speaking a word. The sorrow at the sight before them—the grieving of Mary and the spectacle of the crucified divine Christ—caused vehemence and bitterness in them.

Finally, John drew near to Mary and beseeched her to let the body of her son be taken. As John led her away, she turned suddenly, freeing herself from John's grasp and ran back to her son, where she once more gave her farewells. Gathering herself, she wiped away the tears and went back to the embrace of John as the men lifted the body to lay it upon a leather hand-barrel that was covered with a brown cloth. They carried the barrel with two long stakes with Nicodemus and Joseph bearing the front upon their shoulders and Abenadar and John supporting the rear.

Mary fell into more grief and collapsed into the arms of the other women. Mary Magdalene ran a few steps forward in anguish toward the body of Jesus as they carried Him away. For her, it was with ultimate sorrow as the Lord had so changed her life.

The funeral procession advanced into the sunset with an eerie chant of mourning. The silhouette of the funeral procession was sky-lined against the fiery orb of the setting sun as they strode across the outskirts of the garden of the tombs.

* * *

Lengthening shadows from the small group fell deep into Joseph of Arimathea's newly carved tomb. Nicodemus and Joseph prepared the body with haste, straightening the mangled limbs and folding the bruised hands upon the lifeless breast. They then wrapped it in fine linen and applied the spices they brought. Placing two coins over the eyes and then placing the head napkin over the battered face, they were barely finished when they heard the trumpets sound, announcing that the Sabbath had begun as the setting sun slipped below the horizon.

As they laid Christ's body in the grave, Nicodemus thought of the Lord's predictions and how they had been fulfilled so far. *"Had He not said He would rise again on the third day?"* He saw things in a clearer light now as ephemeral songs of lamentation rose up from the group like ghostly spirits into the twilight ambiance as the thirteen-foot in diameter and two-foot thick stone grated along its trough.

Inside, the tomb was fully bathed in a golden-amber haze. The light began to gradually decrease into a crescent, diminishing until only a finger of light remained to delicately caress the body of Jesus in repose. The light became a sliver, then weakened and grew pale to finally fade into a harsh and suffocating blackness, jolted by a vibrating, hollow thud.

* * *

Annas, Caiaphas, Archelaus, and Gamaliel stood among the golden candelabra, the golden altar of incense, and the table of showbread. Before them, the veil separating the Holy of Holies from the Holy Place lay torn in half on the broken marble floor. This miracle, striking and terrible to the priests, astonished them, given the veil was two inches thick and impossible to tear. It signified an awful and noteworthy phenomenon.

Frightened, Gamaliel cried out, "By His death, these mighty signs have come upon us!"

Caiaphas rent his robe and fell to his knees. "What evil have we done?

A prey to the tortures of his own conscience, Annas wandered off from the group in a guilty sense of right and wrong. He was terribly alone. Dark oppression overtook his soul and gripped it with ferocity. The light from the torches cast dancing shadows against the walls, causing Annas to shudder. "Woe for our sins. Judgment draws nigh."

Archelaus held the two-inch-thick veil in his hands, rubbing it between his fingers with passionate emotion, feeling the weight and observing the thickness. He brushed its surface with his hand, responding to the stimuli of its velvety touch. He stared long and hard at the devastation surrounding him when a sudden thought occurred. He turned to the others. "Did He not say He would tear down the Temple and rebuild it again in three days? What if He were not found to be in the grave? What if the body were to be removed? Might the people accuse us? Will they judge us guilty as we are the overseers of the law?"

All looked aghast at Archelaus.

Alarmed, Caiaphas exclaimed with an emphatic gesture, "We must seal the tomb!"

The
SIXTEENTH
Chapter

THE COMING NIGHT was full of chill as Pilate postured with an impolite and ill-mannered attitude atop the steps leading up to the portico. The flicker of torchlight bathed half of his features in a harsh yellowish-orange and the firelight bleached his blue eye in cold maliciousness, leaving the other half of his features in blue with the eye black in deep shadow. The firelight illuminated the stone steps leading away from Pilate and down below to the brink of the footsteps where stood Caiaphas, Gamaliel, and Archelaus in a haughty fashion of embarrassment, all awash in the brightness of the full moon that seemed large in the night sky.

With agitation, Pilate growled, "What is it that you must vex me so on this forthcoming night?"

Caiaphas, in somewhat discomfiture, was expressive. "Sir, we remember that the deceiver said while He was yet alive, 'After three days I will rise again.'"

Pilate waved him off. "I want nothing more to do with your king and this petty matter. Be gone! Go your way!"

Pilate turned to leave, but Caiaphas was unrelenting. "We make a request that the sepulcher be made sure until the third day, lest His disciples come by night and steal away His body and say to the people, 'He is risen from the dead!'"

Pilate spun around, his eyes burrowing into Caiaphas. A breeze wafted through his cloak, disturbing the flickering torches with a *whoosh* of turbulent combustion that sent sparks into the night air. "Go! You have your watch. Vex me no more with your petty disturbances."

Pilate glanced at Abenadar who stood nearby. "Centurion, make it as sure as you can. Take Longinus and Marcus, along with the others who were on the crucifixion detail."

* * *

Sunset had fallen as three soldiers finished off stringing seven leather cords across the huge stone, securing each end to the solid rock with blobs of clay to seal the sepulcher. Abenadar stamped the blobs of clay with the official signet of the Roman governor. One of the Roman soldiers drove an iron shaft into the rock channel to seal and prevent the huge stone from being rolled back to open the tomb. Present as witnesses were Archelaus, Gamaliel, and some of the chief priests. Malkus, captain of the six temple guards, was also present. Caiaphas had sent them along as further witnesses.

By lantern's light, Longinus read from a parchment scroll an ordinance:

> *Ordinance of Caesar: It is my pleasure that graves and tombs remain undisturbed. If anyone either demolishes or in any way extracts the buried, or maliciously transfers them to other places, or displaces the sealing of other stones, I order, in case of such violation, that the offender be sentenced to capital punishment on charge of violation of sepulcher, as in respect of the gods.*

Longinus placed the ordinance on the stone, slapping clay on the corners of the ordinance, and then stamped the clay with the signet ring.

The
SEVENTEENTH
Chapter

THE BRILLIANCE OF the skyline faded with the sun slipping below the horizon, ending a not so ordinary day. The moon climbed to its heights to look down upon the valleys, fields, and canyons, bleaching the desert and limestone in a silvery glow. Lights twinkled from households that were settling down for the evening, adding a warm glow into each dwelling place. One household was the exception, in which moonbeams filtered through a rough window, revealing the coarse quality of the interior, both softening and enhancing the irregular features of stone and wood.

Shadows fell long and deep even unto the angles and corners. The moonlight's silvery fingers slithered along chinks and crevices of the dark floor to where it found a man covered in ashes, his garments torn and head hanging. Giving full vent to his grief sat Peter, alone in tomb-like seclusion. He was humbled, contrite, and repentant of heart, sorrowful and broken under the weight of sin. Tears glistened down his cheeks with liquid reflections of moonlight.

In an upper room of Martha's house, burning torches threw restless shadows over ceiling and walls. The murky room was enveloped in intense silence. Mary, the mother of Jesus, sat in a corner with the women in a prayer vigil under the soft glow of an oil lamp. Before them were Nicodemus; Joseph of Arimathea; Lazarus, the one whom Jesus raised from the dead; and the disciples, who sat in solemn silence. A few ate some leftover lamb from the Passover. All were perturbed in spirit and filled with grief. John entered. He endeavored to give consolation, but when his eyes fell upon Mary and the other women, he could not restrain his tears and turned to leave.

At the same moment, Thomas and James the greater entered. They searched each other's face in sorrow.

* * *

Late that night, Joseph of Arimathea headed toward home from the upper room, accompanied by a few disciples and women. All were sorrowful as they walked the streets. In the next instant, they were encountered by a band of armed soldiers from Caiaphas' tribunal. They seized upon Joseph, the one they were interested in taking into custody.

* * *

Joseph spun into view, falling heavily on his knees as Malkus, the captain of the royal city and a temple guard, threw him before Caiaphas' seat of authority. Malkus grabbed Joseph by the scruff of the neck, yanking him up to a standing position while at the same time cursing the dead weight of his body. Joseph stood with an unexpressive and dejected face before Caiaphas and the tribunal. With great solemnity, Caiaphas questioned him. "We have heard that you had entreated upon and begged for the body of Jesus to give burial."

Joseph remained passive and unresponsive for a few tense moments. The only sound in the room was the scratching of a deadpan scribe as he, with careful attention to detail, wrote down questions and answers on a large scroll. Malkus slapped the back of Joseph's head as a non-verbal way of saying, *"Answer him!"*

"Why are you angry with me?" Joseph inquired as he directed his gaze toward his accusers. "What does it matter that I buried the body of Jesus? With what reason did you have to crucify a just man?" With great alacrity, he continued, "May His blood be upon you all!"

The scribe stopped scribbling and looked up in shock. All those in the room were troubled and disturbed. Annas, who sat next to the chief priests and elders of the Sanhedrin, huddled together with the others to whisper among themselves to consider what should be done.

Caiaphas stole himself away from the council to stand in front of Joseph. He looked Joseph over with a harsh and malicious stare. He raised a hand as if to strike Joseph, with his palm outward and fingers somewhat curled. Finally, he lowered the hand. To the temple guards, he charged, "Put him in custody while it is yet the Sabbath, and keep him there until the Sabbath is over." The temple guards grabbed hold of Joseph. As they dragged him away, Caiaphas continued with his tirade: "It is only at this time that it is not lawful to do you any harm till comes the first day of the week."

Joseph angrily wrenched free from the clutches of the temple guards. He turned, facing Caiaphas with clenched fists, his lips pressed into a thin line. "The God you have hanged upon the tree is able to deliver me out of your hands!" To his accusers he vocalized his displeasure: "All your wickedness shall come upon you!"

Instantly, there was an audible reaction among the group of his accusers as Annas, Caiaphas, and the Sanhedrin were enraged with exceeding fury. Caiaphas approached Joseph and gave him a back-handed slap across the face, which sent Joseph flying backward. "Put him in the chambers down below!" he shrieked. "Where there is no window. Keep a guard posted!"

With brute force, the temple guards shoved and manhandled Joseph away as Caiaphas shouted, "We shall meet after the Sabbath to plan 'with and of what' manner to put you to death!"

The dungeons beneath Caiaphas' palace were places of dread; many grisly stories told of them. Roughly hewn out of bedrock, the cells were separated by arches and pillars. Holes were chiseled through the arched tops so manacles could be slipped through to shackle a prisoner's hands above his head. In this way, it was easier to beat the prisoner.

The only entrance into the lower underground dungeons, where the worst of criminals were kept, was by a portal in the floor. The guards lowered Joseph into one of the dungeons. By the dim light of the torch, Malkus stepped forward to look down upon Joseph of Arimathea. Wild-eyed and haggard, Joseph stumbled to a corner, where he slunk in utter despair to the floor with a complete abandonment of hope. Gazing straight ahead, his eyes were vacant, dull, and expressionless with his hands folded on his lap. The limestone walls, cold and dank, seemed to close in upon him as the guards retreated with torches in hand. Joseph could only imagine the dark horrors of the hours as the fading light withdrew until he was in utter darkness.

A deep, deep darkness.

The
EIGHTEENTH
Chapter

DEEP, BLACK, unfathomable darkness.

A sound! A disembodied whimpering cry of despair, barely audible.

A flicker, just off to the side, barely noticeable. Orange, then yellow. Deep groans, muted at first. Becoming more intense, cries of despair.

Rustling sounds. Shadows darted past. Flickering orange-yellow light revealed the dark outline of something here and there.

Sparks eddied and floated about. Flames licked upward, welling up and reflecting off two crazed eyes, wild with extreme pain! A cankerworm crawled out from the victim's pupil and down a transparent face. Through the transparency of the face, a skull could be seen, blackened from constant burning. Out of the nose cavity, another cankerworm exited as one more entered the opening of the mouth and another made its way across the face that was completely engulfed in flames. The departed spirit struggled in great, great pain and misery, erupting in a most shrilling scream as though he were being immersed into a cauldron of boiling oil. Suddenly, all hell broke loose.

Ear-piercing, high-pitched screaming, yelling in guttural agony.

Black figures flashed across the foreground with the roar of flames burning in the background, revealing shallow pits brimming with blood-red liquid sulfur, all ablaze with an unearthly fire of spectral blue flames. Departed spirits resided in the holes. When caught up in this flame, they became white-yellow upon combustion of their spirit body. They clawed at their faces and hands, gnawing or tearing at their flesh, weeping and gnashing their teeth as they struggled in throes of tremendous pain and anguish. One could well discern clearly within the bosom of the spirits a skeletal structure blackened from constant burning, the charred flesh still clinging, the eyes blackened sockets, the teeth bared as they burned in the hellholes of fire and brimstone.

Upon further examination and drawing closer with scrutiny, one could see the spirits covered with worms and other vile creatures that gnawed at the vitals, hearts, eyes, hands, legs, and entire bodies; so ferociously they gnawed as to defy description. The worms crawled in and out of eye sockets, nasal passages, and oral cavities. They moved in a sinuous way around the spirit-bodies, eating.

The cankerworm would not die!

* * *

In wicked profanity, these departed spirits cried out, accusing people, circumstances, and others, while cursing the occasion of their damnation. Others cursed their tongues, their eyes, or whatever sin caused them to be damned forever, paying the price for the pleasure of their sins. The loquacious disorder and blasphemy never ceased for an instant. From somewhere, nowhere, and everywhere came the sound of chains being dragged. Gesmas, the bad thief on the cross, came into view, being dragged in chains by demons into HELL, where the nourishment thereof was fire, a fire so hot as to be white with leaping tongues of flame that do not consume.

The
NINETEENTH
Chapter

FLAMES BURNED FIERCELY, sparks streaming high into the cavernous air. Dreadful shrieks, howling screams, wailing, gnashing of teeth, screeching, and crying were constant, all blending into a singular high-pitched and deafening roar. The clamor was continuous in hopeless despair, amplifying to such an extreme as to cause deafness.

Horrendous and horrible! But here, in the infernal regions, there was no such thing as deafness. The mind became increasingly insane with every passing moment.

Once a person was destined to this place by their free will and choice, the departed soul would experience an immense stark landscape that was both appalling and frightful. The mark of God's wrath and vengeance was visible from every direction with dismal dungeons, dark caverns, and fearsome deserts. It was an absolute air of desolation.

In a faint reddish glow, strange and ghostly forms appeared and disappeared in swirling shadows. An alarming falsetto screech invaded the netherworld. The cacophony of shouts and piercing loud cries deadened as the shriek became louder and more terrifying. Something dark and gigantic slithered past into the dark cavern where dungeons and prison cells lay.

Faces pressed against iron bars, their chains rattling with every movement, reminding them of their eternal captivity while staring off hauntingly into nowhere, their faces lit by darting flames. Immediately, a sickening, pungent, and asphyxiating stench of death came that smelled like burning, putrefied flesh mingled with tar and sulfur—a mixture of which there is no earthly comparison.

The total blackness was the ruler of this expanse where no flame or light could penetrate, where the light was always at the point of being snuffed and to where the black darkness was a tangible and visible reality. The flames were hot and yet invisible, thus giving no further luminosity.

Chains clattered and jangled as a searing soul crawled out from one of the cells. There was no need for a cell door on this man's chamber as he could go nowhere, for there was no way of escape. As such, the shackles were of such hindrance as to allow him not to go much farther. This soul was that of the rich man in Jesus' parable:

The rich man recalled with dread and sorrow his actions on the earth with the one poor beggar called Lazarus: *"The rich man, dressed in purple and fine linen, lived sumptuously in the lap of luxury every day of his life, while there laid at his gate a beggar by the name of Lazarus, who was covered with sores and longing to eat what had fallen from his table and could call nothing as his own. Of their days of life upon the earth, the poor man Lazarus lived by faith and walked in the steps of Abraham, while the rich man was thoughtless, selfish and hedonistic in his ways; dead in trespasses and sins."*

The rich man's chains rattled as he laboriously, in constant motion, raised one foot off the blazing hot rock surface, and then the other, always in relentless torment. He thought about death as the common end to which all classes of mankind must yield to and surrender. Death is a fact that all men acknowledge but few come to realize and understand. We eat, drink, talk, and plan as if this life we live is an immortal state of existence. There is a great proverb that says, "He that would live well should often think of his last day, and make it his company-keeper."

The rich man's thoughts wandered once again to his days on earth: *Lazarus' days had finally come to an end, and he was carried away by angels to Abraham's bosom. It wasn't much longer afterward that the rich man also met death, his feasting and opulent living stopped, the lavish living ended, and he was carried away to eternal damnation and torment.*

The rich man glanced around and then up to Abraham's bosom some distance away. A glowing light marked the area. He was in enormous pain and suffering and full of the acknowledgment of his sins as he looked off into the expanse. He now knew the folly of his wickedness from which he had not repented while on earth. He understood the hundreds of thousands of iniquities, debaucheries, and sinful acts he had been willfully and obstinately blind to:

Lust of the flesh
Adultery
Idol worship
Lies
Bearing false testimony
Hatred in his heart
Unforgiveness toward others
Drunkenness
Theft
Haughtiness and pride
Covetousness
Unbelief unto which there is no forgiveness after death.

Hell is a truth known too late! The searing flames of hell left the rich man with never-ending third-degree burns and a thoroughly eviscerated appearance. He was impaired in his ability to think, and he was tortured to such a degree that his eyeballs bulged out of their sockets. The rock upon which the rich man stood burned right through his feet and into his bones, much worse than standing on a rocky surface during midday summer's heat. It kept him in continual motion to stand on one foot and then the other to get a nanosecond of relief. His purple and fine linen clothes were torn to shreds, his whole body covered with sizzling, oozing blisters as if he were meat searing over a hot fire.

In the red glare, his countenance was a mask of agony, haunting eyes sunk deep within their sockets, hollow cheeks, parched protruding tongue and signs of severe thirst of which no man could possibly endure while on earth. Sweat matted the hair atop his head as well as his facial growth and ran in steaming rivers. He was constantly gasping for a breath of air, which was thin and acrid there. The putrid stink of death, revolting and overwhelming, left his soul in a continual state of nausea and gagging. The sulfurous atmosphere burned his nostrils and eyes, causing an extreme migraine headache.

The scorching flames of hell, the total isolation, the rancid and rotting stench, and thunderous, ear-splitting screams of agony, not to mention the tormenting and torturing of demons, was more than the rich man could take, and yet in that place, there was no escape! The anguish, pain, torture, and distress was beyond misery and imagination; beyond anything humanly speaking and into which no mortal body could sustain, but here, he was already dead! The unrelenting and unremitting torment was beyond his sanity and was forever and forevermore.

Before the rich man, there seemed to be a moving shadowy mass of blackened smoke. Suddenly, and without interruption, all of the walls, floor, and stones glowed white at temperatures of thousands of degrees, yet the fire did not incinerate. A molten mass of lava rose out of an immense pit, like a cauldron of liquid bronze, while thick clouds of vapor, steam, molten lava, and sulfurous black smoke surged up from the fearful depths of this great chasm, the sulfuric smoke, suffocating and airless, the heat singeing unto the point of death. But no death happened there, only the conscious reality of a continuous second death, of which there was no annihilation and no completion!

From this pit rose an unearthly groaning-grinding sound, like never before heard. Gnashing of teeth mingled with weeping. A tremendous explosion of vile curses, oaths, and cries of torment followed hissing and screaming. As quickly as it came, the molten white lava receded to leave behind a greasy, green-tinted smoke lit by flashes of scarlet flame.

The rich man looked far away into the distance, to a misty region of light, clouded over by the vapor and smoke. He could perceive two men, Abraham and the poor man Lazarus. They stood on the edge of the misty region. In a choking and guttural hoarse voice, the rich man called out, "Father Abraham, have mercy on me. Send him who is by your side to me, so that he may dip the tip of his finger in water and cool my tongue. I am so tormented!"

The
TWENTIETH
Chapter

ABRAHAM SPOKE FORTH across the great chasm in admonition: "Son, remember in your lifetime you received your goods; and likewise, the poor beggar, evil things. You gave him nothing, nor did you take him into your household. Now he is comforted, and you are tormented."

The rich man looked down in hopeless despair.

"And besides this," continued Abraham, "between us and you is this great gulf so fixed that those here who would pass to you cannot. Neither can they pass to us who would come from thence."

The rich man's view for a moment dimmed. Vigorous ash and spewing molten lava from the pit (the great chasm) surrounded him afresh with blackened clouds of smoke, covering him with sparks and splatters of molten magma that fell upon his neck and clothing. His clothing smoldered afresh, his breath scorched, the taste of soot aflame in his mouth, his throat and lungs as if on fire. The blood seemed to rush to his head as if boiling, causing everything at that moment to seem glimmering red. He cried out, swaggering as if drunk. He staggered in a moment of delirium from one side to the other; his head, neck, and shoulders steamed in broiling sweat, scalding him like boiling water. He screamed with all his might, his breath steaming as if he were on fire within: *"O God, please have mercy! This is a living fire!"* He cried forth even more with foul-mouthed howling and agony, weeping in lamentation, "Father Abraham, I pray, *please* send the beggar to my father's house, for I have five brothers, to warn them about this place of torment lest they come here when they die!"

Abraham answered, "They have Moses and the prophets. Let them hear them—"

"Nay, father Abraham. But if one went to them from the dead, they would repent!" he cried.

More black billows of ash and smoke rose, obscuring the rich man from Abraham for a moment. The rich man could hear the disembodied voice of Abraham, *"If they hear not Moses and the prophets, then neither will they be persuaded, though one rose from the dead."*

New black sulfurous smoke and ash rose afresh. Everything grew redder before the rich man's eyes, his breath failing his lungs, strength failing his bones. He fell drunkenly. Barely lifting his head, he turned his attention to the stark inferno desert where the conflagration seemed to be taking on more and more space. On the horizon was a distant glow. Rushing across this baked expanse, a living white-hot, liquefied magma river called the Styx coursed in a sinuous flow, flooding level places, drowning valleys, raging and roaring, carrying souls in its currents toward the lake of fire.

The molten sea of fire crashed on a rocky beach like ocean waves of magma. A blue flame hovered over and above the rolling, bubbling surface, which periodically shot forth a stream of fire high into the super-heated air, like gigantic fountains. Pillars of flame spread at their summits to arc and sweep out in a feathering golden rain, the blackness penetrated only by a brief flare of blood-gleaming light. The effervescing frothy surface of sulfurous gas and molten magma hissed and shushed with torn sheets of flame that ran across the surface, producing an eerie glow.

Souls walked the shoreline, filled with shouts and uproar upon their lips: "Behold the Judge cometh in the Day of Wrath and disaster, and we shall be thrown into this lake of fire prepared for Satan and his fallen angels!" Likewise, swearing with violent despair followed on their tongues, calling on the names of dear loved ones for whom they would never see again and a God who no longer would heed to their beckoned calls. Stark visages of fear were upon their countenances as evil spirits wandered among them to fill them with anxiety and alarm.

A sudden "BONG" rang out through the caverns. Hollow, deep, and metallic, it gave forth a clear resonate sound of vibrating metal that lingered in the ears with a throbbing sensation. The bells of hell rang loudly throughout the cavernous regions rattling to its deepest depths.

Deep manly voices chanted.

The gates of hell were made of brass and iron with heavy ornamentation of satanic symbols, gargoyles, and mystical imagery. Above the bronze portal were written words, which changed for every reader of differing nationalities and tongues:

> This is the place of no reprieve. Depart from Me, ye cursed, into the everlasting lake of fire, which was prepared for the devil and his angels. Every tree that yielded no fruit shall be cut down and shall be cast into the lake of fire.

Assembled in mass before these gates were a vast host of demons, too many to number. They resembled Neanderthals, except their skins were black and scaly like that of a tortoise. Grisly hair grew sparse upon their heads, their ears catlike and their eyes ranging in a variety of colors such as from yellow to orange and to reddish-orange. Some demons had the look of being human but were nine feet and taller, while others were shorter. Some were grotesque with an Antaean build and extremely fierce features. Others were half-animal, half-human; some reptilian. Wickedly tortuous swords hung by their sides.

The deep masculine voices gathered in satanic intensity. A gong reverberated into a deep hum amongst a conglomeration of ghostly sounds. A vaporous white-gowned spirit-like male of exquisite beauty, bordering on sensuality, materialized from nowhere. Long flowing blond hair framed a fierce countenance with coal-black eyes that revealed deep charisma and witchcraft. The dominions bowed low in awe and worship of their underworld Lord: Lucifer. Satan was now the name given to him by his Creator, the God Almighty, when he was cast out of heaven.

Satan announced to his demonic hordes, "Prepare for this one who is called Jesus the Christ from Nazareth, the one who dared to boast that he was the Son of God!"

A herculean creature of great strength stood next to this one now called Satan. He carried an ornamental sword of silvery fire and had the appearance of great age. He wore a wrinkled face, his complexion white as though smeared with white grease paint. Dark circles framed eyes of dark hatred and malice. He wore a black cape over a long black tunic, belted with a band of ornate silver. He was known Abaddon, the keeper of hell. In a deep guttural voice, he implored Lord Satan, "I think this one designs to ensnare us for all ages of time, and thus into eternity."

Satan rebuked him in ferocious wrath, "I prepared the cross to crucify Him. It is now finished! He is subject to me!"

Demons hissed and murmured with horror. Abaddon glanced about the showground. "The dominions are disturbed. This Jesus of Nazareth called Lazarus forth from the grave!" exclaimed Abaddon in great fear. "One who has such power over death can only be the one and true Almighty God!" As he spoke, there came a rushing of wind with the sound of thunder, rolling and hissing.

A purplish-gold vaporous cloud of light appeared that grew as bright as the sun. Angels of a ferocious countenance of fire, armed with flaming swords, hovered. A great roar and a mighty voice of one accord arose among the armies of hell. Weapons of flaming swords resembling shafts of bluish flame and other swords of hewn metal came forth, ready to fight.

The gates of hell were shut and barred.

A booming voice of thunder shook the land of the infernal regions to its foremost foundations. Michael the archangel gave the command, *"Open now thy gates! The King of Glory, strong and powerful and mighty in battle, enters to set the captives free!"*

Abaddon instinctively unsheathed his sword in rebellion. *"And who is this King of Glory that we shall give heed to?"*

The
TWENTY-FIRST
Chapter

JESUS APPEARED FROM the cloud of light, His body beautiful and lightsome as that of a celestial being. He floated through the air, His long robe waving to and fro as if in a breeze. The robe reflected a dazzling white one moment and then a thousand brilliant colors the next as though sunbeams were passing over it. Circled about His chest was a golden band, His hair and beard as white as wool. His feet gleamed like burnished bronze.

The satanic hosts fell back in terror, a great number falling to their knees in awe while others cowered, covering their faces from this new spectacle of glory. Hell fell silent. Jesus floated down before Lucifer/Satan. This was Jesus as He'd never been seen before—mighty and fierce! Not safe! With a wild and violent ferocity, anger contended with rage. Jesus loomed dangerous and threatening. His eyes burned like flames of fire that pierced right through the dark spirit of Lucifer, whose eyes in return blazed with an electrical blue hue of wrath and hatred.

Charged with vicious, non-human power, Satan glowed with an unnatural aura. Bathed in fiery luminescence, he composed himself and smiled, stretching forth his arms. "The netherworld of the damned receives you." He laughed a sardonic laugh. It ricocheted and rebounded throughout the cavernous vicinities of his kingdom. The demonic hordes laughed with him, more in gesture than in a sense of amusement.

With great indignation, Jesus made the declaration, "Prince Lucifer, thine impious dominions, powers, rulers, and lords are now subdued. No longer is mankind left in thy subjection!" He raised a nail-pierced hand and light streamed through the puncture. The gates and bars of iron broke asunder. Ephemeral trumpets blasted as warring angels advanced. The Mighty Warrior Jesus stepped forth.

The legions and Abaddon fell back in disorder and array. Misery and torments of chaos and confusion increased a thousand-fold, all consumed with the awareness that from this hour forward, the character of Christ would commence acting with a new force and strength. They became with a heightened awareness that in an appointed time, they would be sent to the lake of fire that was meant for their punishment and that of Lucifer's and not meant for mankind. Men and women would suffer these torments if they would not accept the eternal salvation offered to them.

Seized with a sudden inexpressible fury, the demonic host raged against the warrior angels with flaming swords of fire and of hewn metal. The warring angels advanced with the sound of battle cries and trumpets amid a roar of demonic screams and howls. The demonic army met the angelic army in terrifying resistance, fighting as though their very existence was at stake. They clashed in an electrical display of terrible and awful calamity, their armor made incandescent as they came to blows, sparks flying and floating about. The cavern lit up from the conflict as huge sparks flashed from swords as they came into contact with metal against metal. A lingering electrical hue hung in the smoke-filled, condensed atmosphere, as many of the demonic warriors fell before the vast army of God, wounded but not unto mortal death, for they could not die.

Satan raged with wild and violent savagery. Raising his arms, he chanted in an ancient language that coalesced into a riotous vortex of a whirlwind that became stronger as Satan's incantations became wilder and more powerful. His hands suffused with an internal glow and brightened. Lightning bolts of yellow, orange, white, and blue exploded like thunderous cannon fire.

In his cloak of black, Abaddon weaved through the mayhem in towering vehemence, his sword of silvery fire drawn. He stalked among the biers of fallen demons writhing in pain, although no blood could be seen. Abaddon's attention wavered for a moment.

Michael the archangel emerged out of nowhere, his sword imbued with blue phosphorescence. It hummed and from the hilt forward, the blade grew to a hotter incandescence. Sensing the presence of the archangel, Abaddon turned to face Michael. He lunged. Michael barely parried the thrust before Abaddon struck again with a driving force.

Michael deflected the attack. They fenced with composure, skillful with dexterity and extraordinary deftness both in aerial and ground combat. For every move Abaddon made, Michael had an answer. Michael toyed with Abaddon. For all his size and strength, Abaddon moved with speed and poise and with the smoothness of a dancer while battling on the ground and with the agility of an acrobat while in mid-flight.

Abaddon feinted for Michael's head and then attempted a flank cut. Michael spun and then stabbed to the right cheek with Abaddon easily parrying the blow. Abaddon again attempted a head thrust and then went for the midsection. Michael parried, but the cutting edge of Abaddon's blade tore the sleeve at his shoulder.

Abaddon went airborne and came in fast. Michael met him in midflight. They twisted, rolled, reverse rolled, and quarter-turned into a forward roll, each trying to outmaneuver the other with precision thrusts and cuts, baffling in unexpected speed. The point of Abaddon's sword touched Michael's thigh. Michael parried the next blow, and with quick riposte, he struck Abaddon's cheek. For an instant, Abaddon's eyes flamed with anger. Several times they lunged, parried, thrust, and feinted while they touched the ground and leapt into the air as if carried by the wind.

In a series of powerful thrusts and counterthrusts, each was accompanied by a shower of cerulean blue flashes. Abaddon began to show signs of losing strength and resolve. Michael soared high into the air, and with a quarter-turn-half-roll, he swiftly plunged steeply downward to deal a powerful blow to Abaddon, running him through the chest, penetrating his breastplate and driving right on through the root of his extraterrestrial life form, thus rendering Abaddon into temporary paralysis. The wound sizzled as Abaddon let go a blood-curdling scream of pain and agony.

Smoke lingered in the area with the din of battle. The demons, with bloodthirsty savagery of lions, attacked each other.

Jesus confronted Satan, who was in a state of confusion and torment that could not be expressed by human tongue. Face to face and looking as though He would devour Satan, Jesus spoke. "I am He that liveth, and was dead; and behold, I am alive forevermore. I have the keys of hell and of death! All the advantages you acquired in the Garden with the fall of Adam you have now lost! You are a defeated foe, defeated by My blood and the cross!"

In a shaft of pale blue light and subject to a power not of his own, Lucifer sunk to his knees, subject to the Christ. Satan, now under Christ's authority, became aware that Christ's passion and death had despoiled him of his dominion. Satan labored in panic, causing him excruciating pain as he knew it was now over. This was not how he had planned it. He had fallen into the plans of the Almighty!

Jesus entered the threshold of the gates of hell. Smoke swirled at the mouth of the gate as He entered, the light of His glory lighting up the dark recesses, including that of the great chasm as prisoners in their cells scurried to their corners of darkness. Demons cried out in fright at the appearance of Jesus, the legions seized with dread. Serpentine voices cried out and screamed in panic, "It is the Christ! What have You come here to do? Wilt thou also crucify us?" Angels stepped forth to subdue these demonic creatures, confining them as they tried to resist to their utmost, binding them and leading them away.

Jesus wound His way to Abraham's bosom or Paradise, where archangels with a host of warrior angels guarded the misty region of light.

The
TWENTY-SECOND
Chapter

THE ENTRANCE INTO Abraham's bosom was a thick cloudy atmosphere of a luminescent mist, lit by an electromagnetic field that served as an artificial light source. It glowed with the delicate, iridescent hues of a rainbow and dissolved into a seemingly gentle fire seeping into the air. Angels surrounded Jesus and conducted Him triumphantly into this misty region of light as the angelic hosts sang melodic psalms of praise.

Moving through the bank of cloud, shafts of muted light pierced the dense fog. Strange ghost-like forms appeared and disappeared with blips of light flashing through from side to side and end to end. All the way through, harmonious singing of angelic beings faded in and out, pure and delicious to the senses, both enchanting and alluring.

Purification seemed to take place while progressing through the cloud and awakening to understanding things for what they really were rather than what they seemed to be. When emerging from this mist, a person would be transformed in body, soul, and mind and into a state of perfect wellbeing, which a mortal human soul could never achieve while on earth.

The mist took on an ethereal infusion of golden hues that dissipated into an absolute paradise of lush vegetation, the scent so heady that it almost intoxicated the senses, capable of making one overjoyed with a sense of overwhelming happiness and completeness.

This was Paradise.

Welcome to Abraham's bosom.

A slight breeze brought in refreshing air, not like the suffocating, stale air of hell.

Everything was harmonious in this environment. The flowers and vegetation seemed to dance and sway in rhythm with an all-encompassing pleasant hum.

Angels escorted Dismas, the thief on the cross who defended Jesus and of whom Jesus said would be with Him this day in Paradise, into Abraham's bosom. All the just who had lived before the time of Christ were assembled there, including the patriarchs (Moses, Noah, Enoch, Isaac, Jacob, and Joseph); Zacharias, Elizabeth, and their son John the Baptist; the judges (Samson, Gideon, and Joshua); the righteous kings (David, Solomon, Josiah, Joachim, and Jehosaphat); the prophets (Jeremiah, Isaiah, Daniel, Elisha, Elijah, and Samuel); and many others.

Out of the mist appeared Jesus as if coming in the clouds, accompanied by the angelic hosts. The souls of paradise released a great roar of joyous delight and acclamation. They fell prostrate before our Lord and Redeemer, the Savior of the world and mankind.

Jesus stretched forth His arms. His wounds seemed to be so transparent that one could see into their depths. The congregation of Abraham's bosom was mesmerized. Immediately, as though in a vision, they were suddenly thrust back in time to catch a glimpse of the crucifixion. It was poignant and real as if they had been there as witnesses of the dreadful scene.

The
TWENTY-THIRD
Chapter

FIRST THERE CAME the scourging. The scourging post was three feet in height with iron rings projecting from each side and placed near the top. The scourging taskforce, called Roman lectors, were professionals. These soldiers were experts in the fine brutal art of scourging. They were trained to beat a person until the barest flicker of life existed. It was a science and an art. If they slew someone, they too could be subject to scourging or even execution.

The lectors tore off the clothing of the rabbinical teacher Jesus until He stood naked.

They shackled His wrists to the iron rings, forcing Him to be stretched face down over the scourging post, His feet pointing outward, awaiting the "little death" as it was called by the Roman lectors.

A lector grabbed a leather bag and pulled out a short-handled scourging instrument called the flagra, sometimes called cat-o'-nine-tails, a whip made of leather thongs braided together. Woven into each thong were small weights of metal balls, sharp bits of metal, and bone. Nine of these leather straps fashioned the whip, thus the name "cat-o'-nine-tails." The axiom, "Don't let the cat out of the bag," referred to this whip, which was kept in a bag.

With tension, Jesus awaited the first blow with clenched jaws, every bit as torturous as receiving the blow. His skin was fragile and very sensitive from sweating drops of blood, a condition known as hematidrosis, in which severe anxiety releases chemicals that break down the capillaries in the sweat glands. It produces a small amount of bleeding into the glands, thus making the skin delicate and thin.

His body rigid in waiting, the muscles knotted in tormenting cramps, Jesus turned His head with raised eyebrows and eyed the flagra with uncertainty. He caught the lector's eye. With an ugly grin, the lector drew the tails through the fingers of his left hand. The color drained from the Lord's cheeks, and His lips drew tight against the teeth.

The lector raised his arm, and with full strength, he drew it down with a firm outburst of energy, sending all nine cat tails whistling through the air, the leather straps descending and fanning out across the back. The weights slapped Jesus' back with extreme force, causing deep bruises and contusions that broke open with further blows. Each link cut through the skin and deep into the flesh, curling in torturously around the chest and ribs, ripping the flesh, the pain intense.

The first blow took the Lord's breath with an involuntary gasp. Blood dribbled down His sides from pronounced red welts across the skin. Jesus grimaced as the second blow made grooves in the back and half across the chest with a V-shaped glut of small cuts. Sweat burst from the Lord's brow and stung His eyes. He held back a high-pitched scream as the third blow took off skin with a sucking tear, drawing blood from each knot where small metal weights and shards of metal fell. By the sixth blow, the whole back was raw.

By the twelfth, the cuts were deep in the flesh, leaving a horrible red mass, the very juice of life being torn away from the flesh with every lash. Burning tears filled the Lord's eyes as the brutal whips whistled over and over again through the air and across His back and shoulders, buttocks, and the back of His legs with blinding, tearing, and stinging pain. He was practically being flayed alive with the skin peeling back, causing intense, vicious burning with chunks of meat being stripped off at each stroke of the flagra. The Lord's body twitched at every blow.

Blood splattered the lector as he laughed with mocking glee, loving the debauchery of pain and drunk with a thirst for blood. The lector wiped the spatters of blood from his face with the back of his hand, smearing it across his nose and cheek as he paused a moment to catch his breath. Turning to his peers, he said in a guttural voice, "I like doing this." They laughed and slapped each other on the back in mocking jest.

"I *love* doing this!" he grunted. He smiled, passing the tails through his fingers to once more clear it of bits of flesh and blood. "It is my passion!" He spat and danced about, and with a howl, he let go of another powerful hurl, the weights crashing with bruising force into the ribs and outer regions of the Lord's chest. The lector swung halfway around between each blow to give more packed energy behind the swing. Jesus' whole body writhed in agony as He tried to catch His breath in short, spontaneous gasps.

The flogging continued. The lacerations went deep into the underlying skeletal muscles, producing quivering ribbons of bleeding flesh. Some of the veins were beginning to be laid bare, the muscles and sinews exposed. The remaining lashes sent Jesus writhing in grating torment, as He ground His teeth in agony, His self-control breaking. Panting, He grunted out in pain, "Uhhh—Father!" His teeth clenched with blood pouring down His back to puddle beneath Him. He shouted out throatily, "Father—ugggg-hhh—give mu—give me strength!" Another brutal slam of the whip hit his back with brutal force. "Uggghhhh!"

Under Hebrew law, the strikes were limited to thirty-nine, but under Roman punishment, the lashings were limited to one rule, which was that a man about to be crucified must not die. A spark of life had to remain so that the one being punished could feel the full agony on the cross. Men had been known to bite their tongues in two while being flogged. The Savior drew near to that critical point of injury in which He strained to fight off losing consciousness. From the large amount of blood loss, shock set in. The heart raced to pump blood. The blood pressure dropped. The kidneys stopped producing urine to maintain the volume that was left.

The Savior slouched over the scourging post, falling to His knees in a blackened puddle of blood, His back so shredded that part of the spine was exposed by the deep, deep cuts. The post and the stone tiles on either side were blotched and spattered with black-red gore. From the Lord's neck to the waist, the bones were laid bare. His flesh hung in blackened, tattered strips. His limp body was finally cut loose from the post, the smell of blood thick in the air with an odor that was heavy and sweet.

When all was done, Jesus could not move as a result of paralyzing muscle spasms and cramps. It felt as though someone had taken an iron plate with claws and heated it up until red hot from the inferno fires of a blacksmith's oven and placed it on the Lord's back with the tongs imbedded three-inches deep into the chest, ribs, back, and sides—and then clamped tight! The scene faded into the next, to that of the crucifixion itself.

The
TWENTY-FOURTH
Chapter

ABENADAR WAS THE *carnifex servorum* or the centurion in charge of the crucifixion detail. Along with Longinus, Marcus, and one other, Abenadar held down the prisoner Jesus. Longinus placed the sharp six-inch iron spike in the center of the Lord's wrist. He hammered the spike through the wrist about an inch below the palm and through the median nerve, the largest going out of the hand. The nail crushed the nerve as it was pounded in, producing the kind of pain you feel when you bang your elbow and hit your funny bone, only the pain much more amplified. Jesus experienced pain comparable to that of someone taking a pair of pliers and squeezing, twisting, and crushing the nerve. He squirmed and fought not to scream out in pain. It was absolutely unbearable, beyond words to describe, bringing about a new word: *excruciating,* which literally means "out of the cross." Five more hammer strokes, and the spike was deep into the plank with a final blow to the head of the spike to turn it upward so the hand and wrist would not slip or wrench free.

Marcus shoved the saddle, called the *sedile*, which resembled a rhinoceros horn, solid into Jesus' crotch to take most of the weight off His hands. A short upright spike was attached to the *sedile* in such a way as to allow it to insert into the anus. Abenadar drove another spike into and through the feet, again causing the nerves to be crushed, creating a similar type of pain. The cross vibrated with the hammering blows and shudders of the Lord's body.

Anguished cries of the Lord echoed throughout the vicinity.

When finished, the crucifixion detail drew the cross upward and into the hole that was bored into the rock for the cross to slip into. With a jolt, the cross fell into the hole with a trembling and settling thud, sending a world of hurt and pain as the median nerves in the wrists and feet were crushed for the second time. With the arms stretched out beyond their normal length, both shoulders became dislocated, fulfilling the Old Testament prophecy in Psalm 22 that foretold the crucifixion eight hundred years before, saying, "My bones are out of joint."

The wounds in the wrists and hands sent fire down through the arms. Jesus wavered between consciousness and unconsciousness, darkness and pain, and then drifted back and forth between darkness and pain, the fainting only temporarily relieving the pain. As Jesus drifted back into the horrible reality of consciousness, His back, arms, hands, feet, and crotch throbbed with a dull, endless aching, His anus vile, bleeding, sore, and swollen. He defecated and urinated, the body's way of relieving itself under stress, which caused Him extreme embarrassment and humiliation.

The pain accumulated until there was no moment of respite. He tried to blink away the blood and the clammy sweat, redirecting it from trickling into His eyes. He squinted against the sunlight that hurt His blood-filled eyes, His head pounding with a seismic, pulsating headache as He fought off nausea and light-headedness.

Below, the curious crowd waited with bated breath, fascinated by the torture, and glad it was not them suffering on the cross. The macabre scene played out with an exaggerating slowness. Dying should be a private thing, but not there! This was a public execution with the humility of being spied upon by the obscene spectacle of people standing around to gawk at Jesus' naked body and uncovered genitals, while all the while making fun of Him, spitting, and hurling accusations and insults.

Jesus closed His eyes. He became aware of a new sensation. Thirst! His lips were dry, the mouth parched, His blood hot, the skin filled with the perception of a running fever. He opened His mouth, the dryness of which produced the necessity of a drop of cool water.

Cool water, please. Please? were the screaming thoughts agonizing in His mind. "I thirst!" He said aloud. It was fast becoming a mental torment. He tried to swallow, but the dried membranes tore at the already tortured throat. He felt as if he had stones in the sinuses.

Marcus offered Him vinegar, which Jesus refused. Water was denied. His tongue thickened with cottonmouth, which was dryness with no saliva to moisten. His hands and feet were swelling, and the *sedile* dug deep into His genitals. It was impossible for the Lord to change positions. The cramping muscles twitched, the real horror just beginning.

One by one, the muscles in the back knotted in tight cramps. It moved through the shoulders, then the thorax and down into the abdomen. Two hours had gone by with every muscle locked in solid knots. The torment was beyond endurance as the muscles underwent a slow but steady contraction. Each hour was an eternity. The cramps in the neck were rigid, tight, and burned like fire, the head flushed against the vertical beam of the cross.

Flies buzzed around His head, getting into His eyes, nostrils, and mouth. He shook His head, blinking and snorting to keep the flies from entering His nostrils and eyes. He sputtered and spewed to get them away from His mouth, spittle running down His chin and beard.

Tiny blood vessels that fed the nerves squeezed flat, and with the lack of blood circulation, there came a numbing paralysis. There was no end to the suffering. Only the matter of suffering and the equalizing measure of hurt and the slow death erosion of the cells, muscles, bones, tissue, emotions, mind, spirit, blood, and heartbeat.

Birds of prey circled. Hoping, waiting for a meal of dead carcass.

Jesus looked out with blood-filled eyes that morphed into burning coals of fire as He looked out over the immense crowd of those in Paradise.

The
TWENTY-FIFTH
Chapter

THE VISION SLOWLY faded, the silence passionate, and the assembly moved to a solitary act of weeping. Something piqued the interest of Jesus. There was a movement in the vast crowd. The crowd separated like the parting of the Red Sea. Adam and Eve moved through the great throng with a sheepish blush and with the anguish of shame still written upon their countenance. Jesus opened His arms in compassion to them as they approached the Great Lion of Judah.

Adam, whose name meant "reddish-clay" or "reddish-brown," was of olive complexion, like those of Mediterranean descent. His features were chiseled with refinement. He was impressive in stature and muscular perfection. Eve was an exquisite splendorous beauty, regal in attractiveness, both in physical features and the full blossoming of womanhood. She had a light rosy beige skin tone with olive undertones. Her eyes were mesmerizing with an icy blue hue and hair as golden as those of Norwegian descent.

Both fell prostrate in humility before Jesus, who bid them rise. He laid a hand on each of them. "Be not of shame or of guilt, for as it is written, 'The first man Adam became a living being. The last Adam became a living spirit.' As the first man, Adam, you were made as a living soul from the earth; and I, the second Adam, was made as a quickening spirit from Heaven. You were born without a mother and I without a father. And you, Eve, were made from Adam's flesh and bone and not by nature."

Jesus spoke loudly enough for all to hear, "For since by a man came death, by a man comes also the resurrection of the dead. For as in Adam all die, even so in Me shall all be made alive. I have conquered death and have provided a means of deliverance from the first Adam's fall into sin. Come unto Me, all you who were created in My image, who were deceived by the prince of this world and condemned to death. Live now by the power of the cross. I, the second Adam, have taken back dominion from Lucifer, who is now reviled as Satan because no man could have obtained it on his own. I was despised and rejected of men, a man acquainted with sorrow and grief. I was despised and was esteemed not. They cried forth, 'We do not want this man to reign over us!' They had no use for Me."

Jesus paused for emphasis. "They turned away from My miracles, My commandments, and My love for them. I was wounded for your transgressions; I was bruised for your iniquities. I was an atoning sacrifice, not a victim of circumstances. I laid down My life. No man taketh it from Me, but I lay it down Myself. I did all of this for you! 'The Lord hath laid on Him the iniquity of us all.' Heed these words, 'Of us all.' These are words of triumph! They open every prison door. They signify a way out of bondage and entry into the kingdom of God! Enter into His kingdom, My precious saints. Death cannot hold me in the grave! Death hath no more dominion over you, as it does not have dominion over Me! You are partakers in this victory. The cross would be an empty and tragic failure without the empty grave. Therefore, arise with me, saints, in resurrection power. I have come to set the captives free!"

An enormous and unrestrained roar erupted with cacophonous hymns of praise, adoration, and thanksgiving. The Lord took Adam and Eve's hands, and all those in Abraham's bosom arose with Jesus and ascended from hell.

Hell shook with violence, fissures opening with flames and magma. Across the great chasm, Abaddon, Satan, and the great demonic horde saw their defeat with awesome, terrifying fear! Abaddon glanced around in great trepidation, lashing out at Satan, "Now we shall receive large torments and infinite punishment! We are defeated by His death and resurrection!"

When Jesus was laid in the grave, Satan had triumphed. Now he was fearful that Jesus would indeed rise from the grave in resurrection. Turning to Abaddon, he said, "Set a guard about the tomb! Seek to hold Jesus as a prisoner!"

The
TWENTY-SIXTH
Chapter

CAIAPHAS LAY AWAKE in the dark hours of the early morning, listening to the night sounds. In the darkness of the dungeon, Joseph of Arimathea awoke from his slumber to pull his cloak about him. Marcus pulled his mantle over himself against the morning chill. He and another soldier settled down next to two other sleeping guards of the tomb watch.

The tomb detail slept in a semi-circle with their heads pointed in the direction of those on watch, swords in their grip as was the custom for a Roman soldier on guard duty. There were always two on watch while the others slept in six-hour shifts. Those on guard were entailed to be alert and not slumbering, for to fall asleep on watch was punishable by death. The two now on sentry duty were Abenadar and Longinus. Both gathered around a small fire, watching the smoke rise.

* * *

Through the smoke of incense, Pilate offered up prayers to his gods, clearly troubled and confused. Near him, an oil lamp burned with a feeble light, slightly illuminating the stone floor and casting weird shadows upon the walls. Thinking of the day's events, his eyes drifted upward with the smoke to search the shadows that filled every corner of the small inner room. His thoughts wandered. *I fear the wrath of the gods for not sparing this god-man.* An ominous foreboding grew over him as he stared into the darkness. He cast an eye toward the idols. *I fancy, could He have been a species of demigod? Is it possible?*

Shivering, he got to his feet, backing away from the idols in sudden fear of them. His back touched the wall. "I wonder if this man Jesus may have really been the king of the Jews for whom the Magi had come from the East to worship, and for whom I heard of prophecies foretold." He caught himself whispering out loud. He shuddered at verbally announcing his inward expression. Fearing the gods may have heard him, a chill ran down his spine and his skin prickled with bristly goosebumps. Holding out his arm, he rubbed a hand over the raised hairs. His superstitious mind, borne out of the culture of the Roman world and that of his heritage and past, overtook him once more. He surveyed the inner chamber. The shadows seemed to move and then become still again.

Turning away, he rested the side of his head against the wall in contemplation with his eyes raised upwards. *It might have been more prudent to have spared His life.* Glancing back at the idols and burning incense, his notions continued to haunt him. He swallowed his Adam's apple moving up and down with each swallow. A lump seemed to be in his throat. *Perhaps this Jesus was a secret enemy of both of our gods and of the Emperor.*

Dazed, he found himself wandering into the hallway. *Who knows whether His death would not be a triumph to my gods?* He glanced back at the inner room he had just deserted.

Coming up to his sleeping chambers, he heard someone breathing heavily as if in a troubled sleep. He looked in upon his sleeping wife, Procula. She seemed agitated and disturbed in her slumber. He yawned and rubbed his tired eyes.

Procula groaned and wept alternately. *She must be having a dream,* he thought.

* * *

Herod the Tetrarch was having his own disturbed sleep. His wife, Herodias—who had been his adulterous lover while she was the wife of Herod's brother—lay peacefully at his side. Out through the balcony of their sleeping chambers and onto the rooftop of Martha's house, a young teenage lad, Mark, the nephew of Peter, huddled asleep under a blanket. The house moved with a light tremor, awakening Mark. Heavy-eyed with sleep, his eyes caught the twinkling of a campfire through the trees and shrubbery in the distance, in the direction of the garden of the tombs. Down below in the upper room, the disciples, with the exception of John and Peter, huddled together, some in sleep and others awake in sorrow. The insignificant tremor awoke one of the disciples, but only briefly, before he fell asleep again.

In the living quarters, Mary Magdalene, Mary the daughter of Cleophas, Salome, Joanna, Mary the mother of James, and Mary Salome all sat around a long table covered with a tablecloth hanging to the floor with bundles of herbs heaped about them. They were busy preparing perfumes and mixing herbs and spices. Small flasks of sweet oil and water of spikenard remained close by with bunches of flowers, including irises and lilies. The small flasks of oil and the jars of water/spikenard sloshed about momentarily from the small tremor.

Mary, the mother of Jesus, glanced about the room, feeling the slight tremor beneath her feet.

No one seemed to be disturbed by it. Mary went to the window and looked out in grief as the other women busied themselves in their tasks. The crickets chirruped. The leaves rustled in a slight breeze, and the moon was full and bright. She watched as clouds began to obscure the moon.

* * *

The leaves and branches shivered and shifted in the nightly breeze, and flecks of moonlight and shadows of tossing leaves fell across the faces of Abenadar and Longinus. The campfire of the tomb watch burned brightly. The noises of the night amplified until suddenly there was deathly silence. There was no breeze, and the crickets were no longer chirruping. All was silent and ominous. An all-encompassing muteness saturated the area.

Longinus sat attentively in reaction to the silence with a keen awareness that something was amiss. He leaned over to Abenadar who sat motionlessly, "I like not this quietude."

Abenadar nodded.

Together, their senses heightened, Longinus' and Abenadar's restless eyes roamed the trees and shrubbery. Abenadar bent over and touched a torch to the fire, his attention on the surroundings. Moaning seemed to be coming from the darkness beyond the light of the campfire, a low far-off sighing like a low wind. The two soldiers threw a look at each other.

"Maybe it's the gods," Abenadar suggested.

Both chuckled. Nervous and with apprehension, their eyes darted to and fro around the outer rim of the tomb garden and then along the trees. They discerned no movement of the leaves, and not a breath of a breeze. They were tense, coiled, and ready to spring into action at any given moment. The firelight licked the shadows, elongating them.

They heard a sighing moan, far off yet seemingly close by.

Longinus was disquieted. "Maybe they're watching us," he said under bated breath.

Their ease and well-being were quickly draining out of the both of them when the fire suddenly flared briefly, alarming the two.

The
TWENTY-SEVENTH
Chapter

A GENTLE BREEZE stirred the flames of a shepherd's campfire. In a remote spot among the hills, pre-dawn approached the Judean desert landscape where three shepherds gathered for warmth. Above and unbeknownst to them, a miracle of a curious spectacle was happening as multi-hued lights fluttered faintly in the northern sky. The earth beneath their feet trembled slightly but went unnoticed.

One shepherd sitting by the fire straightened, stretched his lanky frame, and sauntered over to a bush close by to gather more brushwood. Another shepherd, squatting on his heels, stirred the kindling to excite the flame. The firewood spit and sputtered, the drift of burning wood scenting the cool night air, the smoke stinging his eyes. The third shepherd raised his bony neck to gaze up at the flying sparks leaping and pirouetting in the night air. Gawking upward, his eyes suddenly held open, his mind stuck in a confusion that he could not describe. He became numb and he had trouble accepting what he observed in the sky as reality. He could not move.

The shepherd gathering fuel for the fire came back and added more sticks to the blaze. He noticed his companion's perplexity. He too, looked upward, his expression giving way to surprise and astonishment. The shepherd kindling the flame, upon noticing the other two, followed their gaze skyward and rose with an involuntary start. All three men pondered the irregular shafts of light with a growing sense of amazement mingled with fear. They were filled with personal insignificance and powerlessness as they were confronted by the extraordinary situation.

Glowing ribbons, gossamer veils, and brilliant rays of light danced and spread, rippling with sky-filling swirls. The breeze picked up and then came to an abrupt stop. For a brief period, there was absolute silence—no sound of wind, and no chirps from night critters. The desert was dead. Then it began.

They heard a slight noise in the distance that was barely audible at first. Gradually, the commotion became definite while it grew intrusively louder. The shepherds listened, the blare becoming stronger and more prevalent. There came a cracking sound like that of a thunderclap.

The dogs whimpered. The sound grew brassier and seemed to be moving closer. It was as if choirs were singing in unison with thunder. The breeze kicked up again. In a few moments, it blew in gusts. Heat lightning flashed in the distance amid the irregular shafts of light. With each flash of lightning, the delicate curtains increased with an otherworldly glow, dazzling in beauty.

The wind gusts grew more intense until they became a mighty rushing of wind, forcing the shepherds to shield their faces with their hands, but all the while watching the chain lightning rip across the gossamer veils of light. Thunder clapped, the lightning increased with the activity of an intense spectacular electrical exhibition of furious power, mesmerizing the shepherds as they stood speechless, listening to the overwhelming sound that now seemed only a few yards away. The dogs whimpered more loudly and dramatically until they were baring teeth and growling.

With each discharge of lightning, a kaleidoscopic symmetrical figure of dazzling beauty appeared, resembling stars or diamonds of various colors with each light dissolving into angels. Soon there was a vast heavenly host of angels, countless in number, men of lofty stature, beautiful in an array of indescribable glory, shining like stars. The heavens were alive and were quickly becoming seven times more luminous than the sun.

Unexpectedly, the noise took a quick turn and could now be felt. At one point, the shepherd's hearts were pounding within their temples, and they felt as if their stomachs would fly out of their mouths. Then, as swiftly as it came, the wind died down and all was quiet. The men's hearts pounded within their chests. The dogs were upset, and they barked with wild frenzy.

Soon there was now a distant sound of voices. The dogs positioned themselves amongst the men, whimpering and curling up on the ground. The voices were singing thunderous praises to the risen Lord and Savior, becoming louder and more melodious.

Christ Is Risen
The world below lies desolate, Christ is risen
The spirits of evil are fallen, Christ is risen
The angels rejoice, Christ is risen

The tombs of the dead are empty
The first of the sleepers
Jesus Christ that was crucified has risen again
Glory and power are His forever and ever.

The melodious strains rolled among the foothills and mountains and then died away. They become like whispers, growing fainter until the light in the northern hemisphere paled into a bright orb like the luster of a pearl on the horizon. It then became softer but much richer than the brightest moon until it was a slight impressionable globe upon vanishing.

The shepherds remained where they were, enchanted by the remarkable spectacle they had never seen before and would never see again. Soon they came out of their stupor. They began to shout and weep and praised God with joy over what they witnessed.

The
TWENTY-EIGHTH
Chapter

CLOUDS SLITHERED ACROSS the full moon like knife blades. The moon slipped in and out of the clouds with eerie shades of brightness and dullness. The garden of the tombs was alive with unreality and spookiness, the shades of moonlight dripping through the foliage of the trees, moving and shivering in the world of light and shadow.

Longinus and Abenadar were on their feet. They were listening, their bodies frozen, their faces pale and unreal in the floating light. Abenadar handed the torch to Longinus. He motioned with a nod for Longinus to check the dark edges of the perimeter. Longinus gave back the torch with the same motion of a mimicking nod and with a non-verbal expression: *"You do it!"* Abenadar curtly handed the torch back to Longinus with an unspoken order: *"Do it!"*

Longinus, with reluctant hesitation, slunk into the outer dark boundaries of the garden, drawing his sword. Abenadar turned and looked about with apprehension, glancing back toward the tomb where the moaning seemed to be coming from. He scratched at the earth with his studded leather boots, testing their traction. Reflexively, he drew his sword from its scabbard with an echoing ring in the chilling air. He gingerly tested its edge. Leaning over, he removed one of the burning logs from the fire and held it up like a torch, all the while letting out a slow breath. He moved with uncertainty in the direction of the tomb.

He was close to the outside edge of the huge stone sealing off the entry to the tomb when the torch dimmed, the flickering growing fainter until it was like a candle flame, barely glowing. The darkness closed in upon him. With apprehension, he looked about, his eyes wide and vulnerable.

Longinus returned from the perimeter, mystified by the same dullness of his own torch. He glanced at the fire, which was now low and flickering. He set the torch down. Without warning, a white flash and a resounding boom of thunder knocked Abenadar and Longinus off their feet.

* * *

Moonlight bathed a balcony in cool blues, washing out any colors. The aroma of fragrant flowers in decorative pots wafted on the breath of a slight breeze as curtains billowed and swirled inward into an elegantly furnished and spacious bedchamber. Moonlight fluttered across the features of a sleeping Herodias who tossed and turned; her breathing accelerated with rapid eye movement under closed eyelids; her face, fingers, and legs twitching; her circadian rhythm interrupted as she woke groggily from a deep slumber—afraid!

She sat up and looked around the spacious apartment. She reached out to touch the sleeping Herod's shoulder. Tossing in his sleep, Herod relaxed; his face contorting into a half-smile—dreaming.

Within his dream, music flowed in a sensual pulse, filling the banquet hall of Herod's palatial palace with the high whine of pipes and the mad strumming of citharas. Lutes, harps, and lyres accompanied angry pounding drums that bellowed forth to the big ring of crashing cymbals, all in quick rhythm to sistrums and castanets.

A feast in the honor of Herod's birthday was underway, his guests being lords, high-ranking officials and officers, leading citizens of Galilee, and others from the foreign lands of Greece, Egypt, and Rome as well as barbarians from the distant republics. Together, they watched a lone woman as she danced seductively, her arms fanning like wings in an up-and-down fashion with quick wave-like echoing movements, as though she were simulating flight with her chin held high. The music slowed to a soft air, and the drummers came in with no more than a soft beat.

Salome, in her seventeenth year, was light in her movement, both sensuous and innocent, and sumptuous in appearance. She was sexually exciting as she lasciviously danced the dance of Ishtar, fluttering a fan in one hand and then raising both arms above and over her head as she pirouetted on tiptoe. She danced with buoyancy and naughty gestures, drifting about and among the tables and couches, arousing the desires of male guests who reached out with inebriated arms, but always coming short with empty hands as she often succeeded in eluding them, never once missing a beat.

Herodias filled the cup of the tetrarch with fragrant, cool red wine. All the while she somberly studied Herod who, with the look of pleasure, was mesmerized in his drunken state of mind. With sudden vehemence, she skewered him with a statement within a question: "Why do you look too much at her?"

Herod looked down at the fair nimbus with a hypnotic gaze. She seemed to be floating without touching the floor, giving a fluid, languid, mesmerizing quality to her dance. Light captured the golden highlights of her hair like sunlight, gleaming in one place and then another. Her eyes were that of crystallized emeralds. She danced with high spiritedness.

Herod's heart melted within him, her beauty stimulating his senses, and he desired her.

Arising from his cushion, he felt an irresistible need to speak of her beauty, "Thy princely daughter. She has nimble toes and dances like a nymph."

Herodias scrutinized Herod with jealous eyes. She rebuked the tetrarch, speaking in a tongue of mournful annoyance: "I see in your complexion that you worship her as a goddess."

Herod ignored her, indifferent to what she supposed or thought. He continued in his acclamation, "Is she not like a butterfly, quivering in the wind?"

Salome came near the flight of marble steps where Herod stood in surveillance. With the precision and skill of a ballerina, she climbed the marble steps with a twirl, her feet touching each step in perfect time. Reaching the step immediately below the top and just before Herod, she hesitated in a breathless moment, teasing the tetrarch, and then bowed with arms outstretched. She drew herself up and threw her head back with her mouth in open enticement, exposing her throat. She slid her hands down to her waist while lowering her head until, with the sinful expression of a downturned face, she looked up with an attempting lure, her eyes fastened on Herod, and then danced backward to the lower level, never missing a beat.

This had an effect on the tetrarch. Running down the flight of steps and onto the marble floor, Herod sluggishly reached out with an overexcited and trembling hand. Extending his open palm, he said, "Come hither to me."

Salome came to a stop, poising herself on her naked toes, and then sprang like a panther, gliding over to Herod. She regarded Herod with a flirtatious twinkle in her eyes and then began to weave a provocatively tight circle of dance around him, enticing him with her cavorting. She whirled close to Herod, face to face, her hips swaying before him, her body flowing like silk, her movements beautifully interwoven. She breathed with a meaningful, effortless grace and intoxicating quality that awakened Herod's sensory desires. Herod's mind grew receptive to physical pleasure. Holding the goblet of wine out in front of him, he caught the rhythm of the music, swaying and moving drunkenly, sometimes in a pace with her and other times out of it.

Her body appeared to melt before the tetrarch. His eyes beamed with excitement on the dancer, quivering with eagerness. Chuckling, he said, "Oh, how whimsical you are." His eyes dilated in a rush of fervent anticipation as they roamed over her hourglass body, taking in everything he could see and imagine. His heart rate increased, his blood pressure rose, and his face flushed. His bodily muscles tensed with aching desire. He expressed his yearning with exclamations of passionate speech: "*Mmm,* how delightful you are!"

Salome leaned to within inches of Herod's face, teasingly flashing her tongue, seduction oozing from her fleshy lips. Herod felt her minted hot breath upon his face and tasted the flavor of her intoxicating aromatic perfume. She also felt the heat and passion arising from him and bore within her both delight and shame. With sudden precociousness, she whispered, "The tetrarch looks at me with the eyes of a hungry lion. Is it not strange that my mother's lover should look upon me with such lust?"

Herod was caught off guard by her precocity and then gurgled, "How sweet the air is, and much wine flows." Salome puckered her lips demurely as she moved closer. Her arms moved up and around the nape of Herod's neck without touching.

Herod's whole body tingled, and his breathing becoming quicker and shallower with emotion.

Moistening his lips, he spoke flowing words with shortness of breath, "Whatsoever is your delight, my child, ask upon me what I may give. Even if it is—" his breath gave way, "—even unto half—" His heart pounded in his throat, his brain fogged with the effects of wine. Gushing forth the words from a dry throat, he impassioned with emotion from the heart, "—even unto half my kingdom."

Salome looked Herod straight into the eyes, her eyes questioning him. A feral look came over her face. Dropping her eyes, she raised them again, timid and yet inquiring. Tossing her hair, she pursed her lips and replied, "Yes, there is something I delight."

With a devious smile, she moved away, but only to come again to pirouette in a cold chaste movement of the feet and body. Her emerald eyes were sparkling and captivating, her gaze was setting Herod on fire with a heat of lust burning deep within his soul. It was an enchanting, unquenchable desire, the kind that arises when something is prohibited, and that seems to be more attractive when it is out of reach.

Herod frowned. Suddenly he was sober, his gaze strange. He tried to focus with eyes as pale as ice. He faltered backward, the goblet of wine falling from his grasp to hit the floor with a loud metallic crash. His mouth fell open. The red wine oozed from his lips as blood to run down his chin, staining his royal garments.

Salome danced cold and chaste before Herod with a silver tray bearing the head of John the Baptist in a slow and enticing dance. Tilting her head slowly to the left, she pronounced in a low tone of voice, "I can see with my own eyes how your red wine is fading."

Salome twirled away from him and to her mother Herodias, who stood by in close proximity, all in her own little world. In doing so, Salome slipped on a pool of blood. The head rolled off the tray and hit the floor with a hard smack, rolling until it thumped against Herodias' feet with the face up, revealing the head of Salome!

At first, Herodias was frozen in horror and then she let out a blood-curdling scream that morphed into a haunting, forlorn wind that filled the palace and dissolved into the sound of beating wings, akin to that of bass drums beating at a low rate of speed.

The angel of death ethereally materialized in a long black trailing robe of sackcloth, its filmy wings fluttering, and its long black hair flowing. His countenance was that of warrior-like fierceness, his skin glowing like burnished bronze. His eyes blazed with a fire of amber as it came to face Herod.

The death angel drew back, unsheathing a long scimitar with a singing ring. He flashed forward, and in one swift movement, the scimitar whistled through the air, smiting Herod. With a cavernous voice, the death angel announced, *"Not many days henceforth when you are adorned as a god, you shall be eaten of worms!"*

The thunderous voice set off an earthquake. The walls of the palace pulsated. Statues fell. Candelabras, oil lamps, and torches tumbled. Herod's throne split in half. Herod's hair turned into red mire filled with worms. A crown of thorns appeared on his head. Long snake-like worms slithered from the orifice of the mouth.

* * *

Herod awoke from his dream with great agony, falling out of his bed. An earthquake was in full force, rattling and knocking over objects and items. With a primal scream and anguished cry, Herod clawed at his throat, exploding across the room in frenzy, tripping over rubble and broken fragments of sculptures and pillars, debris falling all around him. He plummeted to the floor, scratching and tearing at his throat, screaming out in torment, "I'm choking! Give me ice!"

Herodias climbed out of the bed amid the earthshaking, chunks of ceiling crashing down around her. She tried to keep her footing, making her way across the room to calm the mad tetrarch who was still tearing at his throat until it was bleeding and who was still shouting, "Loosen my mantle, quick!"

Herod regained his footing, stumbling to keep his balance. Again he lost his footing in the quake, plunging to his knees, weakened from his thrashing about among the crashing articles and objects. "Quick!" Exhausted, he barely spoke with a whisper, "My mouth—my mouth is like fire!" He lay back, whimpering in madness of mind.

The
TWENTY-NINTH
Chapter

THE SHEPHERDS, WITH a sense of reverence caused by the majestic and powerful event they had just witnessed, now seemed to be paralyzed, their eyes fixed on something happening before them. They shivered from head to foot.

The trees were trembling. The earth before them groaned and lurched on the Judean desert. The ground unexpectedly swelled before them in a dome shape to a height of about four feet. With the split of a thunderclap, a fissure ripped open with a loud and continuous hissing. Fine ash and smoke rose. The depths of hell opened as myriad ghostly spirits of the saints ascended from Abraham's bosom.

The land was now in the full upheaval of an earthquake.

Mark, Peter's nephew, woke with a start as the rooftop swayed. Inside Martha's house, the disciples also were shaken awake. Downstairs, the exhausted women, who had fallen asleep after preparing the spices, were instantly wide awake with alarm as the house wobbled on its foundations.

Joseph of Arimathea stirred as the quake hit his cell. The violence tossed Caiaphas out of bed. Pilate was jolted awake from his sleep in the doorway of his bedchamber. Procula awakened with dreadful fright.

The earthquake subsided.

Abenadar and Longinus scrambled to their feet in shock and alarm. As if by a sixth sense, Longinus whirled around, his skin prickling, aware of something from behind. He and Abenadar drew their swords. The rest of the tomb watch, awakened by the thunderous bolt of lightning and the earthquake, stood close by with trepidation. All together, they stood entranced at the sight before them.

The night sky was of a rosy hue, with an ever-increasing afterglow. It looked as if the sun were rising over the treetops. Two stars appeared on the rise, oscillating with intensity. They swelled into well-defined, sphere-shaped suns, floating and spinning like wheels of fire above the tomb watch, turning the surrounding area from differing shades of yellowish-orange to blue and white. The night air crackled with electrical energy.

The two golden suns wobbled and shuddered and then drifted toward the tomb watch. In the gleam of the two suns, two figures of dazzling brilliance appeared, causing all to turn their backs and shoulders from the intense brightness, causing the tomb watch to be sharply outlined in shadows against the ground. The two figures, being angels, had the forms of men, but with a supernatural quality about them. They pulsated with subtle iridescence. A long filmy train began at their shoulders, flowing down their backs to the ground, giving the impression of wings. In a flash, the trees quivered, as if someone were shaking them.

A sonic boom detonated the air with shock waves. It blew the tomb watch to the ground and carried undulating airwaves that swelled into a flare of blue-white light, shattering into a circle of blinding radiance. It lit the skyline with a brief flash from one end to the other.

Seconds seemed like hours. The tomb watch gave way to a hypnotic, paralyzing trance, unable to move, frozen in abject fear. They squinted against the glare, their faces registering total astonishment and extreme terror as they looked upon the face of the mightiest of the Lord's host. The light turned into a beautiful blue, fading gradually, and then seemed to give off a yellowish cast, embellishing the whole area.

Abenadar turned away, shutting his eyes but keeping his hands before him to shield himself from the light. When he opened his eyes again, he saw the atmosphere had cleared and the landscape had taken on the color of old yellow damask with everyone looking jaundiced.

He looked back at the radiant source. In the brightest center of the translucent void, something moved. It broke loose from its position and lowered itself to the earth to advance threateningly upon the tomb watch as if to crush them with its huge and fiery weight. The sensation during these moments was terrible.

This extraterrestrial being was Gabriel, arrayed in armor like that of a warrior and standing to a full height of thirteen feet. He ambled toward the tomb watch guards, who quaked from head to foot, sinking into deep comas and appearing as dead men. Gabriel changed his course and approached the sepulcher. He cast a strange elongated human-like shadow across the two-ton stone that sealed the entrance to the tomb. He tore the stone from its moorings, carried it to the top of the incline, and took a seat on top of it. Two other angels then entered the sepulcher.

In the pre-dawn light, the body of Jesus lay in repose on the slab of stone. The two angels positioned themselves on either side of the slab, stretching their filmy wings out across the body, touching the tips of their wings like the cherubim on either side of the ark of the covenant.

An intense blast of energy erupted inside the burial cloth as the Lord's spirit and body reunited, levitating the body from the impact and burning an image of the Christ into the cloth. The Messiah laughed as He rose and shook off the winding sheet wrapping His body. The whole sepulcher was lit up by His radiant suspension of energy.

A lion-like roar peeled apart the ambiance of the chamber as a frightening apparition burst from the floor of the tomb. The body of a serpent-like creature with the likes of a red dragon, the head of a human, and the face of Lucifer launched itself at Jesus' feet. The Lord placed His foot on the head of the serpent to bruise it. The apparition disappeared into the floor in a guttural display of agony and a harsh, piercing scream.

One who had the appearance of the Son of God came forth in majesty and glory from the tomb, draped only in a loincloth. His countenance was as lightning, and His skin glistened as though covered with oil. This was the one the priests and elders ridiculed, saying, "He saved others; Himself He cannot save." A host of angels in the form of aerial spirits surrounded the tomb, bowing low in adoration before the redeemer with welcoming songs of praise. With a radiant burst of light, Jesus was gone, the burial cloths trailing back into the tomb.

The
THIRTIETH
Chapter

A FULL MOON brightened the ridge of Golgotha. The three crosses were stark and sharply defined as Mary Magdalene, Mary the mother of James, and Salome passed below carrying sacks filled with spices on their way to the garden tomb. The path before them was flooded with silvery light, fringed by a dark wall of brush with a low shroud of patchy mist slithering across their path.

Suddenly, their attention was caught up by an energetic movement in the bushes. Hearing rustling noises that continued for several minutes, the women looked on in concern. Pastel and whitish in the moonlight, a small shadowy figure sauntered out from the brush, crossing their path to lose itself among some trees. Mary Magdalene let out a sigh, patting her chest in relief to see that it was only a small dog.

The women drew abreast of the garden, ignorant of what had taken place. They spoke among themselves. Mary Magdalene proposed the question, "Who shall roll away the stone?" They looked despairingly at each other.

"Do you know of anyone?" asked Salome.

"Perhaps we should just leave the spices on the stone and wait until someone comes to open it," said Mary the mother of James. They nodded in agreement.

Entering the garden leading to the sepulcher, they stood aghast. Before them, a ground-hugging mist enveloped the soldier's tent and enshrouded the tomb watch guards as they lay in repose, giving them a death-like appearance. Boldly, Mary Magdalene took a few steps forward and drew near the prostrate soldiers with trepidation. She slowly realized that they were out stone cold and not dead. She looked back at the other women who had joined her. Together they entered the garden and stepped gingerly around the tomb detail so as not to disturb them.

As they pressed forward, a current of air fanned the unattended fire. Firelight flickered among the trees in strange shadowy shapes. A log fell, sending up sparks, startling the women. Regaining composure, Mary Magdalene gathered up the burning torch Longinus had used, which still lay near the fire. She paused and then proceeded to the empty tomb, her breathing shallow, and her nerves troubling her stomach with vague nausea.

Drawing nearer to the sepulcher, the torchlight wavered on the stone face of the tomb. Up until now, they had not noticed that the stone had been rolled away. They saw the burial wrappings strewn out from the mouth of the sepulcher and immediately became aware they were facing the black opening of the tomb. They hung back afraid. They looked about with an apprehensive suspicion and then at the guards who were still comatose.

Mary Magdalene gathered her courage and entered the tomb, her heart pounding in her throat. The blaze of the torch crept along the walls of the tomb, the darkness retreating. The rushing flame was like a flag flapping in a breeze, the crackling loud in the enclosed space. The air warmed with the torch's pitchy blaze as it dropped blotches of fire on the hard rocky floor. The space was heavy with the fragrance of spices.

Mary followed the bindings to where the burial shroud lay, encompassing the slab of stone where Jesus' body once laid. The large winding sheet rested on the slab, doubled over with the spices Nicodemus and Joseph of Arimathea had used when wrapping the body. She noticed the head napkin was rolled up in a tight bundle where the head of Jesus had reclined. With bated breath, Mary retreated, her feet scraping with an echoing whisper on the dust-laden rock floor.

Outside the tomb, Mary tried to grasp what had happened. She took in the surrounding environment: the garden, the tent, and the passed-out tomb watch. She recognized Longinus and Abenadar. Tears streamed down her cheeks when she suddenly remembered the other Mary and Salome. She turned. With a trembling voice, she announced, "They have taken Him. I must tell the others." She dropped the torch and raced out of the garden, leaving behind a bewildered Mary and Salome.

Puzzled, both women entered the tomb. They paused, mystified. An indistinct and soft bronze glow filled the tomb. Behind them and slightly to each side, two shapes glittered like sunlight reflecting off dust particles, mesmeric and yet engaging.

"Why do you seek the living among the dead?"

Startled, Mary and Salome whirled around to see surreal shafts of light crisscrossing the interior of the tomb, casting multicolored rays in many directions. The two angels stood on either side of the women in shining garments, shimmering like a mirage. The women were afraid and bowed with their faces to the ground, the rainbow light flickering across them.

The second angel spoke in a soothing voice, "He is not here; He has risen. Remember how He spoke to you when He was yet in Galilee, saying, 'The Son of Man must be delivered into the hands of sinful men, and be crucified, and on the third day rise again.'"

The THIRTY-FIRST Chapter

THE DOOR BURST OPEN, spilling moonlight in through the open doorway. Mary Magdalene stood in a shadowy profile of the entryway, her shadow falling upon an exhausted and sleeping Peter. She scrambled over to him and clawed at his shoulders, her face close to his, screaming, "Peter! Peter!" John, unbeknownst to her, lay not too far away on another cot. He wakened and rose up on one elbow. "They have taken away the Lord's body!" cried Mary. John climbed out of bed hurriedly as an increasingly hysterical Mary wailed even more, "They have taken Him away!"

Filled with compassion, John lifted her away from Peter. Mary buried her head in his shoulders, sobbing. "We know not where they laid Him."

John tried to console and to calm her. "Mary, sweet Mary." He buried his face in her long hair while holding her, gently patting her back. He looked over to Peter, who struggled to gather his senses as he crawled groggily off the cot and into his tunic and sandals.

Grumpily, he asked John if he knew where they had buried Jesus. John nodded an affirmative. "Then we must go and see for ourselves," Peter said.

* * *

Longinus was the first to rouse, completely in a daze. With an ear-piercing screech, he bolted upright as if awakening from a nightmare, his eyes wide and consumed with an overwhelming fear with the anticipation of danger. He moved without delay to arouse the others, going from one to the next and finally to Abenadar. In wild desperation, he shook Abenadar, but there was no response. Hesitating only for a moment, he shook Abenadar once again, not sure whether he was dead or alive. Abenadar finally came to, grabbing for his sword. The tomb watch guards, already on their feet, staggered around like drunken men.

They hurried to the city on trembling limbs.

* * *

Torches moved swiftly through the trees and bushes as if those carrying them were running. The tomb detail fled from the garden tomb. On the opposite side of the bushes and trees, John outran Peter.

Heavily panting, John collapsed on his knees next to the guards' tent, resting his hand on one of its poles. His eyes roamed the landscape while he caught his breath. The mist was thinning. He noticed the tombstone had been rolled away and to the side. He couldn't believe it! He looked about, searching for someone or some kind of evidence of foul play, but there was none. With uncertainty, he got up and came closer to the tomb.

He noticed the wrapping bandages and followed them cautiously to the open cavity of the tomb. He peered inside but did not enter. Whirling around, he fell dizzy to his knees with panic written all over his features. Peter arrived. John glanced up at Peter. Compulsively, Peter entered the tomb. After a beat, he stumbled out, grieving.

John's eyes were fixed on him. "Did Jesus not say that He would come back to life again?"

Peter wavered on his feet and gave John a disheartened look. "Hasten to Bethany, to the house of Martha and Mary. I am certain the others are hiding there. Tell them what we have seen." He looked back at the tomb and then to John with a look of consternation. "The authorities are going to claim that we have removed the body and will cause more trouble."

Mary Magdalene rose from her position in a secluded spot of the garden, weeping in silence as she watched Peter and John leave the premises. Sniffling, she wiped her nose on the sleeve of her garment and directed her steps toward the sepulcher, her garments quite moist from dew and her hair in disheveled masses over her shoulders.

She stopped before the opening of the tomb, mustering the courage to enter. Being alone, she was rather uncertain about whether she should enter. With trepidation, she willed herself to go into the tomb once more.

Leaning across the threshold, her hair fell across her face, obscuring her vision. She heard a soft voice, "Why do you cry?" Brushing her hair back, she noticed the tomb was illuminated with a glowing light.

Mary saw two young men, the same angels as before, sitting on either end of the slab where Christ's body had lain. Astonished and overwhelmed with grief and not realizing they were angels, she choked back her tears while replying, "Because they have taken my Lord away, and I do not know where they have put Him." Nothing more was said as she held the gaze of the two angels until her attention fell to that of the wrapping bandages leading out of the tomb.

Transfixed, she tracked the bandages outside of the burial chamber and into the garden.

Unkempt, Mary's hair was wild and tousled, and her cheeks were streaked with tears. Dazed, she shook with an emotional display of fury and hatred toward whoever had taken the body. She wandered about resembling an insane person, her grief and sorrow mixing like honey and vinegar. Almost on the breath of a wind, she heard an inner voice, or so she thought: *"Why are you crying? Whom do you seek?"*

She turned searchingly toward the voice, her hair floating loosely in a gentle breeze.

With annoyance, she brushed her hair away from her face, throwing it back over her shoulders. As she did so, she perceived an indistinct human shape perhaps ten paces from her, clothed in white radiance, and partly hidden by the shadows of a tree, as dawn was now upon them. Somewhat startled, she thought he was the gardener, yet he seemed vaguely familiar. "If you have taken Him away, please tell me where you have put Him, and I will go and get Him," she said.

"Mary."

She instantly recognized the Lord's voice and fell prostrate to the ground, trembling like a leaf with fear and excitement. Jesus stood before her. Stretching her hands out to Him, she burst out in tears, "Rabboni!"

Mary could hardly lift her shaking hands spread out before her in adoration and worship. Her lovely features and slender form convulsed in emotions far too great to convey. She could not lift her eyes as she stretched her trembling hands out to touch His feet. Jesus motioned for her to be still. "Touch Me not, Mary, for I have not yet ascended unto the Father, your God, and My God. Go and tell the others." In saying this, He was gone.

Mary Magdalene rose, trembling with tears in her eyes. At once, she ran off to tell the good news.

The
THIRTY-SECOND
Chapter

JOSEPH OF ARIMATHEA knelt in the middle of the dungeon in fervent prayer while four angels stood before him, their transparency luminous and shivering with an enchanting light. An orb swirled from the corner of the ceiling, taking form with an intensity that filled the chamber with light as bright as the sun. Joseph opened his eyes and immediately was face down in fear. The form laid a hand upon his shoulder. "Fear not, Joseph. Look upon Me, for it is I."

Joseph raised his head. The angels were no longer there, but the room was lit with a soft glow. Jesus stood before him. Joseph raised himself to a sitting position and said, "Rabboni Elias."

"I am not Elias, but Jesus of Nazareth, whose body you buried in your tomb."

"Blessed be He who comes in the Name of the Lord," replied Joseph. While saying this, a crack appeared in the wall that further opened until Joseph found himself alone on the outside walls of Jerusalem in the middle of a deserted road.

Coming toward him were floating balls of fire, their flames sending out elongated shadows and shafts of light into the underbrush where Joseph now hid, peering out motionless and watching. As the shifting fireballs came closer, Joseph realized that they were torches carried by the tomb watch guards as they converged upon and rushed through the city gates. Joseph emerged from the underbrush, glancing at the retreating figures as he stood.

Pulling his cloak about him, he vanished down the road into the darkness and was all but invisible in the shadows.

* * *

Caiaphas sat on the side of the bed with his elbows on his knees and his hands over his eyes, seized with shaking, taken aback from the earthquake and the previous day's events. There he remained for a long time until an orderly entered. "Rabboni, I am sorry to disturb you, but the tomb watch is here to speak with you. They insist on seeing you immediately."

Alarmed, Caiaphas dressed right away and hurried down to the lobby.

Abenadar paced back and forth in obvious distress. He was uncertain how to explain the night's current events. His eyes lifted to catch a melancholy glance from Longinus and knew that Caiaphas had just entered the lobby. Marcus and the rest of the tomb detail lingered nearby, full of anxiety.

Caiaphas marched over to Abenadar, his expression full of worry and concern.

Abenadar's face was colorless and full of apprehension. He was not quite sure how to describe what had happened, for he knew how Caiaphas and the Sanhedrin would construe their testimony about the resurrection of the Christ. He drew a deep breath, but he could not find the right words. All he could muster was, "The Galilean is raised from the grave!"

Caiaphas remained expressionless, but inside, he was in shocked amazement. He tried to speak, his lips moving, but nothing came out other than a gasp.

Longinus stepped forward. "While we were yet guarding the tomb this night, there was an earthquake—"

"Yes—yes!" interrupted Caiaphas with impatience.

"There appeared to us three gods with the brilliance of a midday sun. They rolled away the stone and entered the tomb and—"

"And we fell as dead men," intervened Abenadar.

Caiaphas watched them, examining them with cold forbearance. "You have gone mad." He turned away from them and then turned back. "Maybe you were drunk or dreaming."

"Verily, the things we saw this night were real. We were not in a drunken stupor, nor of slumber!" exclaimed Longinus.

"As the Most High liveth, I do not believe you!" countered Caiaphas.

Marcus stepped forward. "What they say is true. We are all witnesses."

"You suppose us to be mad," interjected Abenadar, "but of a surety, something greater than nature itself has taken place this very night." He wet his lips. "We had not the time to think or to speak, such were the goings-on."

"The One who had been crucified, He was the One who came forth from the grave. We heard the angel proclaim Him as Majesty and the King of Glory," stated Marcus.

Caiaphas examined them long and hard, clearly unsettled, sensing they were telling the truth. Raising his chin, he closed his eyes and moaned. Lowering his head, he rubbed his temples with his index fingers for a moment and then gazed back at them breathing a heavy sigh. "I regret placing you at the tomb." Turning from them, he clasped his hands behind his back and began to pace, giving them a sideways glance now and then. He stopped pacing and pulled long on his beard. He peered back at them. "If any of these things of which you speak should become public, then all will believe in this Jesus."

Nothing more was said, with the tomb watch becoming restless. They were about ready to leave when Caiaphas halted them. "Wait! Wait!" Caiaphas' voice stayed them. "Tell no one of these things you have seen."

The
THIRTY-THIRD
Chapter

THE SOFT AND ORANGE ruddiness of sunrise embellished the morning with an indulgent warmth and pleasant harmony. Joanna, Mary the daughter of Cleophas, and Mary Salome (not to be confused with Salome, Herodias' daughter) were engrossed in grief, unsure of what was about to transpire. They soon found their sorrow turn from mourning to perplexity when they came around the corner of the garden leading to the sepulcher. In the early morning light, they could see that the stone had been rolled away. Lingering about the place, the women suddenly fell to their faces, seeing they were not alone.

With a countenance of lightning, the angel Gabriel appeared, sitting on the huge stone that had sealed the entrance to the tomb. "Fear not, for I know that you seek Him who was crucified. He is not here for He is risen as He said." He motioned to the tomb. "Come see the place where the Lord lay."

The women lifted themselves from the ground and entered the tomb. The two angels who previously appeared were sitting at the foot and head of the slab where Jesus had been laid, their long linen robes so bright the women were nearly blinded. The women were terrified but also amazed. They bowed low.

The angel to their left announced, "Go quickly and tell His disciples and Peter, 'He has risen from the dead,' and behold, He is going before you into Galilee. There you shall see Him. Lo, I have told you."

The angels took on a fiery luminescence with the air about them seeming to bend. Their heavenly bodies flickered as the flame of a candle in a slight breeze and then dissipated with melting light.

The women left with haste, quivering with joy and astonishment. In their merriment, they almost ran into Jesus. "All hail," He said. Shocked, they fell at His feet to worship Him. He smiled. "Fear not. Go and tell My brethren to go into Galilee, and there they shall see Me."

Jesus faded away, the pathway now empty before them.

* * *

"We thought the gods had come to destroy us. They were more visible than the light of the sun," explained Longinus of the night's events.

Pilate stood immobilized before the tomb watch, pierced to his very soul. "You are full of superstitions; your minds made of cheese." He scrutinized the group in a state of self-conscious distress and agitation. "Certainly, you are full of imagination."

Abenadar stepped forward. "Most sovereign governor, we are bound by oath of testament to communicate to you the facts. These things were beyond the natural. This Jesus is no longer in the tomb."

Pilate seized Abenadar in a hard stare, and then his eyes pounced on the rest of the tomb watch. "His gods have taken advantage of your weaknesses. Can you not see they have conjured up all kinds of magic pictures to alarm you, to take full power over you?" Quavering with anxiety, Pilate concealed his worry to the best of his power. He rubbed his bald pate and turned away in consternation, shaken.

Closing his eyes, he pinched the bridge of his nose, fighting with the rules of administration and feelings of guilt. *Why have I allowed myself to get involved in such a predicament?* he thought. Not wanting the tomb watch to know of his weakness, he strained to maintain control of his feelings. He half turned his shoulder and advised, "I counsel you to keep silence and not recount such silly tales, especially to the priests, for you would get the worst of it from them."

Longinus and Abenadar shared a furtive glance. *Oops!* Pilate dismissed them with a curt wave of his hand.

Sauntering with a brisk step along the corridor, Pilate felt ill. He was flushed, nauseated, and faint. Sweat broke out on his brow. Clearly disturbed and fainthearted, he entered the inner room, his sanctum, and set about offering sacrifices to his idols. "I believe none of these imaginary fables."

He offered more incense, his hands shaking visibly.

* * *

The early hours of dawn tumbled into the room from the window, rendering its image on the floor, casting most of the room in deep shadow. Peter sat with his head in his hands; unmoving, anguished, and numb. Having just left the tomb, he found himself alone; grief-stricken and dazed, and somewhat fearful.

"I will not turn away a contrite and broken heart."

Startled, Peter lifted his eyes. Jesus stood before him. Peter's breathing stopped. The blood rushed to his head as he was nearly in the throes of a faint. "Be not afraid, Peter; it is I. It is not a vision you see, nor am I a spirit, for a ghost has no body as you see that I do. Death no longer holds Me in the grave, for I have risen on the third day as I said I would do." Jesus knelt in front of Peter and put a hand on his shoulder. "Out of fear, you denied me. You have a faithless heart. Be steadfast now. Repent and have not a hard heart, for I have a work for you."

A glistening tear dropped down Peter's cheek, but he sat silent. For the first time, he had no words.

The
THIRTY-FOURTH
Chapter

CAIAPHAS CIRCLED THE soldiers of the tomb watch. "Either you had an understanding with His disciples for carrying off the body of Jesus, or else you have fabricated these accounts to justify your own conduct." He postured with his head raised as he eyed them in a careful, intimidating, and interrogative manner, reading their faces. The soldiers remained silent under his scrutiny. He raised his chin further, glaring at them. "How much did they pay you to take the body?"

The soldiers spoke not a word.

"Are your tongues so swollen with lies that you cannot speak?" Caiaphas waited a moment and then put a hand to his ear. "What? You still won't answer the question?" Still, there was no reaction, so he returned to his seat of authority. "Come, I only want to hear from you. Tell us where you took the body, and we will pay you much more than His disciples did."

"We did not take the body of the Galilean!" stated Abenadar under Caiaphas' querulous gaze. "We were so moved with fear that we were like dead men."

"I will have you punished severely if you do not forthwith produce the body!" erupted Caiaphas. A ponderous silence fell. Archelaus stepped over to confer with Caiaphas, who nodded. Archelaus left the room, and Caiaphas gazed upon the group. "I see you have conceived your stories very well." He steepled his fingers across the bridge of his nose in thought. "Maybe you fell asleep when the disciples came and carried away the body." He placed a forefinger over his mouth in contemplation. "Or is it that you've been beguiled with witchcraft?"

Archelaus returned with an orderly who carried leather pouches, each filled with silver. Caiaphas proffered them. "You are to tell the people that the disciples of Jesus came in the night while you slept and stole away the body." Each soldier was given a pouch. "Do as I say, and all will be well." The tomb watch hesitated in taking the pouches of silver. "Which is it to be? The time for profit is at hand!"

Eyeing the leather pouches, Abenadar expressed boisterously, "Did I not hear tale of a Judas Iscariot who was given thirty pieces of silver to betray his Master? How is it that we say the disciples stole away the body while we slept—how could we know, if we were asleep?"

Caiaphas was about to say something, but he was interrupted by Marcus. "This would contradict what we have already told Pilate."

Longinus eyed the bag of money. "Indeed," spoke up Longinus, "it is of a surety as to what Marcus says." Hearing the clinking together of coins, Longinus accepted the bag with reluctant hesitation, feeling its weight. Abenadar gave him a look of reprimand. Again, Longinus was in doubt as to whether he should accept the bribe. "If Pilate should hear of this, and more so hear that the disciples stole away the body while we slept, he will order our deaths."

The tomb watch looked uncertainly to one another. Each was horrified by the thought of bringing themselves up for charges of sleeping at their posts. After all, what Longinus had just said was true in the matter of dire consequences. This offense would be punishable by death.

"If Governor Pilate should hear of it, we will satisfy him and secure you," Caiaphas countered. Fearing they would silence their testimony, Caiaphas further reiterated, "Pilate would, no more than you, desire to have such a report circulate."

A pouch was handed to Abenadar. He shoved it away, "Gold makes one stupid," he snapped. He then quoted an old Roman proverb: "'A fortune made by a lying tongue is a deadly snare. It leads men to destruction,' and we would be forever in your debt!"

"Ah, perhaps it is so," divulged Caiaphas, giving him an eye, "but also note—does it not feel most gratifying on the palm of your hand, knowing that you may obtain things of yearning?"

Abenadar stared back with a steady look in his eyes, his mouth drawn into a tight straight line. "I, in charge of the tomb watch, will not accept this bribe, nor will I vary our first statement, even in the smallest degree!"

Caiaphas flew off the seat of authority in a heat of rage, filled with uncontrollable, powerful emotions, almost to the point of madness. The intensity of the room was punishing. With an imposition to exercise his will, he exclaimed, "You will do as I have said, or I will have you punished!"

The room fell into silence.

With strong resolve and conviction, Abenadar obstinately countered, "I will *not,* to the *utmost* of my power and conviction, declare this lie to the public or otherwise!"

No more was said. Selling their integrity for a few silver coins, the remaining members of the tomb watch retreated from the presence of the Sanhedrin, taking with them their bribe money. They had come with the startling message of truth and now left with the burden of a few coins, their tongues full of a lying report supported by the priests.

The
THIRTY-FIFTH
Chapter

IT WAS QUIET overall, except for the tramp of feet on a soft path and heavy breathing. A cart rattled and creaked over stones as it swayed from side to side. A man labored, leading an ox and cart bearing a corpse wrapped in linen cloths. Two men shuffled behind with shovels across their backs.

The cart stopped.

The two men stumbled forward to the front of the cart, staring intently, their faces pale. Their dark and anxious eyes looked toward the man who had been guiding the ox and cart. He stood riveted in place with a white-knuckled grip on the wooden cart. His countenance was frozen with a fixed stare. He viewed rubble everywhere and a warren of open shallow graves. Burial clothes were scattered all over.

All three men saw and felt what was before them, curious about what had happened. Above them, Mount Zion rose impressively over the valley of Gehenna. They could also see the Kedron Valley and the Mount of Olives. Running like a vivid scar along a crease in Gehenna was a slimy low spot in a deep narrow glen just outside of Jerusalem. There, for the price of thirty pieces of silver, the corpses of paupers could be buried. This was where the three grave-diggers stood.

In olden times, this valley of Gehenna was the site of infant sacrifices. One nightmare after another occurred on this soil. Children were made to pass through the fire as they were placed in the glowing brass hands of a god named Molech. A fire was made in the belly of the idol, heating the brass statue from the inside. A beating drum drowned out the screams of children and kept their mothers and fathers from hearing the voices of their little ones so that their hearts might not be moved.

Now, Gehenna was a garbage dump of refuse where the lifeless bodies of criminals and the carcasses of animals were thrown, a place of crawling worms and maggots. In this cursed and loathsome valley, perpetual fires were kept burning to consume the filth and cadavers that were continually thrown into the pile of rubbish. The Roman legion used it as a place for the cremation of the dead. It was the only group known to practice cremation in that region.

* * *

The tomb of David was located at the base of the stairs that went down into the Kedron Valley from where the Temple stood. It was positioned alongside a pool fed by the waters of a conduit from Gihon Spring. From the interior of the tomb, the dark silhouette of a man stood in the light of an entryway. Visible from head to foot, the shadowed man held a staff while he watched a double rank of Roman soldiers as they marched past the edifice.

The lofty tomb threw a twilight shadow over the path before it. From the echoes of time, the shaded image emerged from the entrance of the tomb and lumbered down the steps to the street below. Passing from shadow into light, the dark figure seemed to transform into an ancient royal personage, dressed in the royal robes of a king. He then followed the soldiers. As he neared them, he took upon himself a lofty demeanor of unbroken dignity and marched with a warrior's step.

* * *

In the old section of Jerusalem, there stood a young man on a rooftop looking down at the dark, narrow cobbled alleyways and dirty streets of the marketplace, filled with hundreds of shops and bazaars, teeming with humanity. Most of the people were of the poor working class, but there were foreigners as well.

Moments later, the young man, Marcus, found himself among the wares of the bustling marketplace. It rang with the babbling, haggling, and screeching of excited shopkeepers as they enticed potential customers to visit their booths filled with artifacts and oddball necessities. They displayed everything from gold and silver jewelry to tools and whips.

Marcus was soon walking through the back streets of the old Jerusalem marketplace as though he had come out of a dream. Unpleasant smells were overwhelming in the heat, and he could feel the bites of many flies. The odors were of a crowded, unventilated marketplace filled with ordinary unwashed people making their day-to-day purchases. Booths, kiosks, and sukkahs dotted the marketplace landscape with fresh fish caught that morning in the Sea of Galilee, displayed on mounds of ice in baskets. Fly-covered raw chunks of meat dangled from hooks alongside chicken heads cleaned and presented on tables.

Marcus walked through the crowded alleyway, rubbing elbows with people along the avenue as they stopped to talk to each other. He overheard people talking amongst themselves of the previous day's events and heard vendors catering their wares and goods.

A little child wandered alone, crying because she lost her mother in the crowd, not being able to find her in the endless sea of buyers and sellers. The sight of this brought Marcus to tears as he recalled when his own mother gave her life for him ten years before. She had leaned over his bruised and broken body to protect him from the crush of a stampeding crowd as he shivered in terror, watching the Roman soldiers bludgeon to death two thousand people at Pilate's command.

Shaking the horrible nightmarish images from his mind, Marcus passed by bazaars selling clothing and household utensils. Specialized shops sold spices and colorful condiments that added to the aroma-charged air. Many beggars, cripples, and blind people sat around the edges.

Marcus came across a beggar woman propped against a wall. She was starving and clothed in rags and held a small child in her lap who was tugging at her. The mother cried out, "Alms, alms?" Piteously she held out her scrawny hands as Marcus approached. He stopped and gave her a piece of silver from his leather pouch. In a slight way, this made him feel better as he agonized within himself the guilt of having taken the bribe of silver coins.

Men led animals across the way while a group of menfolk squatted in the dirt gambling.

A woman cleaning fish and preparing to fry them on an open brazier in front of her booth scattered the entrails everywhere, some hitting the gamblers who turned to hiss and curse her while others laughed. For the great majority, this was their world of dirt, poverty, disease, and death.

Some of the fish guts hit Marcus. Stopping to brush off the mess, his attention was arrested by a dead body being carried off the streets as if this were an everyday occurrence, a shroud wrapped around the body in a slipshod manner, a stiff leg showing. A few Roman soldiers crossed the path leading a couple of prisoners across the way and into a side alley with the prisoners' elbows bound behind their backs. A Mitanni trader pushed past with a couple of loaded donkeys. Nearly naked children played in the street. Suddenly, everyone scattered and pressed against the walls as a detachment of foot soldiers passed by, led by a centurion who was flanked on either side by his officers. Many grumbled at their presence and hurled insults.

The
THIRTY-SIXTH
Chapter

AFTER THE SOLDIERS marched past, Marcus stopped by a booth to examine tools. A woman bargained with a shop owner across the way. Suddenly, there was much confusion and panic. He turned to see what the commotion was all about.

Out of the intricate labyrinth of alleys and passageways of the old city, the resurrected dead came forth, much in the same appearance as when they were alive but with burial cloths and wrappings clinging and hanging from them. The market crowd gave way in revulsion and dreadfulness. People ran in alarm down the streets in all directions, not sure of where to go. A man ran down a narrow avenue only to encounter dead humans who were now alive; another sprinted in the opposite direction, his progress made ever more difficult as a growing number of the resurrected dead filled the streets.

A merchant dashed through an enclosure that held donkeys, which resulted in a stampede of the animals running, kicking, and braying in fright. The gamblers scrambled in all directions, with one dashing through the booth of the woman cleaning and preparing fish, slamming into her table and brazier, strewing fish and guts everywhere. Another gambler flew headlong through an archway of a bazaar, crashing into a cage full of chickens, scattering them into the street. One of the gamblers turned and plowed helplessly into a pottery shop, causing a deafening noise from the wreckage.

High overhead, from the top of two- and three-story structures, observers could make out the resurrected dead entering a narrow intersection where blind beggars squatted, sensing something eerie going on around them. From a cobbled alleyway, the resurrected dead turned into the market street where rows of dyed wool and yarn hung from overhead, strung along sapling poles. An unfortunate collision resulted between a retreating beggar and a vendor crossing the street with a cask of red dye upon his shoulder. The narrow avenue became saturated in red dye with everyone slipping, falling, and hopping around, trying to avoid being stained. The beggar man picked himself up and ran recklessly past a resurrected woman whose eyes scanned the crowd, looking for someone. Once she found what she was searching for, she started in that direction.

Marcus, wide-eyed, watched the spectacle before him. He found himself repulsed even as he marveled at the spectacle before him as the resurrected dead continued toward the Temple area. Some left faint red footprints in the dust from stepping into the red dye, causing greater alarm and hysteria among the masses. Two men raced toward Marcus. They parted around him, leaving him face to face with the resurrected woman. She now stood before him swathed in grave clothes, her skin pasty white, her hair scraggly, and her matted nails long and curved. He was frightened.

She spoke, breaking the tension. "Marcus."

Upon hearing his name, Marcus could not move. He stood rooted to the ground in astonishment. Thoughts raced through his mind. He looked deeply into this resurrected woman's face. There was a strange familiarity about her. Abruptly, his face registered the full impact of the moment as it dawned on him. He knew this woman but thought, *It can't be!* A guttural scream welled up in his throat, but it never became audible. His lips moved as he glanced around. *I'm aware of my surroundings,* he glanced at his arm, *and I don't appear to be hallucinating.*

The resurrected woman, Rebecca, the mother of Marcus, held out her hand to comfort her young son, who was now sixteen years of age. A blood-curdling scream from down the street alarmed Marcus. He jumped back, crazed and frenzied. "This can't be! You couldn't possibly—"

Rebecca tried reaching out to him again.

Marcus stumbled and fell backward. Rebecca tried to grab him to break his fall, but she missed his shoulders. She captured his cheeks but his face slipped through her fingers.

Marcus lay stretched out on the ground in horror. She extended her hands once more, but Marcus clambered to his feet. "Don't come any closer!" he said in a hoarse whisper.

Rebecca attempted to reach out again. Marcus shrank back. In desperation, she declared, "Marcus, my son, I am not a spirit. I am of flesh. I am real." She stretched out her hand with palm up in an open gesture. For a moment, no one dared to move. Marcus stood back in shock as Rebecca extended her hand nearer with tears forming in her eyes. Marcus flinched. His labored breathing seemed to ease and soften. Rebecca spoke gently. "Marcus, I was raised from the dead." There was a sound of scuffling and voices behind her. She turned.

A curious crowd had gathered, many in awe and bewilderment upon seeing Rebecca. The marketplace became quiet. They had known her ten years before and knew of her death while preserving the life of her only son. Seeing their panic and trepidation, she entreated them, "I—we—have come forth from the grave to bring testimony to the resurrection of the Nazarene, the one called Jesus, who has risen from the grave this very day! We too have been resurrected in His power!"

The
THIRTY-SEVENTH
Chapter

A CLATTERING OF hooves interrupted Rebecca. The Roman cavalry, led by the centurion, had made its way into the market square. They moved in laboriously through the narrow avenue, occupying nearly the whole street. A double rank of infantry brought up the rear, their steady march like heavy machinery that could crush everything in its path. The crowd rolled back and huddled together, close to the edge of the street, as the soldiers and cavalry advanced amidst scattering jests and mockery. Some of the crowd spit at them behind their backs. The horses stamped and reared, becoming unmanageable.

Two ancient men of old seemed to emerge mysteriously from the crowd. The two men boldly pressed forward to the center of the street. They wore garments of days past, and both had the appearance of ancient patriarchs. One held a staff in one hand to assist the tremulous gait of age and to establish the impression of authority. The other patriarch had a hoary beard that descended to his chest. He rotated in a relaxed manner, studying the crowd unhurried while making a gesture of encouragement. He wore the mantle of a prophet and thus spoke to the throng. "I am the prophet Elijah, the Tishbite." An outcry emanated from the people as the prophet continued, "I was taken up into heaven by a fiery chariot." Elijah gestured toward the other ancient one. "This man is Enoch, who was translated by the God of all Ages and who saw no death."

Once again and without warning, the horses began to rear and become unmanageable.

The mounted troops had difficulty commanding their steeds, but the horses continued to romp back and forth in distress. From among them emerged an ancient one of royal personage, holding up a scepter of authority. He blanched not a step as he scanned a determined eye here and there and throughout the vicinity of the crowd.

The centurion, surrounded by the crowd, cried out with a loud, gruff, and brutal voice, "Who is this old clumsy lout?" He looked at the royal personage. "Are you mad, old man?"

The royal personage turned to confront his assailant. His eyes, face, and attitude revealed to all that he was an individual of commanding and august form. With a voice of solemn and yet warlike resonance, he announced, "I am one of the days of old, who commanded the ranks of Israel. I am King David!"

The centurion, his mounted cavalry, and infantry seemed to be held at bay, having no power. Awe and delirium ascended from the crowd as they half encompassed King David, marveling at the venerable grandeur before them. They murmured in low indistinct tones, but with a continuous sound as they became aware of more patriarchs and saints of old—Abraham, Samuel, Joseph, Isaac, Jacob, Noah, Samson, and Elisha—as they ambled into view from amongst the people, simultaneously announcing who they were.

King David continued with his proclamation, "I and the great patriarchs of old are here because it was accorded us to appear once again on earth as witnesses and to declare the resurrection of the One of whom I prophesied, our Lord Jesus, the Messiah."

With many souls being stirred at the words of King David, the centurion cast a severe and cruel eye over the multitude and then held a hard look on King David, beholding him in burning wrath.

In a bold voice, King David continued, "Sing unto the Lord a new song, O inhabitants of Jerusalem—a new song, for He has done marvelous things. He has made known His salvation. His righteousness has He openly shown in the sight of the heathen. His name shall be a byword in these very streets."

The centurion, with his gaze fixed upon King David, sat on his horse in the open space. Uttering no words, he commanded his troops to commence a slow forward march, passing a disheveled Longinus who staggered down the cobbled stone avenue of the marketplace gripping a bag of silver, his expression heavy.

Longinus became aware of the upheaval surrounding him. Looking around, he turned to face Judas of Gaulon. Coming to an abrupt halt, he fell back a couple of steps and froze.

Longinus could not mask the horror he felt! *Did Judas come back to the living to haunt me?* His vision blurred as he rushed forward past Judas, his world in a spiral. He stumbled about, without reason or thought, as though he were inebriated. The leather bag of coins released from his grip to fall on the cobblestones with a metallic clink and clatter. The jangling silver pieces spilled out to lie glittering in the sun.

Longinus swooned and fell into a vertigo spin. The edge of a vendor's wagon rushed up to meet him. He caught hold of its sides, his diaphragm in a spasm, and then he heaved. These last three days were too much for him. Wiping his mouth with the back of his hand, he worked his lips, turning his eyes restlessly about, far and near.

He saw the back of Judas as he strode down the cobbled street toward the Temple Mount. Turning about, Judas looked around the marketplace. Without a moment's hesitation, he scampered down the avenue, meandering until he fell into a brisk walk and then into a trot and then into a run, shouting, *"The Galilean has risen! Jesus is raised from the grave!"* Grabbing a passerby by the shoulders, he announced, "The Galilean, Jesus, is *not* dead!" He shouted even louder for all to hear, *"Jesus has risen from the grave. He is alive!"*

The

THIRTY-EIGHTH

Chapter

THE RIGHTEOUS DEAD went farther into the city, generally in groups, meandering down the narrow avenues in the direction of the Temple to appear unto many, declaring, "Christ has risen from the dead, and we have risen with Him." They bore witness to the truth of the words, "The dead men shall live, and together with My dead body shall they arise." They circulated the fulfillment of the prophecy from Isaiah 26:19, "Awake and sing, you that dwell in dust; for the dew is as the dew of herbs and the earth shall cast out the dead."

On the Temple Mount, sacrifices were underway when an unexpected and most appalling pause came. A high priest surveyed the surrounding area, sensing something was not right. He squinted over the crowd.

Simultaneously, the sacrifices ceased. There was not a sound. Something eerie caused hair to stand on end. Everyone sensed it. Without warning, the doors leading into the sanctuary of the Temple blew open as if by a wind. The entire area warped and undulated, like heat waves creating a mirage. The images of two huge and beautiful archangels appeared as wraithlike apparitions and instantly exited the Temple. A single voice rang out, echoing throughout the whole of the Temple Mount. *"Let us leave this place!"*

Every face revealed new terror and astonishment built by panic. The high priest and his retinue, having not lost their presence of mind, and by their outward tranquility and hardness of heart, strove to maintain the strictest decorum while struggling to calm the confusion and terror. Raising his arms, the high priest proclaimed, "Be not afraid. These are natural events. Do not be alarmed!"

Smoke engulfed almost the entire altar of sacrifice while rising normally from the fire of incense, the offering fire, and the perpetual fire. A vaporous wisp of smoke separated from the altar smoke as the prophet Jeremiah emerged. With a menacing voice, he confirmed unto the people, "I, the prophet Jeremiah, declare to you that sacrifice is at an end. A new one has commenced."

Extreme fear held a relentless grip on the multitude as they swooned in distress. On impulse and as if on cue, there was a general rush to the exits. Several attempts were made by the priests to squelch the panicking crowd who rushed the gates leading out onto the dais and into the Court of Women. Standing at the entrance to the Court of Women was the prophet Habakkuk proclaiming, "Blessed is He who comes in the name of the Lord, for He hath come back from the dead for your salvation. I, the prophet Habakkuk, declare that Jesus the Christ is the Son of God."

The resurrected dead entered the Court of Gentiles, the Court of Israel, and the Court of Women, still in their grave clothes. Some looked pale, and others jaundiced. They stared at the general public forthrightly as many of the people recognized their deceased loved ones and friends.

Charinus and Lenthius stepped out from among the throng, their countenance pale and of a yellow tint. In the company of those running past Charinus and Lenthius, Phinees, a high priest, cast a fleeting look in their direction, as if he recognized them, and hurried on his way.

The priests pushed their way forward in advance of the crowd, trying to maintain order and to prevent the crowd from rushing ahead. The high priest persistently strove to calm the people, shouting to be heard above the commotion, "These are visions. They cannot be real. They come from Beelzebub himself. Do not listen to them, for they will corrupt your souls!"

Pockets of confusion continued to erupt in the court of women where the resurrected dead emerged from everywhere. In the Court of Women, the crowd surged, pushed, shoved, and charged headfirst. Perched on the semi-circular raised dais was Isaiah the prophet. "I, the prophet Isaiah, declare that Jesus is the light of the world and is the Son of God according to my prophecy when I was alive on earth."

Simeon the high priest made his way against the rush of the crowd and approached the dais. A murmur ran through the crowd in low inarticulate voices as many recognized Simeon. Supernatural awe pervaded the complex. "I am Simeon, the high priest, who took Jesus up in my arms when He was an infant in this Temple—"

"I am the voice of one crying out in the wilderness!" A huge gasp fell as the crowd recognized John the Baptist!

* * *

Pilate ran in madness from room to room, almost running into a resurrected individual who accused him, "You have condemned an innocent and righteous man!" Almost out of breath, Pilate ran the length of the hallway.

A resurrected woman upbraided him in a scolding manner, "You unrighteous judge, the vindicator of the ungodly."

Pilate faltered, plunging into a wall, shaken, horrified. The living dead were everywhere, reproaching him with the unjust sentencing he had passed upon Jesus. Many called out to him, "Why did you not listen to your wife, Procula?"

"Why do you follow me?" he shouted out to his resurrected accusers. "Are you the gods of the Galilean?" His voice carried along the walls. Pilate collected himself and continued to take refuge in the inner room, his sanctum where he offered incense and made vows to his idols to invoke their assistance in his distress.

* * *

Herod the Tetrarch hunkered among the rubble and litter strewn about his split throne, torn asunder from the onslaught of the earthquake. His glorious palace lay in fragmented ruin, a testament to his own ruin as he sat cowered, terrorized, and alone.

* * *

In the inner Temple leading into the Holy of Holies, a mortified Annas stood in dazed confusion among the wreckage and devastation, mentally disturbed and aghast. Out of the corner of his eye, he saw a flicker of movement. A strong hand gripped him by the shoulder. Startled, he spun around to see the resurrected high priest Zacharias, the father of John the Baptist, standing before him. Alarmed, Annas was filled with overwhelming fear and remorse, his brain sending out a signal that paralyzed him. His breathing stilled. "You are here!" he whispered.

"You have slain the prophets of old. You also killed me and my son, John the Baptist, and now you have executed the Son of God!"

Annas's memory flashed back, fading to the time when he stood in the Camp of David, which was between the Altar and the steps leading up into the Temple sanctuary. He recollected all too well, with the prestige accorded to him by his office, the slaying of this one before him. He recollected how he witnessed Zacharias being slain by the sword after he was tortured by Herod for not giving up the whereabouts of his son, John the Baptist.

Back to the present, Annas broke like glass, his state of being and mental health giving way to a grave disorder that impaired his capacity to think and function.

The
THIRTY-NINTH
Chapter

THADDEUS, ELIUD, THOMAS, Nathaniel, Luke, Cleophas, and James the Lesser exited from John Mark's place of residence. Thomas implored the group on their way out, "The commands of the high priests have again been made known not to harbor us, or to supply us with food. Maybe we should depart and go our separate ways."

Luke, a meticulous and fastidious doctor, nodded in agreement. "I think you are right, Thomas." He looked over at Cleophas. "I shall go with you."

"Yes," remarked Cleophas, a companion of Luke who was also a follower of Christ.

The two began moseying along the country road leading to Emmaus, which in Hebrew means "hot spring," a village located about seven miles from Jerusalem. It was late in the afternoon and the road was busy with merchants and travelers. Luke carried a leather bag slung over his shoulders, hanging low on his hip. Cleophas walked alongside carrying a stick. Both were lost in thought.

It had been a bad week for both of them. With their heads hung low, their conversation was laden with doubt, despair, and disappointment. Already that morning, they had heard reports coming out of Jerusalem that the Lord's body had been removed. The women who had visited the tomb early at dawn were saying they had seen the Savior.

A traveler with white hair and beard drew near to the duo from a side path while they were in the midst of conversation concerning these things. The two wayfarers slowed their pace so the stranger, who appeared wise and yet youthful, could pass them by and go on ahead, but the traveler also slackened his pace and stepped out onto the road after they had advanced.

After ambling onward for a moment longer, Cleophas and Luke continued their conversation in lower tones over the scenes of the trial and crucifixion. Mournful and shaking their heads, they talked about Jesus' betrayal, arrest, torture, and execution, as well as the mysterious tale of the resurrection and the plain fact that the body was gone.

"We had hoped—" lamented Cleophas.

"Verily, we had hoped—" repeated Luke.

They paused in their discussion. Then Cleophas further expressed what he had on his mind. "It troubles me, my dear Luke. I was certain that Jesus was the One who would be our deliverer from this awful Roman tyranny." Luke nodded in affirmation, stopping by the roadside to gather some herbs, weary in grief and hopelessness. "I believed in His ways," Cleophas continued as he watched Luke gather the herbs. "I believed in His teachings, His doings. How could you not, with all the miracles He performed—especially with the raising up of Lazarus." Cleophas' eyes grew misty. "How could it end this way?"

The enigmatic sojourner drew closer. He overheard the two comrades debating whether the reports they were hearing bore any truth or were just of imaginary hope.

"I do not know, my dear friend," said Luke solemnly while examining the herbs. His kind eyes bore a hint of weariness as he held up the herbs to inspect them more fully. "I am as baffled as you are." Putting the herbs into a leather pouch, they continued on their way. "I do not pretend to understand how it could be so and how it could be such."

The traveler caught up with them and was upon their heels. He then asked them a question: "You seem to be in deep conversation about something. What is it you are bandying about?" The question stopped the twosome in their tracks, their faces sullen and downcast with a dark sadness. He continued, "Why is there such sadness in your hearts?"

Cleophas was quiet a moment. Sizing up this stranger, he replied, "Are you the only sojourner in this country who has not known the things that have come to pass here in recent days?"

"What things?" inquired the stranger.

Cleophas and Luke swapped glances. They were mutually baffled as to why this strange visitor had not heard of the past few days' events, but they were also curious about his identity. "Things concerning Jesus of Nazareth, the Galilean," answered Cleophas. "The young rabbi was a prophet mighty in deed and word before Yahweh and all the people. Surely, you must be a foreigner in our land if you have not heard of Him."

The stranger smiled.

Luke acknowledged the strange traveler's polite, astute manner and explained further, "Jesus was a thirty-three-year-old rabbi. We were expecting much from Him." Luke stared off into the distance, recollecting the words of the Lord. "He stirred us to believe that things could be different, not only in this life but also in the life to come." He turned his attention back to the stranger. "He taught a whole new way of thinking about life and the afterlife. But in the end," Luke shook his head in regret, "the local authorities dismissed His philosophies and arrested Him for His radical claims and for being a rebel against their political and religious agendas."

"We were hoping," interjected Cleophas, "that He would be the One to redeem Israel, but it is now the third day since they crucified Him." Cleophas became melancholy. "When He was crucified, we were utterly devastated. He had been powerful in speech and action, enough for us and His disciples and followers to devote our entire lives to His atonements and beatitudes." Cleophas sighed. "Now we find ourselves questioning how this man, who suffered Himself to be so humiliated, could be the Christ we were looking for."

Luke further iterated, "We thought we knew enough of the prophecies to believe that He was the long-awaited Messiah who would bring about a military campaign and set Israel free from Roman dominion. He was the only one who could bring liberty from our enemies and set up His Kingdom. But now, the one we thought was the Messiah is dead." Luke paused a moment to ruminate. "Before His death, we were hopeful our circumstances would change."

"Indeed," nodded Cleophas. "And we have received news this morning that is only making things worse," he grumbled.

"How may that be?" asked the stranger.

Cleophas threw a quick glance at the stranger. "This morning, some of our friends have been hallucinating, saying His corpse has come back to life." He shook his head. "It's all too confusing and discouraging."

They walked on a little farther, somewhat lost in their thoughts. "Yea, we believed one thing, but now another has happened," said Luke after a moment. He kicked a stone out of the path, "Verily, some women from our group were at the tomb early this morning and did not find His body. They came back and reported they had seen angels who announced He was alive! Some of the group went to the tomb and found things just as the women had said."

The stranger listened to their complaints before speaking. He looked upon them with compassion, not reprimanding or condemning them. Finally, he spoke as a teacher would speak when trying to get the attention of his pupils. "How foolish you are, and how slow to believe in your heart all that the prophets have spoken."

Both men raised their heads, somewhat perturbed but at the same time perplexed.

"Why do you find it so hard to believe everything spoken by the prophets? Was it not so clearly predicted by the prophets that the Messiah would have to suffer these things before entering into His time of glory?" As they walked toward the setting sun, the stranger began to expound upon them the scriptures, from Genesis to the Minor Prophets, that signaled the Messiah's arrival. He revealed how the Son of Man had been present throughout all the ages. He recounted the truth of scripture so they could hear His voice as He challenged their thinking and with the knowledge that they would tell others who believed the same way.

The
FORTIETH
Chapter

A BLACK WIDOW hung in her web in a small window. Suddenly the web shivered and a fly buzzed as it became captive. The black widow's spindly legs negotiated the open-mesh framework of the web toward the fly. Having no stomach of its own and thus rendered incapable of digesting, the spider embraced the fly and pierced its torso with her tiny projectiles. It injected its fine mixture of acidic liquors until the fly's insides were broken down and were cooking with various enzymes. The black widow drank of the warm soupy innards until the fly, which appeared to be whole, was nothing but a hollow corpse.

Simon the Zealot stood alone in the looming darkness, isolated in heavy shadow by the corner of the window. Disheveled, he leaned with a half-bent arm against the wall, resting his forehead against the sleeve of his forearm. Bitter were his feelings as his eyes constricted, observing moodily the scene before him, struck with the notion that he was like the fly in the spider's web, caught in a web of deceit.

Little was known of Simon, except that he was called the Canaanite. He had once been a member of the famous Zealot party, a fierce advocate of Jewish home rule, and an enemy of Roman supremacy. He had become zealous for the kingdom of Christ and believed Jesus to be the Messiah, who he thought in time would become king over the Israelites and drive out the Romans. Now, doubts and anger were raging in his mind. The torturous thoughts of Roman rule came back to haunt Simon. This evening of the first day of the week, he and the other disciples were gathered together with the door locked for fear of the Jews and their own lives.

In anger, Simon kicked the wall and turned his attention back into the room where oil lamps and candles flung a meager light over the upper room of Martha's house. Longish shadows fell ghostlike across the floor and walls. Eight disciples and other followers, including Mary Magdalene, Salome, Mary the mother of Jesus, and Martha, sat around a low table, motionless in sorrow and defeat, not touching the remnants of the Passover meal before them. Anxiety and grief were deeply etched in their features. Some buried their heads in heartache.

Simon paced back and forth. His eyes shone with a fierce brightness; his lips quivered with anger and fear whenever he thought of their situation.

Three mighty knocks interrupted his vigil. He stopped pacing and looked questioningly at the others. An immense, frightening silence filled the room. Finally, since he was the closest to the door, Simon pulled back the bolt. Thomas, James the Lesser, and Nathaniel rushed in through the doorway. Pushing through the door, Thomas exclaimed, "We heard rumors in the streets that we are being accused by the authorities of removing the body from the tomb."

Indignantly, Simon snapped, "Did I not tell you this would happen?" He slammed the bolt back in place. Looking back at the group, he thundered, "We have nothing—nothing, and for what?" Fuming, his eyes swept each individual, looking for any signs of affirmation, but they simply looked back in silence. "Jesus deceived us! Do you not see?"

No one said a word. All was quiet until James the Lesser, with his eyes cast downward as if he were in shame, spoke with a whispering voice, "Verily, I have to agree. Certainly, he was a good man, but he was not the Messiah we were looking for."

Matthew spoke up, "Mary Magdalene has said that she has seen Jesus, and He is yet alive."

"She has left her senses and returned to the seven devils from which she was delivered!" cried Thomas with a sudden outburst. Everyone looked at him.

Mary Magdalene raised her eyes, anchoring on Thomas with a firm look, her eyelids fluttering and filling with tears. "You have the split tongue of a horned viper!"

Thomas drew the back of his hand across his nose and turned his head the other way, his countenance expressing embarrassment for his sudden outburst.

"The other women saw Him early this morning," interjected John.

"More idle tales," voiced Thomas, more or less to himself.

"Did Jesus not say on many occasions that He would rise from the grave on the third day?" protested John.

Thomas gave him a look and then his face darkened as if the passing shadow of a cloud had fallen across it. "Your heads are like bladders, your mouths spewing out piss!" In a fit of anger, he pulled back the bolt on the door and was gone!

Nathaniel closed the door and bolted it. Remaining in the shadows of the room, he drew in a deep sigh. Turning to face the group, he spoke in a hoarse voice, "Maybe we should leave under the guise of darkness and go north."

"Why north?" asked Matthew.

Nathaniel shrugged his shoulders, "Fewer patrols."

The
FORTY-FIRST
Chapter

FOOTPRINTS LEFT AN impression in the dirt road, leading through a tunnel of trees, down a slope, and across a field. The sun seeped through the trees in an amber burn. Birds nestled in the green foliage with an occasional flapping of wings. In the distance the voice of the Master could be heard: "They shall see My Servant beaten and bloodied, so disfigured one could scarcely know Him."

It was toward the end of the day. The strange traveler, Cleophas, and Luke stopped by the wayside to take in the spectacle of the setting sun that touched a nearby stream, setting it ablaze with a fiery reflection.

"He was wounded and bruised for our iniquities," explained the stranger. "He was beaten so that we might have peace. With His stripes, we are healed. He was buried as a criminal but in a rich man's grave." Cleophas and Luke stood transfixed. This man's doctrine of religious axioms was unparalleled beyond anything they had ever heard explained upon these scriptures. "When His soul has been made an offering for sin, then He shall live again."

The stranger gazed with longing into the vivid sunset that washed the sky in blazing shades of scarlet, orange, and red. Brilliant streaks blazoned the entire landscape with a surreal diffusion of saffron. The clouds were splashed with reflecting red and orange, putting the entire sky in a lucent glow with a little blue light scattered from the upper levels of the atmosphere.

The three men surveyed the beauty with an awestruck gaze as the blazing sun fell beneath the horizon, painting the firmament with deep lavender above the fading light of the dazzling sunset. The sky darkened as the firelight of campfires, torches, and lanterns glimmered on the hillsides and valleys. The stars lit up as a patchwork of celestial sparkles that danced in the evening glow. The stranger readied himself to leave in the opposite direction from where Cleophas and Luke were traveling. "I bid you farewell, for I must be off," he said.

By this time, the two men had warmed up to the charismatic stranger. Cleophas reached out and grabbed him by the sleeve as he tried to leave. "Lodge with us, for this day is far spent and the evening draws nigh." The stranger looked toward the horizon, nodding his head in assent.

* * *

Pilate was in full dress uniform, the red mantle flowing from his shoulders. As was his habit, he stood with his right hand on the hilt of his sword. He was in the audience of Caiaphas, Archelaus, Gamaliel, and some of the chief priests of the Sanhedrin that Caiaphas had summoned to be witnesses of his proclamations. In superstitious fear of the gods and not wanting to be held accountable for crucifying the Christ, and for which Tiberius might request a hearing, Pilate had been stirred to action. It was imperative that he prove that neither he nor his men were derelict in their duty during the watch of the sepulcher.

Already in a heated argument, Pilate was even now forthwith in his exclamations. "...And I have already learned from the tomb detail that this man-god, the Galilean Jesus, rose from the dead. You desired me to be associated with you in this crucifixion, but it was YOU who determined this! I am guiltless concerning the blood of this—this god-man!"

In a calm exterior of outward emotion, Caiaphas shot back, "Why should we believe the soldiers who guarded the sepulcher? Do we believe, as they say, that an angel rolled away the stone? Perhaps Jesus' own disciples made allegiance to them and paid them money so that they, by themselves, took away the body. Perhaps they were floundering in a drunken sleep. From a thing's possibility, one cannot be certain of its reality."

Pilate thrust himself forward in cavalier fashion down the steps. "Thou son of a wild boar, do you know the Roman punishment for such a dereliction of duty? From head to heel, the guard is tied to a post, stripped of his garments, and then burned alive in a roaring fire started by his own garments! From a thing's reality, one can be certain of its possibilities!"

Being fully possessed with the idea that a scandalous appeal to the Caesar Tiberius might be imparted by Caiaphas or the Sanhedrin, Pilate once again took up the stance of the hand upon the hilt of his sword as a nonverbal impartation of his power. And by setting himself upon his usual occupation, he divulged the high priest with a proverb. "There is a saying in my country: 'A horse is half a ton of raw power, but place a bridle and bit in its mouth, and a hundred-pound woman on its back, and you can make it dance.' My men live to serve, and serve they truly do. They ceaselessly serve me and Rome. Paying my men so they can perform for you is a cause of concern, not only for me, but for them as well. You have placed their lives in jeopardy!"

"Nonetheless," replied Caiaphas with a smirk, "they took a large sum of money from us and now declare to the people according to our instructions."

Irritated, Pilate moved away from Caiaphas and started back up the steps. He stopped. Half turning, he bellowed, "Add little to a little, and soon you will have a big pile. It seems to me that you should have taken the body on the third day and paraded it around the streets of Jerusalem rather than pay my soldiers to say that while they slept, the disciples of Jesus came and stole away the body."

Caiaphas, in a ruffled state of dignity, could not motivate himself to protest further, but he stood at ease, though he was unsure how he should exonerate himself under Pilate's roof.

Pilate noticed his wife, Procula Claudia. He saw her in the corner listening with some quiet dismay. His thoughts reverted back to when she had hastened to meet him on the terrace behind Antonia:

She was agitated and pale with her hair slightly skewed and covered by a long veil that fell with a gracefulness over her shoulders. She entreated her husband, Pilate, not to give up Jesus. "You must not give up this righteous man to the Jews, for I have been troubled through the night by visions in my sleep."

Pilate was troubled by her words. "I have already, by my own convictions," he told her, "beheld this Jesus to be innocent, for I have seen through the deception of his enemies." He drew the ring of his authority off his finger, giving it to her. "I promise you, Procula, that nothing shall induce me to condemn this man who gives mysterious answers to my inquiries. I give you the ring of my governorship as a pledge to my promise."

Becoming wistful and reserved, Pilate turned in the direction of Caiaphas. "Procula, my wife, believes in the visions of the night as they appeared to her regarding this Jesus as I was about to deliver Him to be crucified."

Caiaphas eyed him in a severe and reproach fullness. "Did we not tell you that He is a conjurer?" Arrogantly, Caiaphas lifted an eyebrow, "Behold, He has caused your wife to dream and to see visions."

Pilate, having enough of Caiaphas and his unreasonable pretense of superiority, descended the steps in fury. Coming nose to nose with Caiaphas, he focused his attention on the high priest with narrowed eyes. With an exaggerated motion of the lips, and knowing his words would gnaw, he declared with heated passion, "You may consider this. It has been reported to me by narrow places and by high roads that this Jesus has been seen bodily in Galilee, in the same form, with the same voice, and with the same disciples." The words spewed out of his mouth in a rage, "And not having changed in any way, He is like a flame in the wind, preaching with more boldness than ever before about His resurrection," he gestured toward the heavens, "and about having an everlasting kingdom!"

Caiaphas remained stone-faced, seething with an overpowering rage, tightening like an old leather wine bag filled with new wine, losing control.

The
FORTY-SECOND
Chapter

THE PUBLIC HOUSE was quadrangular and tidy. On reclining cushions surrounding the table sat Cleophas, Luke, and the stranger, who had taken a seat at the end of the table as their guest. A steward placed before them a simple meal of honeycomb in a woven basket, a large cake, and a Passover loaf. A bone knife lay on the tabletop. The stranger took the knife and divided the cake into three pieces and laid them on a small plate. Then he broke the bread and stood, raising his hands above his head to bless the food. The other two felt obligated to stand. They watched the stranger while he raised his eyes to heaven. There was something familiar about the way he prayed.

They closed their eyes in turn, but when they opened them, the stranger's sleeves were rolled back, revealing nail prints in his wrists. His appearance had changed. His hair and beard no longer appeared white but golden brown. Cleophas' and Luke's eyes were now opened. Both exclaimed at once, "It is the Lord!"

Jesus smiled at them and gave them bread. Raising His hand to His mouth to partake of the bread, He vanished. They stood looking at the place that only seconds before had been occupied by the One whose body had lain in the grave. His disappearance left them with an understanding that in His timing, He will reveal all things.

Cleophas and Luke hurried into the dark of the night, leaving their meals untouched, their weariness and hunger gone. They scrambled over hills and valleys, slipping and sliding on smooth boulders, stumbling and falling over rocks, tripping over stones on the pathways, all the while excited in their conviction to tell the others what they had just seen and heard.

* * *

James, the half brother of Jesus who would later become a disciple and would write the book of James, wore a simple brown cloak. He wept in silence over a rough table when there came to his senses a ghostly whisper, *"James."*

Paying no attention, James continued to weep in anguish over the unjust and cruel death of his half brother. He felt that Jesus had been a good and righteous man, but that He had delusions of grandeur. It angered him when his half brother claimed to be the Son of God. James even scoffed Him for it! Neither James nor his siblings believed Jesus to be the Messiah. They were not supportive during His early years of ministry.

Once more, he heard a light and airy whisper, *"James."*

Lifting his head, James glanced about the room. He rose up from the bench, brushing the table sideways. Groping around in the darkness, he stumbled about in the dim twilight shadows, searching for a small oil lamp. Once he found it, he lit it with trembling fingers. He then raised the lamp, bringing it close to his face so that he felt the heat from the small flame. Turning his head sideways to avoid being seared, he lowered the flickering oil lamp. The light touched his features, casting elongated shadows up and down his face, highlighting the chin, nose, and brow.

James shuddered as he saw, at the dull outer edge of the lamp's glow, something in the gloom—a shadow of something or someone. He shaded the back of the flame with his hand to throw the light forward. His eyes adjusted. He could make out an indistinct face and chest. He gasped. "Who is here?"

The figure advanced, with the upper body and then the face coming into the vague light. James shivered, backing away.

"James, my unbelieving brother of our mother Mary." There was a pause, and then Jesus took another step. James stumbled backward for each step Jesus took forward. James' eyes fell to the ugly wounds in Jesus' wrist as He raised His right hand in nonverbal communication. "Please don't be afraid." Jesus took another measured step forward so he would not alarm James more. "Peace be unto you. It is I. Be not afraid."

James took another step back while Jesus reached out with a piece of bread. With piercing eyes, Jesus looked straight into James' eyes, as though He were reading his every thought. "Have you not made an oath to not eat nor drink until you had seen the One who has risen from among them that sleep?"

It was at this moment that James became aware of His identity. "Jesus!" James smacked into some shelves full of miscellaneous items, knocking them onto the floor.

Jesus reached out with the morsel of bread, breaking it in half to offer a piece. James hesitated and then reached out to take the bread, still not sure if this apparition was real. The Lord took a bite to assure James that He was indeed flesh and blood. "My beloved brother, eat your bread, for the Son of Man *has* risen from among those that sleep."

James struggled to find his voice. "I—I was so wrong. I believe now. It is all true. You truly are who You say You are."

"Study what has been taught in the Scriptures, for you have much to learn," Jesus instructed. "Teach and lead the people here in Jerusalem."

James turned to pull a leather wineskin from off the shelf. "I am honored to join in with Your work." Turning back, he said, "Would You like some wine?" He saw that Jesus was gone. Observing the piece of bread lying on the table, he retrieved it, turning it over in his hand, pondering what had just happened. The bread was proof that the Lord had indeed been there in His physical body. Frowning at first, James took a bite and then smiled. It was truly the Lord's resurrection that brought James to faith in Christ.

The
FORTY-THIRD
Chapter

JESUS STOOD ON the landing at the top of the steps leading into the upper room of Martha's house. Approaching the door, He raised His hand, which dissolved into a bluish transparent glow as it moved toward the latch. His pulsating body suddenly broke into dazzling irregularity of light as He passed through the barred door and on to the other side.

The drafty old upper room smelled musty of stone, wood, dust, and age. It was dark with a few lit candles and a crackling cooking fire that cast shadows across the room.

Cleophas, still trying to catch his breath from running seven miles, gave his story as he paced among the group: "And just as we were conversing about His death, He appeared to us while we walked along the road to Emmaus. We wondered who this stranger was. He spoke with such sincerity and gentleness that we were full of hope. We invited Him to sup with us and to stay the night where we have just chatted and eaten with Him." Cleophas continued, unaware of the presence of Jesus in the room: "Verily, I tell you, He was very much alive, just as you are!" Cleophas stood behind Luke where he put his hands on Luke's shoulders in a gesture of shared common knowledge.

Luke nodded with emotion. "Aye, it is as Cleophas says. Our hearts were throbbing with joyful expectation. We did not suspect that the one who walked by our side was our Lord. He never referred to Himself, but spoke as another person. We thought He had come from another town." Luke smiled in recollection. "We were indeed walking in the presence of the resurrected Christ and did not even know it! Yea, the Lord is indeed raised. We recognized Him as He broke bread."

There was a contemplative moment in which no one spoke. Jesus seemed to glide among them unnoticed as He observed those present, knowing of each one's future.

First, there was the impulsive Simon, also known as Simon Bar Jochanan or Cephas in the Aramaic, who Jesus renamed Peter, which means the Rock. Peter had repented with bitter tears for denying the Lord and was to become one of the great leaders of the church.

Then there was James the Greater, who was ambitious and short-tempered and was a favorite companion of Peter and John. He would be the first of the disciples to give his own blood for the gospel by being to put to death by King Herod Agrippa.

Next was John, the son of Zebedee, who was ambitious and judgmental. He was the beloved disciple whose head had lain upon the Lord's breast during the Last Supper. He once wished to "call down fire from heaven on a village of Samaritans." He would live on to write three epistles and the book of Revelation.

Also present was Andrew, who brought his brother Peter to Jesus after saying to his brother, "We have found the Messiah." Later he would be crucified on a diagonal or X-shaped cross.

There was also Philip of Bethsaida, the first disciple to whom Jesus had said, "Follow Me," and who told Nathaniel to "come and see" the promised Messiah. He had a questioning attitude and had wondered aloud how Jesus could feed five thousand. He was to suffer martyrdom at the Heliopolis in Phrygia where he would be flogged, imprisoned, and later crucified.

In addition, there was Bartholomew, also known as Nathaniel, who at first rejected Jesus by saying, "Can any good thing come out of Nazareth?" But upon meeting Jesus, he exclaimed, "Thou art the Son of God, thou King of Israel." He was the one the Lord singled out as an "Israelite without guile," because Jesus respected honesty. Nathaniel/Bartholomew would encounter death by first being skinned alive and then beheaded at Derbend on the Caspian Sea.

Matthew, who was the tax collector, now sought treasures in heaven. He would later write the first gospel called Matthew. He would meet death by a halberd (a pike fitted with an ax head) in Nadabah.

Let us also not forget James the Lesser, the son of Alphaeus, who would later be called the "Pillar of the Church" and would die by being thrown off the pinnacle of the Temple and then stoned and clubbed to death.

There was Judas the brother of James, called also Lebbaeus or Thaddeus, who would eventually write the last epistle Jude in the New Testament. He followed Jesus because he believed in Him, not always understanding the details of God's plan. He was later to be crucified at Edessa.

These were the women: Mary Magdalene, Salome, Susanna, Joanna the wife of Chuza (Herod's steward), Martha, and Mary the mother of Jesus.

Cleophas shook his head, chuckling, hardly able to contain himself. "Were not our hearts burning within us while He talked with us and while He opened to us the scriptures?" Mary Magdalene and the other women chuckled, along with Luke, knowing what the others did not want to believe.

The disciples' eyebrows furrowed, rolling their eyes in disbelief and anger, agitated by the gentle laughter of the women, Luke, and Cleophas. Stricken by pain and hurt, their emotions were swirling as they locked in conversation. They recounted the tales of the women, the bizarre account by Mary Magdalene and even that of Peter, who had told them of his brief encounter with the Lord, saying that he, too, had seen the Christ and that He had indeed risen. Now here they were, hearing the same story from Luke and Cleophas, respected brothers and disciples.

"These accounts are simply too strange to believe," uttered Simon who happened to glance over at Cleophas, whose eyes widened and grew alive. Simon's hair suddenly stood on end with a tingling, cold chill as he became aware of the presence of a divine entity. He turned. Color drained from his face and became deathly pale.

The
FORTY-FOURTH
Chapter

NATHANIEL, LIFTING A cup to his lips, suddenly dropped it on the tabletop. He got up, his own face haunted by fright. He seemed unable to take his eyes from the twilight shadows of the room where Jesus stood in their midst.

A moment passed, a naked breath of time held in suspension. Simon stepped back, falling over Thaddeus, who tried to get up from the table. One man screamed and another shrieked. Eyes widened. Elbows flew as all bumped into each other. Someone fainted, but no one had the wherewithal to fling open the door and run. Stumbling into each other, a few ran to the wall. An intense intellectual battle raged in their minds, their hearts and eyes at war with their brains, their reality turned upside down and rearranged.

John fell to his knees in an act of worship. Cleophas and Luke remained where they were, much less alarmed than the others. No one moved. No one spoke. The men were struck with terror, supposing they were seeing a ghost. They were all sweating and scared as the image spoke to them, His voice sounding familiar.

"Peace be unto you." There was a moment's pause. "Why are you troubled, and why do doubts arise in your mind?" Jesus observed the group, taking in each individual. "Look at My hands and My feet. It is I! Touch Me and see—a ghost does not have flesh and bones as you see I have." He held up his hands, the nail prints clearly visible, and the wounds not festering but fresh. He lifted His robe to show His feet. Still, no one moved; all were filled with wonder. Some still remained undecided about whether He was of the flesh or a spirit. "Do you have something to eat?" Jesus asked so that they would know and believe that He was indeed in the flesh.

Mary Magdalene scurried over the fire, grabbed a piece of broiled fish and then took some honeycomb from the table. She gave it to Jesus, who popped a piece of fish into His mouth, chewed, and swallowed in front of them as they all stared.

All were holding their breath. Jesus was indeed alive, appearing before them in the flesh and talking to them. It didn't make rational sense, but right before their very eyes was a supernatural power in human flesh that had overcome death. The form in front of them was not imagined but was His actual physical presence. Deep passionate emotions cried out, giving voice to the heart. Someone relaxed his grip on another. Simon quit cowering in the corner and inched closer. Cleopas and Luke stood straight and shrugged their shoulders, "See? Now you see and hear Him as well."

Jesus laughed. Chewing on the broiled fish, He explained to them, "You now actually see fulfilled the words of which I so often spoke concerning the prophecies written about Me by Moses and the prophets and in the psalms about My sufferings that must be accomplished." He swallowed. "You could not then believe that I was going to really suffer and die, and afterward rise again." He took some honeycomb. "You now see that it is true. It was written long ago that the Messiah must suffer and die to rise again on the third day."

Divine impartation permeated the souls of those in the room with the understanding of the scriptures. Jesus cast an eye over the group. "The message of salvation is that there is forgiveness of sins for all who turn to Me, and that repentance and remission of sin should be preached among all nations. As the Father hath sent Me, even so I am sending you."

Jesus laid down the remains of the fish on the table. "Go and preach to all nations, beginning here in Jerusalem." He blew on the group and told them. "You are witnesses of these things. Receive now the Holy Spirit. The sins of those you forgive, they are forgiven, and anyone's sins you refuse to forgive, they are not forgiven."

Jesus retreated to the shadows. "Don't begin telling others yet, but tarry here in Jerusalem until you are endued with heavenly power from the Holy Ghost whom the Father has promised and I shall send and impart to you."

The upper room filled with a golden warm haze. Jesus raised His hands in salute with a gesture of the Kohane blessing. Both arms were held horizontally in front at shoulder level, His hands touching at the base of the thumbs with palms forward, the middle and ring fingers parted, the thumbs pressed against the hands to form the Hebrew letter "Shin," which means "Almighty God." And with this, He spoke once more, "Peace be unto you." His hands grew transparent, His body shimmering with a subtle bluish glow as it dissipated into floating particles and then dissolved until He was gone, leaving all in the upper room pondering what He had just said and the mission He had given them.

The silence was heavy. Steps were heard outside the room, scuffling on the stone treads of the staircase, and then a knock. Cleophas pulled back the bar. Thomas entered, shameful of his previous outburst. He looked around the room, sensing something different. The ambiance of the room had changed.

"We have seen the Lord!" cried Simon.

Thomas could see there had been a change in everyone. He could sense they were filled with elation and were no longer fearful. Earlier, the room had been filled with individuals weeping in grief, and now they were joyful, ready to leave the upper room in confidence, having a mission to accomplish and a message that would transform lives. Still, Thomas could not bring himself to believe. "Except I shall see the nail prints in His hands and put my finger into the imprints, and thrust my hand into His side, I will not believe!"

The
FORTY-FIFTH
Chapter

MARTHA AND HER sister Mary lit lamps around the room. Thaddeus, James the Lesser, and Eliud entered through the doorway with Mary, the blessed mother of Jesus. Martha walked over when she finished lighting the last lamp and went to greet them along with her sister Mary. Lazarus, their brother, excused himself from the other guests to welcome those who had just arrived.

A shadow fell across the entranceway. Thomas stood gazing over the group, not sure if he wanted to be a part of this company of friends. Upon seeing him, Lazarus went to receive him, but Thomas passed him by without salutation. Lazarus reached out to touch Thomas by the sleeve, but Thomas waved his arm away. The others who saw this gesticulated with their hands in protest of his rude actions. Lazarus waved off the impoliteness. He then walked over to a lamp that was suspended from the ceiling and began to draw it down with a rod. Upon lighting it, he pushed it back up and retreated to close the door. In doing so, he passed Mary Magdalene and one more lady as they entered.

Peter and John greeted the two women. Peter positioned himself under the hanging lamp with his back to the door. John and James the Lesser placed themselves on either side. To their left and right stood the other disciples. The gathering, arranged for praise and worship, knelt in prayer and then stood to sing praises and psalms.

Suddenly, the door opened of its own accord as if blown ajar by the wind. The lamps and candles sputtered, the hanging lamp flickered. Everyone turned as Jesus crossed the threshold. He was clothed in white garments and a white girdle. He directed His steps through the group, looking to each person. They all fell back on both sides.

He smiled and said, "Peace be to you."

Thomas stood with mouth open, much frightened. Stepping between Peter and John, Jesus went straight to where Thomas stood. Thomas drew back with apprehension and shock. Jesus reached out to him with His right hand. "Thomas, reach hither your finger and behold My hand." Thomas could not possibly move even a half an inch. Peter gently nudged Thomas forward.

Jesus took Thomas's right hand firmly in His own. "Tell Me who I am." Thomas could, without a doubt, feel the warm flesh and gentle pressure of the handgrip, while he beheld the nail-scarred wrists. He could feel the divine blood flowing into his hand. His body tingled. He could feel the power. It flowed from Jesus' hand into the hand of Thomas, who could feel the love streaming from the heart of God into his.

Thomas slowly released the breath he held, tears spilling down his cheeks, giving Jesus an expression of overwhelming wonder along with astonishment and disbelief. Jesus took Thomas' right hand and pressed it into the wound of His right side. Thomas' heart pounded like a sledgehammer as he slumped backward, sinking involuntarily as though unconscious. Jesus fixed His eyes on Thomas and would not let him go, drawing him back up to stand.

"Look into My eyes, Thomas, and tell Me who I am." Thomas heaved with emotion, his torso shaking with sobs. He touched the Lord's face. "My Lord and my God!" Thomas kissed Christ's hands, the hot tears flowing like a river. For the first time, he realized the full impact of the resurrection and the power that even raised Lazarus from the dead after four days of being in the grave. "Thomas, because you have seen Me, you have believed. Blessed are they that have not seen, and yet have believed."

Thomas felt completely defenseless and humbled. Jesus looked over to catch the eyes of Lazarus, whose gaze saw Him as the life and resurrection. Jesus smiled, with Lazarus smiling in return, both in full acknowledgment of what the other thought.

Jesus walked among the group. "Go into all the world and preach the gospel to all creation. He who has believed and has been baptized shall be saved, but he who has disbelieved shall be condemned." He stopped before Mary Magdalene and took hold of her hand. She was full of emotion. He proceeded to His mother, Mary. She remained in perfect rest, absorbed in calm, deep recollection. He placed His hands on her shoulders and bent over to give her a kiss on the cheek. "Is there something to eat?"

She motioned for someone to get something while He continued around the group. "These signs shall accompany those who have believed. In My Name they shall cast out demons, they shall speak with new tongues. They will pick up serpents, and if they drink any deadly poison, it will not hurt them. They will lay hands on the sick and they shall recover."

An oval dish was brought to Jesus with remnants of a loaf of bread and some fish. Jesus took these and turned to all those around Him and blessed the food. He distributed it, starting with Thomas and Peter. Peter knelt before the Lord as he took a morsel. Jesus laid hands on him and then passed the plate on to the next person. As Jesus watched them, His image grew misty and blurry.

The
FORTY-SIXTH
Chapter

AN ETHEREAL outline of a man materialized, standing on a rock that jutted out into the Sea of Galilee. He stared into the distance of the placid lake, which was bathed in the glow of a large full moon on the horizon. Torches produced a glow on the water from a fishing boat on the lake.

Little by little, the horizon lightened with the gleam of a new day as mist wafted across the surface of the waters. The sea lapped at a drifting hull as a hand tugged on a casting net. The fisherman then leaned over to haul in the mesh with meticulous attention. Torchlight illuminated the water to mirror the reflection of Peter. Two other figures close by reeled in the anchor, their muscles rippling, their wet bodies glistening in the torchlight and the dawning day. The boat bobbed peacefully on the docile water as mist covered the vessel.

The mist parted to expose a horizontal strip of a face. The eyes were static and unblinking. They were watching the eyes of Jesus. Soon the mist once again shrouded His eyes from view.

Out of the swirling fog, the boat drifted in a gentle motion, the fishermen worn out from an unsuccessful night of fishing. They rowed toward the shore. Through the mist, about three hundred feet from the shoreline, the fishermen became aware of the mysterious stranger who remained motionless on the rock watching them. The stranger, Jesus, finally cupped His hands and yelled out to them, "Any fish, boys?"

The fishermen glanced at one other with several shouting back, "No."

"Cast the net on the right hand side of the boat," Jesus shouted, "and you will find some."

The men turned to one another with rolling eyes, some shrugging their shoulders, despondent in their weariness. Despite exhaustion and fatigue, they ventured back out onto the sea. The sun rose with a glow of soft pink and orange, silhouetting the fishermen—Peter, John, James, Andrew, Nathaniel, Thomas, and James the Lesser—against the morning blush.

The fishermen cast the long net called a seine to the right side of the boat. Weighted with lead sinkers on one side and with floats on the other, the seine had long ropes fastened on two ends that were many yards apart. The ends were brought together to form a circle. Some of the men dove into the water to bring one portion of the weighted edge under and around to form the bottom of the net. After performing these tasks, the men dragged themselves back onboard, water dripping from their wet skins. Suddenly the boat tipped, nearly toppling them back into the sea as the seine was drawn under with a heavy strain, sinking like lead weights into the depths.

The men heaved and tugged. As the seine drew nearer to the surface, they observed a heavy shape in the net. Straining to bring in the mesh, they were excited and animated. John leaned over to take a closer look, nearly losing his balance as he saw the water boiling and the net teeming with wriggling and thrashing fish. The men toiled under a great physical effort to bring the net aboard, but it became apparent they would have to tow the seine into shallower waters before drawing.

John looked ashore in the direction of the stranger. The boat teetered as Peter climbed aboard after adjusting the net for drawing. Glancing up, he saw John staring at the beach. "What is it you look after, brother?"

"It is the Lord."

"Huh?" Peter looked ashore, gazing through the dawn's haze. Naked, he rummaged the deck for his clothes, not taking his eyes off Jesus who stood on the shore at the water's edge with the gentle surf lapping at His feet. John felt the boat sway a little before hearing a splash! He turned to see the hind end of Peter as he plunged into the cool waters of the sea.

Swimming back to the surface and rising out of the water, Peter was hit with a vivid memory.

*   *   *

The sea boiled with a fully raging storm. It was wild with spray and spume, the atmosphere laden with electricity. The sea was heavy and treacherous with twenty-foot waves rolling high. The wind blew with a gale force of up to sixty knots, the rain strafing sideways and torrential.

A blinding glare of lightning was followed by a sonorous peal of thunder vibrating the waters. The top of a mast rose out of the rough seas, followed by a twenty-six-foot fishing vessel. It appeared to spew from the deep to be thrust upon the crest of a white-capped wave. Now and then, gesticulating human forms in the boat could be clearly outlined for a second or two in a glow of lightning, only to be vanquished in the succeeding blackness.

The disciples fought the violent rolling and pitching waves, rowing hard and struggling against the wind. Though several of the disciples spent most of their lives on the sea, they were afraid. Another black wave rolled toward them, erasing them from view as they moved into the trough.

Numerous lightning strikes illuminated the waves in sheets of fire as the sea roared. The rhythm of lightning revealed the person of Jesus. In wild bursts of eerie light, the Lord's hair and clothing were whipped by the hard-bearing wind. In the distance, He could see the floundering sailing vessel, large enough to hold fifteen people, as it reached the apex of the next wave.

In the same instant, lightning flared across the black rainclouds and the disciples observed a human shape on the water. From their position, at first it seemed to be a dark moving speck. The crashing waves over the boat caused a foggy mist that hindered their vision, so the approaching figure was terrifying and surreal. With each flash of lightning, the dark speck drew closer and more discernible until they could see that it was a human, although barely visible by the mists of the storm. Peter was terrified. A blast of wind strangled out his cry, "A ghost!" as it whistled through the tackles and ropes.

The sailing craft slid through the trough of another wave to separate them from the specter. Upon climbing the face of the next wave, they reached the lip where they heard a *shush* as the roof of the crest passed over them like a waterfall. They were drenched in spray and spume while lightning bursts exposed once more the frightening anomaly before them on the water.

The disciples were as superstitious as any fisherman in believing the sea inhabited spiritual creatures. In the Jewish culture, it was believed that to see a spirit on the waters at night, particularly during a storm, foreshadowed pending doom and death.

John shrieked, "A water spirit!" as the fearsome apparition approached. It passed them several yards away, the hair and clothing thrashing fiercely in the wind and rain. The disciples screamed in unison above the din of the storm with absolute dread and horror, *"We are going to die!"*

The apparition was Jesus, who knew they had every reason to be afraid. First, they were not expecting Him. They had left Him ashore to be alone to pray after feeding the multitude of five thousand. Next, they were four miles out from land. No ordinary man could walk on water as if on land. Above all, they were in the midst of a fierce storm, and He was walking faster than they could row.

Jesus looked their way, riding the waves parallel to them. By way of a sign, He was heralding to them the phrase "passing by," which in Jewish idiom meant "God's way of saving and protecting." In the same manner, He impressed upon them the scripture from Psalm 93: "Though the waters rise and the seas roar, greater is the might of the Lord."

To their astonishment, they could hear His voice above the gale: "Take courage; it is I. Be not afraid!" The voice had a familiarity about it. *Was this water spirit truly speaking to them?*

It fell upon Peter's mind that it could be none other than the Christ Himself. Standing up in the boat and holding onto the mast with one hand, Peter tried to take a closer look through the barraging downpour. The rain stung his face as he called out, "Master, if it be you, bid me to come to you on the water."

"Come," was the reply with Jesus reaching out a hand, beckoning him.

The
FORTY-SEVENTH
Chapter

PETER, QUAKING WITH fear, launched out of the boat, only to fail and be thrown back again as the boat climbed another crest. Looking out onto the raging sea, lightning struck the waters in furious wrath, and waves rolled and crashed. The growling thunder was one continuous low and incessant murmur.

Jesus could not be seen anywhere. *Maybe it had been a ghost or a water spirit.*

As they crested again, Peter was the first to see Him. Pointing, he cried, "Over there!" Gathering himself together and with strong determination, Peter put a foot over the edge of the boat as a wave hit him with a devastating slam, washing him back into the vessel. Undeterred, Peter ventured back out as the others looked on with amazement.

Peter stuck one leg out over the side and set his foot on the water. It didn't sink! He stepped out with the other foot. Standing, he was baffled, scared, and ecstatic. The feeling and footing were solid, yet fluid. The cold water slipped around the soles of his feet and between the toes, rushing up and over his ankles. Holding on to the edge of the boat for support, he could see Jesus smiling at him through the green mist of spume and rain. His hand was outstretched, encouraging him to step forward, much as a father would encourage his son to take his first step.

With audacious faith and courage, yet with trepidation, Peter stepped out onto the water as the boat crested over the top of another ferocious wave. It caused him to almost surf down the side of the wave and crash into an oncoming upsurge. Having not gone under, and having a solid yet adaptable liquid footing, Peter walked and nearly climbed the next wave. He seemed to airdrop on the descent, landing on all fours, catching himself before going under the heavy waves. He took another step and then another, wobbling and then balancing as he went up and down the waves. He was learning to roll with the surf and breakers while he deliberately and continually kept his eyes on the Lord. The wind and rain tore at his person and garments. He was walking on the water—just like Jesus! He shouted above the din of the storm, *"Look at me. I'm walking on the water!"*

Jesus laughed with excitement. *"Come on, Peter!"*

Peter ambled toward Jesus, arms spread out trying to maintain his balance, as the disciples in the boat watched with intensity. The storm and waves boomed. The storm seemed to intensify, the sea broiling and frothy, the gale-force winds mounting and screaming like a banshee with a loud, piercing cry.

Forked lightning ripped across the sky. The windswept rain was penetrating, stinging Peter's skin like prickling needles. Peter could barely see. He was forced to take in shallow breaths as the wind and slanting torrent were enough to drown a man. The violence of the storm reached epic proportions.

A blinding flash of lightning licked the waves with white fringes of fire. An ear-shattering *bang* of thunder penetrated the inner ear to such a degree that everyone went deaf for a moment. Peter felt the concussion of shock waves. The air expanding and contracting produced a partial vacuum, briefly sucking the breath from Peter's lungs. A sulfuric smell lingered briefly, leaving a taste in his mouth as his ears rung.

Looking about, Peter was only a few yards away from the boat, but it seemed awfully small and distant. It slipped out of sight as he was now well down in a trough. He gasped despairingly at the black-green, white-capped wall of water with ragged edges and tumbling peak as it shut out everything around him. Peter regarded the surrounding wall of darkness and shouted, *"What am I doing? People can't walk on water!"*

The wave slid under him, lifting him up and into and through the surging crest.

For a moment, he could see Jesus, who seemed too far off to be of any assistance. Peter saw nothing but black churning water all about as he was buffeted by the strong gusts. Taking his eyes off Jesus, he was now in the flesh, and he was afraid! Suddenly, the swirling black water beneath Peter's feet let go.

Hearing a hissing sound to his left, Peter turned in time to see an ominous breaking swell crash into him with enormous power. Gulping, he flapped in a wild frenzy as the cold water swallowed him, sucking him under with a boil of upwelling and whirling turbulence. Thrashing about underwater, Peter was desperate for air. His thrashing became frantic. Through a lingering flash of lightning, he could see the fluid shape of Jesus high above him on the surface, wreathed in a watery image of fire.

Managing to get his head above water, Peter gulped, taking in more water as another wave engulfed him. Forcing his head above water a second time, he gasped desperately, reaching out tenuously, crying out in desperation. It was imperative for him to remain above the surface or he would drown.

With the uplifting action of a rolling wave, gazing with hope and despair in his eyes, for a fleeting moment he caught a glimpse of Jesus. He waved frantically with the last of his ebbing strength, crying out, "Lord save me!" only to see the Savior dropping off into the boiling crests and out of sight. Another wave pounded Peter with sheer force, plunging him into the black briny depths of the sea. Once more, he fought to the surface, his face breaking suddenly through the white fringe of a wave. Upon its crest, his eyes searched the tormented waters, then the sea rushed over him and under he went, his hope of Jesus saving him dying within him.

Peter was in grave danger. He fought with a mad aggressiveness to get back to the surface, but it was becoming vain. His movements were becoming weaker.

Peter's eyes protruded, staring wildly. He bordered on blackout with small gold and purple spots appearing before his eyes. This forewarned that death was near, a signal that the brain was losing oxygen and about to shut down for holding his breath too long.

Finally, his eyes bulged, his struggling subsided, his eyes rolled. He was hit with spasms as he, in his last awkward movements, began to drown. His mouth at last opened as the last element of life was deprived of him. Gurgling bubbles belched from his mouth, trickling upward.

His stare fell vacant, with all going silent.

Whoosh! Suddenly, with a rush, Peter was being pulled up from the watery grave. The violence of the storm was abating. A hand was firmly holding on to his, not letting go.

* * *

Jesus grinned as He helped Peter gain a foothold on the rocky bottom of the seashore.

The
FORTY-EIGHTH
Chapter

THE FISHERMEN PULLED in two groups on each end of the ropes, many yards apart from each other. Gradually, they drew the seine toward the shore and into shallower waters. Jesus, having a good time, watched the disciples finish landing the fish on the beach with small nets or by hand. He chuckled as they emptied the seine, counting the large fish as they separated them into rows according to their kinds. There were about eighteen varieties of fish in the Sea of Galilee. Most prevalent were sardines. There were also slender barbells, which had whiskers like barbs near the mouth, similar to a sturgeon or catfish; well-fleshed biny, which included three species of the carp family; and the large fish musht, meaning "comb," representing the appearance of their fins. Jesus was delighted as the fishermen/disciples stood in wonder and amazement after tallying 153 fish.

It had been dark when disciples ventured out onto the sea to ply their trade early that day. They cast their nets numerous times during the morning hours, only to find them empty with not even a single fish. Doubts and perplexity filled their minds, but now their nets were nearly torn with the copious amounts of fish! It was truly another miracle wrought.

These disciples had made their living off the sea. They were primarily occupied with catching and selling fish, as it was important to commerce in that region. The fishing industry commonly provided brine used for seasoning and oil for fuel. The skins were used for writing surfaces, and the bones were fashioned into writing implements, hooks, needles, and hair ornaments.

Jesus motioned for them to follow Him. "Come, let us eat."

Approaching the small bonfire, they saw fish hanging on large upright sticks at the edge of a flame, which allowed for slow roasting without scorching. Tired from their toil, the men reclined around the fire in a sense of awe. The sweet scent of fresh-baked bread hung in the air, causing their mouths to water. Jesus played host as He broke the bread and gave them each a piece along with a portion of fish. He stretched out to enjoy the meal. The fish was tender and tasty with a smoky flavor.

No one dared to ask who He was, for they already knew. Still somewhat timid and a little awed by the One who sat before them, the disciples scrutinized Jesus as He took a bite of fish and started chewing. The Lord was amused as they watched Him eat. He could sense their fascination as they silently questioned whether He was of the flesh or the spirit. He asked them, "Do you still wonder within yourselves whether I am of spirit or of flesh? Does a spirit consist of flesh and bones? My body, which was perishable, is now imperishable by the resurrection. This same physical mortal body you now see has been transformed into an immortal body, being made a glorified, spiritual body. I am undeniably that of flesh, not like a ghost that is otherworldly, neither here nor there, and having no body of its own." No one said a word, being transfixed as they were. Soon, there was a rustling followed by smacking and boisterous laughter. The men loosened up and they began to enjoy their time with the Savior.

The Lord threw the remains of the fish back into the fire. Leaning back on His elbows, He stretched out His feet and watched the fire spit and crackle. His eyes gleamed in the firelight. Jesus was having a good time with His disciples. Sitting up, He raised His knees to His chest, wrapping His arms around His legs. Having looked at the fire for some time, He tilted His head back and closed His eyes, heaving a sigh. Opening His eyes, He studied Peter. He was concerned about whether Peter loved Him with his whole heart, soul, and mind.

Throwing His gaze back to the sputtering and crackling fire, Jesus asked Peter in a low tone of voice without sparing him a look, "Simon, son of Jonas, do you love Me more than these others?" Though the Lord spoke in a light tone, it was very much in earnest. He deliberately used Peter's real name, Simon, reminding Peter of his frailty of mind and human imperfections. It caught Peter's attention.

A somewhat embarrassed Peter looked up and replied with a modest smile, "Yes, Lord." Self-consciously, Peter glanced about the group, his eyes falling on his brothers, Andrew and John. Turning back to the Lord, he said, "You know that I love you."

Feeling a deep sense of shame as the Lord had referred to Peter by his given name and not the one the Lord had given him, he wiped his nose on his sleeve and looked back into the fire. The flames blurred in his sight as his eyes grew misty. His face fell flush. His meditations were known only to him, or so he thought, for the Lord knew Peter's murmuring reflections of the soul.

Why did He use my real name and not the name He had given me? thought Peter. He threw a sidewise glance at the Lord and returned his to gaze to the fire. *He has given up on me. I am nothing but a stupid fisherman who denied Him three times, just as He said I would.* Peter stiffened with tightened lips and grinding teeth. *He was right! I am such a fool—such a fool—a bigger fool than Judas.* Involuntarily, Peter flinched with a grimacing scowl. *And now He wonders whether I love Him.* He glanced at Jesus and then back into the fire. *How dare He treat me like this after all I did to protect Him in the garden?* Softening, Peter's eyes again grew misty. *He humiliated me when I tried to protect Him!*

The Lord glanced at Peter, who couldn't see past his own hurt and self-pity. There was a long silence. Straightaway, Jesus saw a vision of Peter and John at the Gate Beautiful.

The
FORTY-NINTH
Chapter

FRIENDS SHUFFLED along the streets of Jerusalem, carrying a crippled man, who made been lame from his mother's womb, to his destination at the Gate Beautiful. They left the lame man lying on his mat near the steps leading up to the Temple, a prime begging spot for alms. It was common for the people to see this lame man every day, never giving him any thought other than to give him alms. No one ever expected anything significant happening in this man's life.

Peter and John, who had become good friends by this time, were on their way to the Temple. It was the ninth hour, the hour of prayer. Both men were exact opposites in nature, with Peter being impetuous and a man of action and John being a dreamer. When the lame man saw that they were about to enter the Gate Beautiful, he asked for alms with an eye cast downward, "Alms for the lame?"

John glanced at Peter, who in turn observed the crippled man, noticing his downcast appearance, for he never had any hope of walking. Gazing upon the man, Peter saw that he was about forty years of age and had deformed feet. Peter scanned the steps that went up to the Temple and thought of how this lame man lay on the outside of this marvelous structure and could not go inside.

The Gate Beautiful was near Solomon's porch. It was large and magnificent and was made of a valuable precious metal called Corinthian brass. It was more pompous in workmanship and carvings than any of the other gates, with columns to either side inlaid in silver and gold.

Peter looked back down at the lame man. *Here is a tragic story,* he thought, *being at the Gate Beautiful and not being able to participate in prayer or other activities of worship.* Prompted by the Holy Spirit, Peter fixed his gaze upon the lame man and said, "Look at us," for no beggar would look in the face of anyone he solicited.

The lame man timidly looked up into the eyes of Peter. Seeing that Peter gave him his full attention with personal, immediate, and direct eye contact, he fully expected to receive something from him. He asked again, "Alms for the lame?"

Peter replied, extending his right hand, "Silver and gold have we none, but in the name of Jesus Christ of Nazareth, rise up and walk!" At this moment, Peter exercised a great deal of faith at the cost of looking foolish, for if the man tried to stand and wasn't healed, he could be accused of victimizing the unfortunate.

A crowd of curious onlookers gathered about, intrigued. The lame man grabbed hold of Peter's outstretched hand with more strength than Peter expected. He clung to Peter as he stood. Just about falling over, he clutched John's arm in an effort to stabilize himself. Shaking, he stood up further on his own. He continued holding on to Peter and John when a loud crack could be heard as the leg bones snapped into their joints. The lame man almost tumbled but regained his awkward balance. With many hearing the sharp pops, the gathering crowds held their breath, hardly able to believe what was happening before them.

The lame man let go of Peter and John and fell back to the ground with the crowd crying out in alarm. The man seemed to be in pain, but then his shrunken feet began to expand, enlarging with new growth of muscle. They straightened with more loud pops as the twenty-six bones of the feet, ligaments, and tendons snapped into place from the ankles to the heels to the instep of the feet and then to the toes. Right before everyone's eyes, the shriveled feet developed.

The lame beggar of a man, huffing and puffing, grasped hold of Peter and John.

Sluggishly, he bumbled his way back to his feet with a look of astonishment. Atrophied muscles of the soles of his feet began to regenerate. The ligaments and tendons were reforming, the Achilles tendons strengthening, muscles in the thighs and legs, and even up into the pelvic and loin region, were gaining strength.

The lame man shouted, laughing and crying at the same time. Standing up fully, he still clung to Peter and John and then let go. He stood there for a few uncomfortable moments and then took faltering steps like a newborn colt. This was new for him, for he had never stood or walked in his life. He let out a loud, piercing scream. *"I can walk!"* He chuckled and then continued to laugh and cry loudly.

The formerly lame man sprung, flexing and extending his legs. Standing for a minute, he raised one foot and then the other. Spellbound, he leaped off one foot and then the other. Unable to contain himself, he jumped a second time. In open glee and showmanship, he started walking and leaping and then shouted at the top of his lungs, "Praise the Most High! I can walk! Look—look!" He ran back and forth. "Look! I can run! I can leap!" He laughed with joyous praise. "I was lame, and now I walk!"

Running back to Peter and John, he exclaimed with passion, "Thank you! Thank you! Thank you!" It was through Peter's faith that the lame man was healed, and he knew it, for this man had no faith. He had expected to receive money, but instead, he received something of far greater value.

The man proceeded into the Temple Courts, walking, leaping, and praising God! All the people, five thousand in attendance, took notice of the cripple, as they knew he was the lame beggar who sat at the Gate Beautiful. Others ran over to see for themselves the lame man who could now walk.

Peter and John stood at the portico of Solomon, being full of amazement and filled with wonder. It was truly a miracle. Here was the lame beggar now leaping and running. Peter spoke to the crowds. As many as five thousand came to the Lord that day.

The
FIFTIETH
Chapter

JESUS FELL BACK into the posture of poking at the fire with a stick while Peter nibbled on a piece of fish, looking into the blaze, the firelight playing off his glimmering eyes. Jesus spoke softly to Peter, "Feed my lambs."

Mulling over the words, Peter lifted a heavy gaze from the fire, directing it to the Lord's face. The Lord cast His eyes upon Peter once more, their eyes meeting. The Lord's eyes bore into Peter's with the question still in His heart: *Does Peter love Me as his Lord and as his Savior? Does he love Me sacrificially, enough to lay his life down for Me?*

Peter withdrew his eyes, looking at the flames in the fire. When he raised them again, he found the Lord still watching him. Jesus once more raised the question, "Simon, son of Jonas, do you really love Me?"

Peter wiped a hand across his mouth. *Here we go again,* he thought. Brushing his hands against his garments, he glanced sideways at the others, a little perplexed that Jesus had once again singled him out from the group. Looking back at the Lord, he replied, "Yea, Lord, You know that I love You." Jesus smiled slightly, looked back down, and continued to stir the fire.

Peter pulled on a lock of his hair. He felt low like a snake in a rut. *Why does He question me? Doesn't he know I'm loyal?* Peter examined himself. *I'm not loyal. That's why he's asking me. He doesn't trust me. I'm a deceitful idiot! I'm a coward and a liar, and He knows it! He knows how much of a hypocrite I am! I ran and now He is questioning me.*

Putting the stick aside and wrapping His mantle about Himself, Jesus stood up and shook His legs energetically, as if they had fallen asleep. He stretched and brushed the sand off His clothes. He remained standing there, contemplating once more. Peter regarded Him somewhat awkwardly. A lingering question still held in the Master's eyes. The Lord's gaze shifted to Peter as if He felt the stare. Nonverbally, Jesus motioned with his eyes for Peter to follow Him as He ventured to take a walk along the shore. For a second time, Jesus saw a vision before Him.

* * *

Women prepared the body of a woman named Dorcas for burial, her body washed and wiped with a mixture of spices, her hair and nails cut. Prayers from the scriptures were being chanted while the women finished wrapping the body in linen strips of various sizes and lengths.

Peter was led into the upper room amid the prayers and weeping of friends who were gathered around the room. They showed him garments Dorcas had made for the poor, for she was a seamstress and was well known for her good endeavors. He looked around, moved by the grief of those present. Speaking with a gentle but firm voice, he asked them all to leave the room so he could be alone with the deceased. After they left, he knelt and prayed, facing away from the body so he could focus his entire mind upon God. Following a brief interlude, he turned toward the body, finding her face, feet, and arms already turning black with death. Using her Jewish name, Peter spoke in a mild voice, "Tabitha, get up!"

Dorcas' eyes fluttered under closed eyelids. Her heart began to beat at a normal rate. Her stomach twitched, and then the chest began to rise and fall as she breathed on her own. Her fingers moved and then her toes. She took a deep breath and then opened her eyes, mumbling words. When upon seeing Peter, she sat erect. Peter extended his hand to her and raised her to a standing position.

He summoned her friends; who upon seeing with their own eyes the miracle, gasped in amazement, nearly speechless. In the background, altogether invisible to the group, Jesus stood in His Spirit form, watching.

Up until this moment in the future, Peter had believed his mission was to convert the Jewish people. This event was pivotal in Peter's life, changing the direction of the early church. He realized he had a more profound role to play in human history and that his ministry was both to the Gentile and the Jews.

* * *

The sound of feet scrunched in the sand of the beach. Jesus regarded Peter with more attention than beforehand. "Then, take care of My sheep."

Walking on a tad farther with perplexity and solemnity, Peter was in a self-contained state of mind, plagued with persistent anxiety as to why Jesus would ask him these questions. The Lord placed a hand on Peter's shoulder, causing an involuntary start as though a ghost had just passed in front of him. He stopped and looked up at the Savior, who looked back at him with immeasurable tenderness. Observing Peter with closer scrutiny, Jesus once more asked the same question but with more gentleness, "Simon, son of Jonas, do you really love Me?"

The
FIFTY-FIRST
Chapter

PETER WISHED HE could run away. He knew three times he had denied knowing the Lord. Three times he walked away from Him. And now, for the third time, he was being asked the same question. Hurt and grieved, Peter's countenance expressed deep humility. It was more than he could bear. He stammered in shame and humility, "Lord, you know all things. You know that I love you."

Jesus fixed a careful gaze upon Peter, whereupon he became uncomfortable and plunged his eyes to the ground. And again, time melted away and Jesus saw into the future:

* * *

Peter slept between two soldiers, double-chained. He was awakened by something or someone unseen shaking him. When he opened his eyes, a light filled the room.

An angel stood before him. "Quick, get up!" Immediately, the shackles fall off Peter's wrists and feet. "Put your garments and sandals on." Without question, Peter did so. "Wrap your cloak about you and follow me."

Peter obeyed and followed the angel along the corridor, though he didn't believe it was actually happening, thinking it was a vision. They passed the first and second guards, eventually coming to the iron gates leading out into the city street. The gate opened of its own accord as Peter walked through and onto the street. He sauntered the length of the lane with the angel by his side. Standing in the quietness of the dark avenue, it dawned on him what has just happened. It was not a vision!

Peter had been placed in prison to be executed the next day by Herod's orders. Herod was on a rampage, persecuting Christians, and having James, John's brother, put to death. Not too many days after Peter's supernatural release, Herod gave a speech at a festival honoring Caesar with a large gathering of high-ranking officials. His robe, made of woven silver, was ablaze as the rays of the rising sun touched the robe, dazzling the crowd. With an awe of reverence, mingled with fear and trembling, the crowd shouted out, "We have in the past honored you as a man, but now we honor you as one with a nature greater than any mortal being!" As Herod made his speech, those gathered said among themselves, "This is the voice of God, not a man."

Herod, upon hearing their words, gloated in the admiration. Immediately, an angel of the Lord struck him down as he accepted the accolades. He was instantly struck with acute pain in his stomach, and he slunk off the stage. Within five days he was dead. He had been eaten alive by maggots slithering through putrefied open wounds. They were of such a loathsome, revolting stench that no one would come near him. It was an agonizing, painful death.

* * *

Peter walked alongside the Lord on the beach with an air of speechlessness. He appeared anxious and ashamed, his eyes fixed on the ground. Jesus spoke in a barely audible voice, "Feed My sheep."

Peter glanced back to see John following, nearly colliding with the Lord, who had stopped suddenly. The Lord wrapped an arm around Peter's neck and drew his head down close to Him. His eyes pierced deep into Peter's soul, "Truly, truly, I say unto you, when you were young, you used to gird yourself and walk wherever you willed."

Peter could feel the tension in the Lord's strong arm around his neck, swelling with the passion that possessed Him. Closing His eyes, the Lord drew Peter forward until their foreheads touched. "When you are old..."

Looking into the future, Jesus knew there would come a time when Peter would lay down his life for Him:

* * *

Birds of prey circled in the hot brazen sun and swooped in low to where a sun-blackened body hung upside down on a freshly cut pine cross that bled fresh pine sap. The body on the cross was stark against the brazen sky as the ground fell away to the other side.

The bleak, bird-torn, naked body sagged toward the ground by gravity, hung with nails through the wrists. All the weight pulled at a nail through the arches of the feet at the apex of the cross. The smell was overwhelming, as it would be on a hot and humid day, the stench of rotting flesh coming off the extremities of the body, in addition to the odor of excrement from evacuated bowels and the release of urine.

Perhaps a day or two earlier, Peter had hung there bleeding and agonizing with each breath as his life flashed before his eyes. Pain wracked his entire body, his head pounding and feeling as if it would explode any minute from the prolonged rush of being upside down. It had been Peter's choice to be crucified upside down, not feeling worthy to be crucified on the cross in the same manner as his Lord. His death would be swift.

Crows gingerly pecked at the carcass and eyes, which were already half-eaten and devoid of life. Flies buzzed everywhere, having made their home in the moist and open wounds, particularly those around the nails where they had been stretched from the weight of the body and gravity. Blood oozed down the arms to congeal in the armpits while a crusty discharge of pus remained around the sores due to infection.

* * *

Back on the shores of Galilee, with eyes still closed, Jesus continued speaking to Peter, "You will stretch forth your hands and another will gird you and take you where you would not wish to go."

Jesus knew that Simon, son of Jonas, in his natural flesh, could not partake of what was to come. But He knew the reborn man Peter the Rock could! Jesus had sanctioned Peter to replace his three-time denial with a three-time affirmation, that he did indeed love the sacrificed lamb, the Lord Jesus Christ.

Opening His eyes, Jesus held on to Peter earnestly and said with deep feeling, "Follow Me!" He released His hold. Peter, deeply moved and overcome with emotion, seemed to be held under the Lord's power. Never before had he seen such passion as when Jesus uttered these words.

Out of the corner of his eye, Peter saw John approaching. "Lord, what about him?" Jesus looked back, seeing the future of John.

* * *

The disciple sat outside a cave on the island of Patmos, hungry and ill-treated. He wrote on papyrus the words of the Lord regarding the revelation the Lord Jesus Christ had just given him in a vision.

* * *

Turning back around, Jesus resumed walking. He said as he looked ahead, "If I want him to remain until I come, what is that to you?" Again He said to Peter, "Follow Me."

The other disciples had by now caught up to them. The morning was glorious as shown on the face of each man. The bright sun of life shined on them with a renewed glow of wellbeing and strength for the coming days. It was a new beginning, another chapter about to unfold in their lives. Together, they strode off into the magnificent daybreak and onto a path that led to a fertile valley.

The
FIFTY-SECOND
Chapter

ENTERING FROM A path, Jesus and the eleven disciples came upon a meadow full of green grass on the Mount of Olives where five hundred witnesses were gathered. Fluffy white clouds dominated the sky in celebration of a day that would be like no other. Jesus sat on a prominent rock that jutted out from the side of a hill elevated above the crowd. Peter took a position opposite Jesus as He addressed the crowd.

"I utter grave words concerning the sufferings and persecution that will follow Me upon the earth." Upon Jesus' words, the future unfolded before the Lord, known only to Him for the moment, about the church facing rising persecution:

* * *

Official witnesses and executioners dragged a man out of the city of Jerusalem. They took off their coats and laid them at the feet of a young man named Saul from Tarsus, later to be known as Paul the Apostle.

Stones whistled through the air, striking the first martyr Stephen, who prayed, "Lord Jesus, receive my spirit." He dropped to his knees, crying out, "Lord, do not hold this against them," and with that, his body fell into an eternal sleep, his spirit united with the Lord.

Great persecution broke out against the church. Saul continued to destroy the church, going from house to house, dragging off men and women and putting them in prison.

On the road to Damascus, Paul was supernaturally confronted by Jesus Himself saying, "Saul, why do you persecute Me?" Paul was blinded for several days by the event until he recovered. After three years in the wilderness, he began preaching.

Later, in a chamber lit from the soft firelight of candles, many were listening to the Apostle Paul preach the gospel. The church grew despite the tribulation.

* * *

On the Mount of Olives, Jesus continued, "But be of good cheer, for I have overcome the world." Someone coughed and others stirred, but all were quiet as the Lord continued, "Do not go into Jerusalem, but wait for what the Father has promised. John baptized you with water, but you shall be baptized with the Holy Ghost not many days hence."

Simon the Zealot asked the Lord, "Are you going to free Israel from Rome now and restore again the kingdom of Israel?"

"The Father sets those dates, and they are not for you to know," Jesus replied. "But when the Holy Ghost comes upon you, you shall be witnesses unto Me, both in Jerusalem and in all Judea, and in Samaria and to the uttermost ends of the earth about My death and resurrection."

While the Lord was speaking, unknown and unseen to those present, vaporous apparitions of angels, the ancient patriarchs, Marcus' mother, and others who had been resurrected from the dead during the crucifixion gradually came into view, first appearing like watery mirages weaving into focus.

"And these signs shall follow them that believe in My name. They shall they cast out devils. They shall speak with new tongues. They shall take up serpents, and if they drink any deadly thing, it shall not harm them. They shall lay hands on the sick and they shall recover."

Jesus stood up, lifting His hands to bless them. "All power is given unto Me in heaven and in earth." While He spoke, He became resplendent as a beam of silvery sunlight. "Go therefore and teach all nations, baptizing them in the name of the Father, of the Son, and of the Holy Ghost."

A shining circle, glancing in all the colors of the rainbow, fell upon Him. It seemed to overtake and immerse the crowd as He continued speaking, "Teach them to observe all things whatsoever I have commanded you." He now shone brighter than the glory about Him. He laid His left hand on His breast while raising His right hand. "And lo, I am with you always, even unto the end of the world." Turning fully around in all directions, with an outstretched hand, He declared a blessing upon the whole world.

The rays of light from above united with His emanating glory. He gazed upward, His eyes burning with the glow of a bronze fire. Gradually filling with a deep excitement and anticipation, His outward expression remained still; only His eyes projected any emotion He felt. Filled in quiet awe, His eyes narrowed against the strong light and then closed. Raising His hands above His head as if to receive fully the inflowing energy, His hands shook with the force of full energy. A resplendent, radiant beam of golden light burst down and enveloped Him.

Rising, He shone with brilliance as He ascended toward the light source, dissolving into the light from above.

The crowd was immobile.

First His head dissolved then His body. His feet, which seemed to glow like burnished bronze, then disappeared into the celestial glory and into the cloud. It looked as though one sun liquefied into another or as the sun's rays would shine through a crystal globe. The angels, along with the vaporous patriarchs and the resurrected saints, rose from all sides, together with Jesus, as though sparks were floating into a flame. Only two angels remained visible.

From a bird's eye view, something like dew fell with a shower of light upon all those watching until they could endure no longer the dazzling light. The disciples and those closest were forced to lower their eyes, while many others threw themselves prostrate with their faces to the ground. Martha stood alongside her brother Lazarus. He had his arm around Mary, the other sister, her head buried in his chest. Martha gazed upward at the glory before her. Mary the mother of Jesus remained motionless, looking straight forward.

After several minutes, the splendor began to diminish. The whole assembly fell into deep silence as they gazed up into the brightness above them, which remained visible for some time. Their meditations were disturbed only by a deep voice, "Men of Galilee, why do you stand here staring at the sky?"

Their attention being suddenly averted, they saw two angels in their midst that they had not noticed before. The second angel stated with clarity, "Jesus has gone away to heaven and someday, just as He went, He will return."

Immediately, the angels vanished into the fading brightness in the skies above them, the glare already fading like daylight retiring before the darkness of night. A slight breeze blew upon Mary, who stepped forward. She held a fixed gaze upward for a long time in contemplation of the child she bore and who was indeed the Son of God.

The
FIFTY-THIRD
Chapter

AS IT WAS in the house of Caiaphas when Jesus was arrested, the Sanhedrin and chief priests were once again gathered. At the time of His arrest, they met throughout the night and had argued points of law, looking for evidence of criminality to convict Jesus. Now they were residing in the Hall of Hewn Stones as a twenty-three-member panel, functioning as a lesser Sanhedrin, convened to hear witnesses. The Hall of Hewn Stones was built into the north wall of the Temple Mount with a half section inside the sanctuary and the other half section outside. Doors provided access both to the Temple Court and to the outside on the Temple Mount. The sitting places, all hewn of stone, were positioned so members could sit in a semi-circle so that they might see each other. The *nasi* (high priest) sat in the front center. Two secretaries chronicled various opinions expressed by the members, and in this case, the eyewitnesses.

As a rule, the Sanhedrin generally no longer met in the Hall of Hewn Stones as it was restricted by the Roman Empire as a way to remove judicial power to impose criminal penalties. However, if there were non-related hearings such as bearing witness to testimonies and matters regarding doctrine, heresies, issues, affairs, business, and other events of a religious order, the Sanhedrin could proceed to this hall, where seventy-one members of two courts sat. Twenty-three members of one court sat inside the sanctuary at the entrance of the Temple Mount. The other twenty-three members sat outside at the door of the Temple Court where the other half-section of semi-circular rows of hewn stone was situated.

Reports were continuously being brought to the priests about the populace seeing the resurrected dead, or as they called them, "The Risen Ones." Now, the panel deliberated in the anterior segment of the hall, questioning the validity of the witnesses who had been called forth to give testimony. Caiaphas presided over the assembly as the *nasi*, the official head of state. Annas was the *ab ben din*, the second official head of state. They were listening to the testimony of Malkus, the Captain of the Royal Guard.

"I know nothing personally," Malkus claimed, "only what I have learned from the soldiers of the tomb watch."

Caiaphas nodded dismissively, relieving Malkus from his duty as a witness. He called on Isman, the commander of the royal guard, to come forward. He, too, further reiterated what Malkus had just testified. "I also only know what was spoken to me. All the soldiers of the tomb watch are convinced that Jesus was resurrected by supernatural power and that He is alive."

Caiaphas was flustered. As Malkus and Isman exited, they passed Nicodemus, who lingered near the entrance. Three other men from Galilee— Phinees the priest, who had recognized Cherinus and Lenthius at the Temple; Ada, a rabbinical teacher; and Ageus, a Levite—approached the council for questioning by Caiaphas and Annas.

Caiaphas acknowledged them in a monotonous tone and opened the inquisitorial examination with considerable boredom. "Testify to us," he stifled a yawn, "what you have seen and heard."

Ada, the rabbinical teacher, was the first to bear witness under oath. "Humbly I speak that we saw with our own eyes the one from Galilee, who was crucified, to be alive. He was speaking with His disciples on Mount Olivet."

Ageus the Levite, who stood without emotion near Ada, further authenticated the testimony. "Afterward, we saw Him ascending unto the height of the heavens."

Caiaphas leaned over to speak with Annas in hushed overtones. "I am finding myself disturbed. Reports of these doings have become commonplace."

Annas nodded in affirmation. In a draconian manner, Annas rose from his seat in a feeble slouch. Squinting and half expecting the eyewitnesses to be mad, he touched the end of his beard in a concerted manner. He began his interrogation. "In the presence of the Most High," he waved a hand in dramatic fashion fully about the Sanhedrin, "and in the presence of the masters of Israel, do you affirm whether these things are of a true report?"

"If we do not own the words we speak," responded Ageus, "then we should all be guilty of our own sin!"

Annas sat back down with bewilderment, slumping into his seat, arms resting on the arm supports of the chair. With a grave expression, he leaned forward and resumed anxiously stroking his beard as if in deep thought while the Sanhedrin muttered amongst themselves. He leaned back and over to the ear of Caiaphas, declaring in a hoarse whisper, "Reports of His resurrection keep surfacing among these reputable Jews." Caiaphas nodded.

As the two conversed, Nicodemus stood within spitting distance, his eyebrows narrowed over his green eyes in meditation. In the gesture of a wise man making a decision, he rested an elbow on his wrist, caressing his beard with his thumb and forefinger. He narrowed his eyes further as if trying to see an answer to the disbelief in the room. He stopped stroking the beard and stepped forward, interrupting Annas and Caiaphas in the midst of their mumbling whispers, arresting their attention.

"We have a tradition according to the question of whether these men speak truth." Caiaphas motioned for Nicodemus to continue, half in curiosity and half in wanting to hear fresh revelation. Nicodemus glanced about the semicircular chamber, "Does not our law say, 'By the mouth of two or three witnesses, that every word shall be established'?" Viewing his audience with calm composure, Nicodemus hesitated for a moment so his question could take hold. Many babbled amongst themselves, and more than a few nodded in affirmation. "Yea, thus have I expounded, and thus have my brethren expounded, and thus have I taught, and thus have my brethren taught, so that we may know the truth."

With his head bent low, Nicodemus moved about the hall with his hands clasped behind his back. Looking up, he held his head high with serenity and continued, "By these three testimonies, we have heard from the mouths of three witnesses. These men, as well as many others, have declared that they have seen Jesus alive and ascending into the heavens." He shrugged his shoulders. "Should this not, then, be the truth of their testimonies? Should this not be reason enough that these men speak the truth and we should believe these testimonies? Perhaps Jesus *has* risen from the grave as was foretold in scriptures."

Numerous Sanhedrin adherents voiced their sentiments while Caiaphas remained unsatisfied with his head lifted high, his chin jutting forward, exposing his throat in an arrogant fashion of superiority. He did not like—

"You may be under a great astonishment," Phinees the priest interjected, "to find that many have said that Jesus is alive." A hush came over the assembly. "Which is more of a surprise, that He should raise up from the grave or that He *also* raises up others along with Himself?" Various members of the assembly traded furtive glances. Phinees continued, "Those who have risen from their graves have been among us and have been seen in the streets of Jerusalem. As aforesaid, does this not provoke the notion that such an event has never occurred before on the earth?"

As the Sanhedrin set off to blathering once more, Gamaliel approached Phinees. He asked curiously, "Tell us, do you know of any who have risen from their graves, for we have heard many reports." Upon hearing the question, the assembly grew quiet.

"Yes," Phinees stated. He threw a glance across the assembly. "We all knew our blessed Simeon, the high priest." Many nodded in agreement. "This same Simeon had two sons of his own, Lenthius and Charinus, whom we all knew well. We were present at their deaths and funeral." Looking toward the back in the direction of the doors leading out from the Temple to the outside, he continued, "Lo, they are amongst the risen ones." He pointed. "And they are within our midst to give testimony."

The
FIFTY-FOURTH
Chapter

FIRST THERE CAME a silence of consternation, then undertones of disbelief followed by whisperings uttered in low and inarticulate mutterings. Caiaphas manifested strong reservations. Everyone's attention was diverted by two men entering. Caiaphas let out a drawn-out breath of astonishment and half stood. All slouching forms straightened. Everyone's head came up at once. Many members of the Sanhedrin were up out of their seats to catch a glimpse of the two men dressed in rough attire and grubby tunics, a striking contrast to the sophisticated opulence of the Sanhedrin and leaders of Israel.

The two kinsmen walked through the assemblage as all stepped to the rear to form a narrow pathway. Archelaus, who stood with the assembly, cowered as he drew back into the crowd, nodding to Lenthius and Charinus as they looked in his direction, acknowledging him as they passed on by. All the others dropped back in fright and alarm, disquieted in heart, soul, and mind, all filled with incredulous wonder.

Nicodemus fell back with everybody else as Lenthius and Charinus moved through the collection of unprepossessing souls, focused and confident. He marked the effect on the community of the Jewish Supreme Court, smiling at their dumbfounded expressions with their mouths agape, their eyes wide open, and their eyebrows raised. An ingratiating smile spread across his face.

Lenthius and Charinus approached Caiaphas and Annas with boldness not seen in the other witnesses. Caiaphas could hardly restrain himself. Gasping, Annas held his breath, breaking out in a cold sweat. He rose from his seat sluggishly, moved by fright and alarm. He studied the two men with a whitish owl face, his parochial eyes scanning their entire beings. The veins in his neck pulsated visibly, his breathing shallow. Lenthius, in turn, gazed back stonily. Being mystified and afraid, Annas held out before him a book of the law, which he raised in front of him with grimness, as if it were a talisman to ward off evil. Charinus cocked his head to one side, eyeballing the book and saying, "There is no need to be afraid."

Lenthius turned his attention to those around him, examining their faces. A good number were caught gawking. Archelaus edged back a bit farther, anxious to be hidden as he was embarrassed to be one of those captured in the scrutiny of Lenthius' gaze,

With respect and deference, Annas hesitated as he approached the two men with tense muscle movements. His lips trembled while he announced in a broken voice, accentuated in various tones, "Tell me—uh us," he stammered, "what you have been—uh, what you have seen." He shivered with faltering words, "What you have—um, how you were raised from the dead."

He looked on with apprehension as Lenthius and Charinus gave off the impression of being annoyed. Annas licked his lips, his mouth dry. After what seemed to be a long and terrible moment, the two brothers closed their eyes as though in prayer.

Charinus' eyelids fluttered and then opened. Looking straight into the eyes of Annas, he declared, "We have not come to announce the mysteries of God."

Lenthius raised his eyes, his gaze falling upon Annas and Caiaphas. "We have come to declare and glorify the resurrection of our Lord Jesus Christ and Savior, seeing that He hath raised us from the dead at the same time as Himself."

Annas strained to remain in control of his inner being. "By Adoni and the Most High, who spoke to our fathers by the law and the prophets, do you believe Him who raised you from the dead to be—to be this Jesus from Nazareth, a Galilean?"

"We are here to bear testimony," answered Charinus, "and to give proof along with others who have been raised from their graves, that Jesus Christ is the truth, the life, and the resurrection, and that *no man* can come unto the Father, but through and *by Him.*"

Lenthius surveyed the congregation with the air of an expert witness, raising his voice to be heard by all. "Jesus Christ is the only way to Heaven. Apart from Him, there is no other way, and by no other means!" Turning once again to Annas and Caiaphas, he stated in a voice louder than before so that all would be able to hear. "You condemned Jesus out of jealousy. He cast away your traditions, declaring you 'vipers' and 'hypocrites.' You condemned Him out of fear that the people would follow His teachings." Lenthius rotated in a full circle so all would hear, "What is wrong is that you have wicked and perverse hearts."

"This you must repent of!" elaborated Charinus. "This Lamb you have slain is the One spoken of in the prophecies, from Isaiah to King David. It is He who was to be slain for all mankind, the sacrifice being made for all who have sinned and come short of the glory of God. He died so that *you* might be saved. He is resurrected into the newness of life; therefore, having overlooked the times of ignorance, God is now declaring that all people everywhere should repent, because He has fixed a day in which He will judge the world of righteousness through a Man He has appointed, having furnished proof to all men by raising Him from the dead."

"His resurrection is proof of His deity and that He is the Son of God, overcoming the power of death!" ended Lenthius.

Diffidence and apprehension invaded the assembly with a few smiting their breasts, a number escaping the hall in great distress, others timorous with feelings of aversion and anger, while a minority experienced remorse and concern.

Annas seemed to be suffocating. He looked about frantically, growing more confused by the abhorrence he felt. The dread he had before returned. His lips parted and shaped words without a sound. He dropped to his seat, beaten, faint-hearted, and mixed up, sorely under conviction.

Nicodemus stood in awe and wonderment. "Verily, all these things were wrought by God."

Archelaus, with temerity in his voice, asked himself, "What is this extraordinary thing that hath befallen us in Jerusalem?

Caiaphas sat with his head and body erect, shoulders squared, hands spread out on each knee, and bearing down until his fingers separated further apart and the knuckles turned white. With an ever-increasing glare, he seemed to be turning many things over in his mind. Boring within him was a single thought: *I shall have no rest, day or night. Shall peaceful sleep ever come to my pillow?* He sat with fixed angry eyes for a few more moments, and then he relaxed with a frown, the skin wrinkling beneath the lower eyelids. He covered his forehead with a large brown venous hand, as though he had a headache. Sighing, he whispered, "I am weary."

The
FIFTY-FIFTH
Chapter

MANY FOLLOWERS OF Jesus and numerous righteous Jews of various dialects and nations had come to Jerusalem for the Shavuot ceremonies, otherwise known as Pentecost, meaning 50 days. This took place during the appointed time of Shavuot or the Feast of Weeks, which was ordained by God in Leviticus 23. It was 9:00 A.M. on this holy day as large crowds arriving for morning worship scaled the broad staircase of the southern stairs leading up to the massive double gates.

Longinus, on traffic control, loitered on the large plaza next to the foot of the stairs where literally hundreds of thousands of worshippers and travelers mingled during the major festivals.

The disciples themselves were found to be continuously at the Temple courts, waiting for the day of Pentecost as Jesus had told them to do: *"Tarry here in the city of Jerusalem until you are endued with the power from on high."* On this particular day, they were all in one place inside the synagogue in Solomon's porch with their hands lifted in praise, adoration, and prayer.

A rustling sound like a great wind was heard as throngs entered the gates and the magnificent passageways leading to the floor of the Temple Mount and out onto the Court of the Gentiles. The *whooshing* sound of wind grew until it caught the attention of the crowd as they came together in bewilderment, Longinus along with them.

Crowds can display various personality traits, which can lead to either chaos and danger or merriment and festivities. The whole nature of an event can produce either mass panic and harm or lightheartedness, laughter, and joyous celebrations of singing and dancing.

Perceiving a disturbance among the people around him, and before he could rationalize, Longinus felt a push from behind. A sense of panic welled within him as he realized pandemonium could be unfolding. Before he knew it, he was propelled with the swarm of humanity. The crowd rushed to the synagogue in the direction of the powerful wind as it descended with an ever-increasing roar.

The intensity of the noise amplified. The rushing wind filled the synagogue. Where the disciples and followers were worshipping, a unique sound reached their ears like that of a hurricane cracking and breaking everything in its roaring path. It tore through the ornate archways and through the great house of six rib-vaulted bays with three standing columns supporting and separating the spaces. Six pillars flanked the walls with Corinthian-style columns, the spiky leaves adhering to their bulk, ending in scrolls at the ceilings. The domed ceilings were elaborate with carved vines, rosettes, flowers, and geometrical patterns. The rushing wind crashed through the bays with a mighty bellow like the rushing of subterranean water crashing over a waterfall, the furious gust vibrating the three standing columns. The six pillars flanking the side walls quivered in the ferocious turbulence.

The atmosphere was imbued in a saffron hazy glow as pollen-like particles floated in the shimmering air. The fiery particles held no agitation in the deafening airstream having an urgent breath-like whisper together with a strange echo that resolved into *Receive*. Just as the first Adam had received the breath of physical life, so the second Adam, Jesus, brought forth the breath of spiritual life, which was generated by the Holy Spirit, implicit in the wind.

The bizarre and brilliant floating fiery particles turned into spits of white flame. Longinus entered the synagogue. He looked up to witness a shower of cinders falling, which developed into a fine rain of fiery drops. These came down in varying degrees of intensity, falling upon the heads of the disciples and others in attendance. They appeared to have fire atop their heads, and they were all overwhelmed with joy.

They all threw their heads back, raising their eyes with eagerness, while streams of light flowed into their mouths like burning coals of fire. The people drank in this fire and inhaled. When they exhaled, flames came forth, like a person's breath on a cold winter day.

The effusion of holy light pervaded the assembly. All were full of emotion, intoxicated with joy and confidence. Mary the mother of Jesus stood in perfect calm, dressed in a large creamy white mantle. A blue scarf, ornamented with embroidery, was thrown over her head and held firm by a white silken crown. She seemed to be the only one who retained a quiet, holy self-possession.

Crowds of over three thousand were amassing within and without the synagogue, astonished to hear the disciples miraculously speaking in foreign dialects and idioms. At first they heard indistinct murmuring, but then the various foreign groups began to understand the dialogues of their own tongues, including those of the Parthians, Medes, and Elamites. Also heard were the languages of Mesopotamia, Judea, Cappadocia, Pontus, Asia, Phrygia, and Pamphylia. The dialects of the regions of Italy and Greece were heard alongside the idioms of the Cretans and Arabs.

Longinus was baffled as much as anyone else as to what was taking place. Someone near him expressed amazement: "They speak with tongues of angels!"

A Grecian simultaneously voiced his confusion: "Are not all these who speak Galileans?"

A neighboring Egyptian replied, "They speak in our own tongues; they speak of the mighty deeds of God."

Longinus was amazed and perplexed. Regarding the Egyptian and the Grecian, he asked, "What does this mean?"

An Italian behind them mocked, "They are full of the sweet wine."

Peter addressed the crowd. "Men of Judea, and all who live in Jerusalem, let this be known to you and give heed to my words. These men are not drunk as you suppose, for it is only the third hour of the day, but this is what was spoken of through the prophet Joel when God said, 'And it shall be in the last days that I will pour out My Spirit on all mankind. And your sons and your daughters shall prophesy, and your young men shall see visions, and your old men shall dream dreams. Even on My bondslaves, both men and women, I will in those days pour forth of My Spirit, and they shall prophesy. And I will grant wonders in the sky above and signs on the earth below; blood and fire, and vapor and smoke.' You may recall the sun darkening, the moon turning to blood red, silhouetting the crosses during the crucifixion. The sun shall be turned into darkness and the moon into blood before the great and glorious day of the Lord shall come. And it shall be that everyone who calls upon the name of the Lord will be saved."

Peter's eyes wandered over the crowd. "Brethren, I may confidently say to you regarding the patriarch David, that he both died and was buried, and his tomb is with us to this day. Because he was a prophet, he looked ahead and spoke of the resurrection of Christ, that His soul was not left in Hades, neither did His flesh see corruption. This Jesus hath God raised up, and we are all witnesses. Therefore, let all the house of Israel know assuredly that God hath made that same Jesus, whom you crucified, both the Lord and Christ, the Messiah. Having received from the Father the promise of the Holy Spirit, He has poured forth this which you both see and hear."

Longinus shouted out, "What shall we do?"

"Repent, and each of you be baptized in the name of Jesus Christ for the forgiveness of your sins, and you will receive the gift of the Holy Spirit. Be saved from this perverse generation."

The bold preaching of Peter to a Jewish and Gentile audience was powerful as listeners were cut to the heart, including that of the Egyptian, the Grecian, and three thousand others.

Longinus fell to his knees. The crowd surrounding him seemed to fade away as a radiance of light enveloped him. "Jesus," he said, "forgive me a sinner, such as I am. I repent and turn away from my wicked ways, to repeat my sins no more." Looking upward and closing his eyes, he willed a response to receiving the baptism of the Holy Spirit, his expression remaining emotionless, his mouth closed and even. But nothing happened.

Finally, in open surrender, he raised his arms above his head. Raising his face further upward, he opened his mouth as spits of fire encircled him. He inhaled deeply to receive. Upon exhaling, a vaporous flame shot forth from his mouth with each syllable of a word spoken, as he received the baptism of the Holy Spirit with the evidence of speaking in tongues.

The

LAST CHAPTER

A VERTICAL SHAFT of sunlight fell through the portal of a dome like the finger of God, engulfing a solitary figure in a spectral glow, igniting the surface of his golden armored *cuirass* (breastplate) with a metallic yellow aura. His snowy white silken tunic gleamed in the sunlight. His scarlet mantle, tied over the *cuirass*, caught the beam so he seemed to be sheathed in an outline of blood, giving him a near god-like appearance.

The sunray came through a light well in the center of the dome. This central opening to the sky was a cylindrical space atop a hemispherical dome rising 142 feet above a marbled floor. The dome was part of a larger structure called the Pantheon, meaning "house of all gods." This was commissioned by the Roman General Marcus Agrippa, the son-in-law of the Roman Emperor Augustus, as a temple to represent all the gods of Rome. The portal had been designed by the architect Apollodorus of Damascus in an effort to achieve a fiery demonstration of the all-seeing legendary gods of Rome. This sphere of light not only represented perfection, but also the heavens. It was meant to give forth a star-burning illumination to all. For those who worshipped the gods, it set them on fire with a divine infusion of the watchful gaze of gods and goddesses.

Circles and squares were an underlying theme of the interior design of the building. The marble floors consisted of a series of geometric patterns that were in contrast to the concentric circles of the squared coffers of the dome. The floors were a beautiful example of Roman mosaics, using the same materials, colors, and patterns as in the rest of the building. Four different types of marble were used in the flooring to represent the four corners of Rome. For the most part, white marble was decorated with either red, dark purple, or black marbled squared outlines. There were also several solid-colored gold marbled squares with dark purple-black circles inside.

The perimeter walls of the rotunda that the dome rested on rose to a height of three stories. It had the same awe-inspiring inner diameter as the height of the dome, making the structure a perfect globe shape. Statues of the worshipped gods, representing all of Rome's multiple and superstitious beliefs, occupied a series of carved-out niches within the circular walls of the Pantheon, surrounding all those in attendance. The main niche facing the huge bronzed entrance doors was the most important feature of the Pantheon, for it housed the master of all gods—Jupiter Optimus Maximus. The statue itself rose twenty-five feet above the marbled flooring.

For now, the Pantheon was being adapted for use by the Roman senate as a place of high court. The great and awful Emperor Caesar Tiberius sat above the senate on a makeshift throne for his seat of power.

Situated throughout, and on either side of the emperor, was the Praetorian Guard, the supreme military bodyguards of Caesar. Their uniforms consisted of deep scarlet neck scarves and thigh-length tunics tied together with golden epaulets. They also wore dark blue trousers laced with vertical scarlet stripes on the outside of the leggings. In addition, they had Greek-styled helmets trimmed in black and gold, complemented by scarlet plumage atop their headgear. They also donned silver breastplates ornamented with a scorpion, the emblem of the Praetorian Guard, representing Scorpio, the astrological symbol under which Emperor Tiberius was born. The remainder of their full military attire involved ornamented greaves, gauntlets, and an ornate belt. This belt was the hallmark of a soldier, unique by a swath of several hanging leather straps embellished with small metal disks and fancy terminal pieces that would jingle as the wearer walked. At last, they wore leather boots. To signify they were the Praetorian, their oval shields were black and gold with the insignia of the moon and stars. They held no weapons when in the presence of the Caesar and the senate.

Pilate, the lone figure standing in the shaft of sunlight under the portal of the dome, stood inattentive before the senate and Caesar as questioning was underway. Gazing in awe about the chamber, Pilate was impacted by the immensity of the space. He was filled with a sense of wonder as he recognized his small stature in contrast to the enormous building, with its triangular pediments, the gold-plated dome centered over the rotunda, and the Corinthian columns.

As he surveyed the gods, Pilate felt he was on trial, not just before Caesar and the senate, but also before these demonic entities, the gods whom he worshipped, and that of God Himself, for why he had crucified the god-man. The voice of one of distinguished origin was speaking, beyond Pilate's conscious mind. It grew in tenor, *"And because of your transgression, the darkness and the earthquake have happened all over the world"* to gradually amplify to a clearer and bolder voice, "By daring to do such a deed, you have ruined the entire world!"

The voice, loud and penetrating, thundered through Pilate's brain until his blood froze with an increasing awareness that Tiberius was speaking to him. Sudden panic swept over him, mindful that his inattentiveness could cost him his life.

Turning his attention back to the matter on hand, Pilate caught a view of Emperor Caesar Tiberius standing near his judgment seat. Surrounded by the statues of the divinities, it seemed that Tiberius reflected the light of the heavens off the gold-plated bronzed bricks of the dome, thus imparting power unto Caesar, producing in Pilate more angst to his tragedy. Pilate's heart pounded hard in his chest, the blood rushing to his face.

Tiberius' upper body leaned forward while shaking an angry fist. Raising an index finger, his eyebrows leveled in anger over enlarged eyes, his face turning a furious red. He spoke with a voice of clarity. "Why would you dare to do thus?" he questioned with a stentorian voice that caused Pilate to be more uncomfortable than he already was. "Why would you crucify a god-man who would have come to Rome to heal me of my disease and discomfort?"

Tiberius' voice echoed throughout the Pantheon. Pilate rubbed the back of his neck and drew in a nervous breath. Expelling air with a sigh, he broke out into a cold sweat. He could see the senate displaying the same expression as that of the divine emperor: serious, stern, and disapproving. Arms and legs were crossed. Hands were clasped. Some showed signs of interest, but they displayed hostility through downturned lips and furrowed brows.

Pilate was fearful with a sinking heart, afraid the gods might expose to the emperor his conduct and crimes as procurator. He recalled his endless corruptions, abuses, pilfers, scandals, and malevolent injuries, along with his multiple sins of grievous cruelty and executions without trial. Anxious that he might compromise himself in speech, he resolved in his heart that he must be careful in giving his responses so he would not uncover any of his wrongdoings. It could mean a demotion along with exile to the outer regions of Rome, or even his death, if he said the wrong thing.

Not being able to see Tiberius and the senate clearly through the sunny haze, Pilate dared to take a step forward beyond the column of sunlight, but before he could manage the first step, he was halted by the harsh voice of Tiberius, "You may stay where you are. No reason to venture further!"

Pilate's body trembled. Straightening himself, he raised his chin and cleared his throat, as he always did when he felt awkward. His face was gloomy and his lips compressed. He began his speech, but it was as if someone else talked for him, for his voice seemed not to be his own. With an easygoing, persuasive, calm manner, he began, "If Your Excellency will permit, I would ask the senate and the all-powerful Caesar to recall an incident that took place over ten years ago. This was an uprising among the Hebrews, in which two thousand Jews were killed under my auspices on the Temple Mount." He fidgeted with the hilt of his sword. "I ask you to recall, because it was by this incident that I was obliged, for fear of another insurrection, to yield to the wishes of the high priests, to the Sanhedrin, and to the will of the people who tumultuously demanded the death of this god—"

"When they delivered this Jesus to you," interrupted Tiberius, "why did you not secure Him and send Him to me and not consent to crucify this god-man who wrought such great mira—"

A slight quiver ran throughout the Pantheon at the mention of the god-man, interrupting Tiberius in mid-sentence. He grew quiet along with everyone else. A vibrating, pounding tremor struck, rattling the foundation and the gods in their alcoves for a long minute and then diminished.

Golden dust motes trickled into the beam of sunlight where Pilate stood. No one dared to move or even draw a breath. A melodramatic hush of silent suspense saturated the assembly. No one spoke.

Tiberius staggered back in abject fear and lowered himself into his seat of judgment. His face, which had been angry red, was now pale, with a suggestion of panic in his bulging eyes. Timidly, he studied the gods resting in their niches. His blinking eyes were glassy. He hesitated to say more, lest something else should happen. But he felt compelled to express his inner thoughts, even to the exclusion of everything else, so he spoke again. His voice displayed his disturbance. "It would appear by such miracles, that this god-man, this Jesus—"

BOOM! A low, resonant rumble echoed throughout the Pantheon.

Again, no one moved. All were afraid, all eyes were riveted on the gods, and they were all caught up in their own superstitions. Abruptly, they felt a dull vibration.

With a sudden great upheaval, the infrastructure shuddered, pulsated, and then convulsed in violent popping, cracking, and breaking! The walls screamed into a hissing roar of scraping stone upon stone, the floor grinding in a vigorous jarring and jerky movements. The decibel level was deafening with weighty falling objects and breaking rock. The effigies of the gods swayed, toppling with a massive BOOM.

The sculptured god of Jupiter fell forward in slow motion and toward Pilate with a startling, heavy CRASH, exploding with jarring impact followed by a buffeting shockwave, sending huge clouds of white and gray dust into the air.

The earthquake growled off into the distance. The jolting movements scattered in all directions, finally dissipating into minor rattling that eventually grew quiet.

Shafts of sunlight pierced through clouds of swirling dust and cut through the billowy atmosphere, piercing like torches in a fog. Through the dusty haze, the dim shapes of fallen statues could be seen, their fragments scattered on the marble floor. On the other side of this chaotic mess, the senate, Tiberius, and the multitude of the house bore signs of terror and astonishment. Aftershocks soon followed. Walls shivered and more chunks of plaster crashed to the floor, filling the air with new swirls of dust filtering through the sunbeam.

All was still. Quiet.

Pilate smashed into view through swirling clouds of white and gray dust, appearing wraithlike and ghostly, coughing, sputtering, and spitting out flotsam. Isolated rays of sunlight danced around him, casting him in long shadows in the hazy air. Tiberius' disembodied voice floated toward Pilate, reverberating in a tremulous singsong rise and fall, *"Who is this One that was crucified? His name has brought all ruin to the gods!"*

Pilate gaped through the cloudy air at the devastation. Beads of sweat trickled down his forehead and brow, cutting rivulets over his dust-covered face. His stormy blue eyes mirrored the wafting dust like billowing white thunderclouds.

Turning his focus upward into the foggy shaft of penetrating sunlight, Pilate's voice was thick and rough, his words coming out as though he were being strangled. "Astounded by this terror, and with utmost trembling, I am convinced, your Most Divine Excellency, that this Jesus of Nazareth of whom we speak is a deity who is *greater* than all the gods we venerate in Rome!"

Epilogue

FASTER THAN THE speed of light, through a quadrant of seven stars, three of which are close together, an intergalactic traveler journeys toward the middle star. In fact, it is not a star, but rather a cloudy region of emerald, illuminated by several massive and hot stars. As the traveler draws nearer, one can see that it is an angelic being.

As the angel reaches this emerald-tinted curtain, it first ascertains three stars shining through a vast corridor of gas and dust nebulas. It is a colorful and awe-inspiring spectacle, twenty-thousand times larger than our solar system, twenty-four light-years wide and fifteen hundred light-years from Earth. Beyond is a gap through which a much brighter expanse can be seen, with four bright and dazzling stars in a tight cluster. Called "The Trapezium," this area illuminates much of the surrounding nebulas with mesmerizing reflections of blue, violet, red, and green, the latter color being dominant.

A black path extends from this region as a passageway through which the angel proceeds north toward an even brighter region. This is illuminated on both sides and has the appearance of massive wings; these wing-like borders are laced with expanses of red and blue-violet. Dense nebulous clouds, billions of miles across, hide an incredible source of vivid light from an unknown source.

Beyond these vast veils and through intergalactic swirls of gas and cosmic dust, the angelic traveler passes through this colossal region known as the Great Orion Nebula. It proceeds toward a black hole looming large and massive in the distance. Objects zoom past, one close enough to reveal that it is an also angelic being heading in the same direction. Flying crossways are other extraterrestrial beings, angelic in origin and born of fire.

Crisscrossing the busy thoroughfare are a number of angels embarking to farther destinations, coming out of the portal the original angel is journeying toward, carrying with them various information, answers to prayers, instructions, and commands from Elohim, the Mighty One.

An entity flashes by overhead toward the gateway of eternity, the doorway to forever, where past, present, and future hold no bounds and come together into one band of time. It is one dimension over another, side to side, over to end, and top over the other, an era, an age, an epoch stretching into infinity, where one day is as a thousand years.

A large faint cloud looms ahead.

Upon entering this large and dim gaseous storm cloud, the angel observes a gravitational lens effect, much like that of a halo or ring, causing a fairly bright distorted image of the cloud. Rose-amber in color with a smattering of blue bursting outward, the cloud is continuously enfolding in itself until fire and continuous flashes of light issue forth with varying intensity. The core of this interstellar cloud appears as glowing metal in the midst of a fire.

Passing into, through, and out to the other side, the angelic being rockets through faster than the twinkling of an eye. The storm cloud becomes increasingly dense with vapor-like fog swirling into a fine golden rain. This dissipates into a blue mist that becomes clearer the farther the angel advances beyond the rainy golden veil. The angel finally enters an expansive crystal heaven, so beautiful that no human could fathom.

About this expansive crystal heaven radiate jewel-like suns that gleam in many oscillating shades, colors, and hues. The angel acknowledges these as other angelic beings. Floating in the atmosphere without moving far from their positions, four indistinct human shapes loom large, gleaming like burnished bronze. Their legs are straight, and they have cloven feet similar to that of calves. The beings have four faces and four wings. Two of the wings stretch upward from the middle of the back and touch each other at the ends, and the other two stretch downward and cover their bodies. Under the wings, these creatures have human-like bodies and hands. Resembling living fire, these angelic beings are the cherubim, the great and mighty ones, the guardians of the great throne of God.

Each of the cherubim has four faces—the front being the face of a man, the right side of a lion, the left of a bull, and the back of an eagle. Wherever they move, their faces never turn. From a distance, burning coals of fire appear to be moving in between and around them. The fire is bright with an issuance of lightning coming forth as energy, in a continuum of bluish flames.

With great speed, the angel draws nearer to see the burning coals taking on the shapes of glowing, brilliant torches, which are actually living creatures darting to and fro among the cherubim like flashing spirits of alternating currents. Beneath each cherub is a wheel within a wheel, like a gyroscope, so it can move in any direction, appearing as sparkling pale-green passing into blue, yellow, and white. The wheels have something like rims and spokes, the rims being filled with eyes around the edges. The spirits of the cherubim are within the wheels, so that wherever they go, their bodies do not rotate, bend, or curve.

The cherubim move forward with the roar of a sea hitting upon a shore, then upward into what looks like a crystal heaven, but what is actually the Crystal Sea, having the consistency of glass with seven unbroken gradations of transparency, the whole being of smooth alignment.

In the expansive distant regions of the Crystal Sea resides the immense, colossal Blue Sapphire Throne. No matter what angle or depth of the Crystal Sea one could be passing through, the Blue Sapphire Throne can be seen in different perspectives.

From the lowest perspective, the Blue Sapphire Throne simulates a hologram with visible immeasurable depths. As the cherubim soar upward and through diverse transparencies of the Crystal Sea, the Blue Sapphire Throne varies in appearance as though seen through refractions, like a light bulb through differing degrees of transparency.

After they pass through the divergent depths of the Crystal Sea, the cherubim arrive on the surface that seems to be of one transparency, solid and unyielding, stretching forth as far as the eye can see. The shiny sea appears as polished glass with a clear whiteness bright and reflecting, gleaming and sparkling.

In the distance, the magnificent Blue Sapphire Throne oscillates with the intensity of a star, scintillating with the brilliance of a diamond. It also blazes with carnelian redness like the fiery rays of the ruby. Unapproachable light issues forth from the throne in fiery splinters of flashing whiteness, piercing through anything or anyone in its path.

Ponderous thunder rolls in the distance.

A spectral halo resembling a glowing rainbow encircles the Blue Sapphire Throne with beautiful emerald rays dominating its seven-hued wonder. All is ethereal purity and majestic peacefulness. In a straight line to the Blue Sapphire Throne, the Crystal Sea of glass mirrors this surreal imagery with the appearance of glass mingled with fire.

Changing direction, one would see the back of the Great Orion Nebula and realize where the vivid light comes from. The massive wings of the nebula, its borders laced with red and blue-violet and much of the surrounding area with mesmerizing reflections of blue, violet, red, and green, are in effect the reflections of the Blue Sapphire Throne.

Beyond the Blue Sapphire Throne is like looking into eternity, a doorway to forever where there are perpetual uninterrupted days among timeless worlds. It is like a mirror reflecting a mirror with no variation of time. Eternity is something on the other side of nothing, an abstract continuum of time after a particular time. It is beyond the state of mind and intermingles with an instant, a moment, and an era.

Before the Blue Sapphire Throne is a golden lampstand, a candelabrum with seven pipes and lamps and seven torches of straight jet-like flame. This golden candelabrum evokes the image of the seven-branched menorah or lampstand in the Temple. These torches are arranged around a large golden bowl containing a reservoir of olive oil. The bowl is held up by the lampstand and is carved on either side with images of olive trees representing anointed ones or "sons of fresh oil" who stand by the Lord of the whole earth.

Two golden olive branches or olive clusters stem from the lampstand. They drip olive oil into seven golden pipes. The oil flows through the pipes into the lamps that top with spouts. A fountain spray of olive oil emanates from these seven spouts, and the tips of the spouts light the torches.

The inbound angel appears from the long distance, traveling at an enormous rate of speed. Passing over the golden lampstand, it sees below the seven spurting spouts of streaming flame, which take on the shapes of flaming personages representing the seven spirits of God.

The angel leaves behind the golden lampstand to approach the golden altar. Underneath it are smoky ghost-like martyrs who have died for their faith and call out airily, *"How long, O Lord, holy and true, will it be before You judge and avenge our blood on them that dwell upon the earth?"*

The angel crosses the vast Crystal Sea of Glass, reaching the golden altar of incense with four horns at the ends, a replica of the altar in the Temple sanctuary. A creature of light stands before the golden altar and is holding a golden censer. The angel is not transparent but rather three-dimensional of purest white. Shining through its whiteness is a beautiful iridescence displaying every color of the spectrum. The creature of light's countenance is as bright as the sun with a multicolored halo and eyes blazing like lamps of fire. A golden band wraps around the waist. From the back of the shoulders flow long trains, giving the appearance of wings. Its feet are like pillars of fire.

This angelic being throws incense on the burning coals in the golden altar of incense. Aromatic smoke rises, representing the prayers and praises of the saints. In the smoke can be heard whispers, groans, exclamations, shouts, praises, and adorations.

The angel arrives above the golden altar of incense and descends alongside numerous other angels. The angel dips its hands into the aromatic smoke from which it extracts a lump of yellowish-orange glowing coal. The angel then continues its voyage, traversing the expanse of the Crystal Sea to finally alight before the Blue Sapphire Throne. It has the glowing embers still in its hands to present as a real offering before the Great Throne.

Spears of lightning and resonant thunder erupt from the Blue Sapphire Throne.

In the thunder can be heard voices as if many people are speaking simultaneously. It's altogether great and terrifying! Seated upon the Blue Sapphire Throne is the living body of a sun, an extraterrestrial life form, emitting a continuous glow. The well-defined sphere gives off light and heat. In the nucleus appears the likeness of a man. The upper part of His body glows like metal surrounded by fire, and the lower part is like fire with a radiance of energy all around Him.

Fiery manifestations emanate from Him in different hues of light, from the delicate pale shade of a soft warm glow to the white-hot intensity of a sun. Surmounting and arcing solar flares are far-reaching and expansive but not blinding. The warmth and heat can be felt, but not wholly. More remarkable is that this brazier heat and light penetrate but do not cause pain.

This living Being is:

God in all His majesty.
The Mighty One.
The Father of lights!

Myriad sounds fill the heart and mind, with joyful sounds and melodies satiating the air. The most amazing sound is the *whooshing* of wings, a beautiful and pleasant resonance, like a deep symphonic cadence that never stops. It is form of never-ending praise, leaving one awestruck, wanting only to listen, and with a sense that it comes from above.

Before God's throne, the angel carries the glowing embers as an offering of prayers and praises. In the midst of a multitude of angels, masses of saints dance, bow, sing, and worship before the Blue Sapphire Throne in the accompaniment of music that is different from anything heard on Earth. It has nonstop intensity and an endless variety of songs being sung simultaneously, but without competition. It comes from every direction, some instrumental, all musical, yet comprising melodies and tones never heard before. It embraces the soul with exhilaration, as if one is part of the music, played in and through the body. A golden-ruby light, originating from the throne, pulses with myriad shades and hues according to the level of praise.

The angels vary greatly. Some have wings and some don't. Some appear to be male and others appear as female with great beauty, all dressed in resplendent garments encrusted with jewels in their apparel and armor. The angels also have varying degrees of brightness.

On four sides of the Throne stand four brilliant and enormous living beings called the seraphim, each dotted in front and back and under their wings with eyes. Each seraph has six wings—two covering its face, two covering its feet, and two being used to fly. These burning ones are as beautiful as lightning, emitting bright bursts splaying outwardly until even the angels cannot look upon them. The flesh of each seraph is alive with flame through veins of fire. It has spears of lightning in place of eyelashes and incandescent flaming torches for eyes.

The first of the living beings is in the form of a lion, the second with the likeness of an ox, the third has the face of a man, and the fourth has the shape of an eagle with wings spread out as though in flight.

Additional seraphim hover around the throne having human faces and hands with six wings—two to cover their faces, two to cover their feet, and two to fly. They sing with human voices the *Trisagion*, which means the eternal praises of God. Certain seraphim lead the multitude of saints in praise and worship, teaching them new songs, developing new songs, and singing unto the glory of God. The chords, strains, descants, and airs blend into a harmonious synchronization that comes from every direction, a cacophony of noise that melds with each voice or instrument. This would be a confusion of sound on earth, but here, an amalgamation of hundreds of songs never before heard, celestial tunes surpassing anything ever heard before—hymns of praise, contemporary and ancient chants, end-to-end librettos, lyrics, and stanzas—come alive with musical tones of living colors never perceived or known to exist.

Around the Throne are seated twenty-four elders on twenty-four thrones, clothed in white raiment with crowns of gold upon their heads. The twenty-four elders fall before the Throne of God, also called the Throne of Grace, worshiping the One who sits on the Throne. They cast their crowns before the Blue Sapphire Throne, which represents multi-faceted divine wisdom, intelligence, and omniscience.

"O Lord, You are worthy to receive glory and honor and the power, for You created all things, and for Thy pleasure, they are and were created."

From the right hand of the Father who sits on the Throne comes forth the Son of Man. He is now exalted to the place of highest honor in heaven at

God's right hand. He emerges from the fiery mist of the Mighty One as a divine being in human form. He appears as a white shimmering vision, disappearing and reappearing from and into the fiery mist.

He reemerges from time to time heading forward, disappearing and reappearing as though He were an illusion. First with one arm, then one fiery leg, then a fiery head without a body, then a fiery body without a head, as though He were coming out from the midst of a fire with no real outline in the extreme detail of light.

Melting away again, He resurfaces at the edge of the throne, His head an effervescent flaming light, His body an orange fiery glow. He wears a white robe circled with a golden band across the chest, His hair as white as wool, His eyes like a flame of fire, His feet gleaming like burnished bronze. His face shines like the power of the sun in unclouded brilliance.

Here is the **SON OF GOD** in all **HIS MAJESTY!** The **LORD JESUS CHRIST!**

THE END TO THE BEGINNING

"I am the resurrection and the life. He who believes in Me will live, even though he dies; and whosoever lives and believes in Me will never die. Do you believe this?" (John 11:2)

AFTERMATH

IN THE DARK regions of hell, in the land of the damned, chaos and disorder are enhanced a thousand-fold. Satan has been in bewilderment for some time and has set about to propose to his demonic dominions his new plans. He calls them together and sets himself up in a preeminent location, flanked by Abaddon. He is bitter with anger! When he saw the Christ come forth out of the grave in triumph, he knew his kingdom would have an end and they would suffer eternal punishments. With a flaming recovery, this dark prince of the air exhorts his demonic brethren. He paces back and forth in furious wrath.

"You have followed me throughout the many ages since the creation of man. You who have seen how I was deceived by the man-god, Jesus! I have *hated* Jesus before He assumed flesh! I *hate* Jesus for being more adored than me by the rest of creation. I have now been dethroned of my power, and the keys of death have been taken from me. I am *not* worthy of this low position, nor do I *deserve* the harsh punishment I have been dealt! And neither do you! I shall try to destroy Him by gathering all the forces of government on earth against Him. I will rule the earth through governments and man, and man and government shall worship me. I will take down His creation and bring humankind to these very depths of hell to burn eternally.

"Now follow me! Now is the time to take wrath against God! We shall seek new ways to hinder and prevent the work of God through greater deceits and temptations. We shall prey upon mankind's lust for pleasure. We will play his sexual appetites and make him drunk with the juices of the grape and barley until he rapes, kills, and destroys. We will plunder families, destroy marriages—which are the backbone of society—and lock men and women in sexual perversion and the pursuit of idolatry. We will cause men to have hatred for each other through racism.

"The passion of the flesh and the natural inclinations still remain the same in man. We will begin strenuous warfare against mankind by proposing new attractions, exciting them to follow their passions in disregard for humanity, and indulging them in hedonism, debauchery, and decadence.

"By idolatry, we shall bring them to idol worship through sports, music, and the arts of the humanities. We will cause men to worship images of women, to crave and kill with lust for them, taking virginity by either their own lusts or through rape. We will cause abortion to kill off the race of man, we will establish new religions and religious institutions that will worship us as gods, and we will make men believe there are many roads to heaven. We will warp sound doctrine and make known our doctrines, the doctrines of devils, and make men believe the ludicrous. We will establish sects and heresies.

"We will deceive the nations and bring poverty so that the poor will be subservient to the most perverse and depraved of the human race, out of which we will choose leaders and teachers, and subject them and mankind to all errors. We will teach men not to believe in creation but that creation *created* itself. Men are easily duped to believe such heretical nonsense.

"We will spoil the preferences of children even from their conception and birth; we will induce parents to teach wrong doctrine and to be negligent in their duties as parents, both in their instruction and education, causing them to become abusive as mothers and fathers and thus bringing hatred between them and their offspring.

"We will bring adultery and fornication and cause man to worship and adore himself. We will bring hatred and enmity between husband and wife, causing strife in the home. We will sow seeds of discord, hatred, vengeance, pride, and sensual thoughts and the desire for riches or honor. We will suggest sophisticated reasons to hate God and this Christ. We will weaken the passion of the cross and the resurrection, causing men to believe it is mythology and tales. We will compel man to *want* to come to hell, believing it is all merrymaking.

"I will place many of you in authority over regions and governments. With my wrath, I will persecute those with a vengeance who proclaim and accept Jesus Christ as their Savior. They will be ridiculed, punished, jailed, and tortured. Our most unrelenting battle will be against those who will soon be called Christians and followers of Christ. I will bring about a new church that will institute the use of idol worship of the gods of old and of Rome. In this new church, I will strive to sow belief in man and not in God and to not to trust God but to trust in religion. I will give these new church leaders ambitions, to make them lovers of wine and of the liquors of strong drink; I will bring covetousness, sensuality, and deadly hatred, among other vices. We will induce the faithful to ingratitude and prayerlessness and to believe false doctrine. We will weaken their faith and bring about malice and irritation to God and His laws. We will do everything to weaken righteousness and all that is spiritual and divine. We will make them sleepy, dull of hearing, lukewarm, and careless. We will syncretize differing religions into one, mixing their doctrines into that of Christianity.

"We will deceive, steal, and destroy through pharmaceuticals that they will not give up, and together we will induce suicides and mass murder. We will cause man to spit in the face of God and not to believe He exists! And thus now, *we will lose neither time nor occasion for executing my commands!*"

FINALE

JESUS THE CHRIST appears on a white horse, His eyes like flames of fire. On His head are many crowns that gleam with the brilliance of radiating stars. He is clothed in a robe dipped in blood. On His thigh is written a name: King of kings And Lord of lords. Michael the Archangel booms forth a clarion call: "Faithful and true, and in righteousness, He doth judge and make war!"

* * *

A multitude of inbound aerial lights appear. The lights draw closer, their appearance like that of forms of light energy, radiating many colors as if a rainbow had exploded. The airborne lights descend to settle around a silvery form that suddenly materializes like a silhouette in a mist. The lights surround the silvery silhouette, which is Jesus riding on the white horse. The angels take on human-like shapes, emitting prisms of light as though embodied with a thousand tiny diamonds.

The angelic beings escort Jesus into a luminescent electric blue sky. They drift toward the massive Orion nebula and pass through on their way to Earth for the return of our Lord and Savior.

* * *

A succession of lights that appear as fiery stars races toward the angelic army. With a blinding flash, demonic hordes engage in combat with the angelic host to try to disrupt their progress to Earth.

* * *

The King of kings and Lord of lords with the saints and His angelic army look as if they are on fire, bright and dazzling, as they enter the earth's atmosphere. They appear with a remnant of the angelic army as they battle the demonic defense force.

Behold, He comes!

QUESTIONS/ANSWERS, FACTS, EVENTS, AND THEORIES

The Sequence of Events of the Resurrection (Matthew 28:1–15; Mark 16:1–11; Luke 23:56; Luke 24:12; John 20:1–18) (compiled by Dr. Johnston M. Cheney, *The Life of Christ in Stereo,* Portland, Oregon: Western Baptist Seminary Press, 1969, pp. 204–214).

Matthew, Mark, Luke, and John seem to contradict each other about the women's arrivals at the tomb and Jesus' post-appearances. In reality, they are just different eyewitness accounts. While a single witness may see an occurrence one way, another bystander may observe it a different way, leave out details, remember it in a different manner, or just not include certain facts. Dr. Johnston M. Cheney put the events into sequential order.

Successions of Events

Earthquake: The angel of the Lord descended from heaven and rolled away the stone. The tomb watch fell as dead men, probably into a comatose state out of fear. They were not dead because a few of them ran to tell the chief priests and Caiaphas of the night's happenings. They were bribed to say that Jesus had not raised from the dead but that the disciples took Him.

Dawn: Mary Magdalene, Mary the mother of James, Salome, and certain others with them arrived at the tomb to bring spices and ointments. Mary Magdalene ran to tell Peter and John that someone had rolled away the stone and took away the body of Jesus. Peter and John ran to the sepulcher. Mary went back into the tomb and saw the two angels. She saw Jesus in the tomb garden and thought He was the gardener. Jesus told her to go tell the others.

After Sunrise: Johanna, Mary the mother of James, and the other women came to the sepulcher after sunrise wondering who is going to roll away the stone. They saw the two angels who said, "Why seek the living among the dead?" On their way to tell the other disciples, they encountered Jesus.

Three Days and Three Nights in the Tomb

Many question the accuracy of the Bible or Jesus' statement, "Just as Jonah was three days and three nights in the belly of a great fish, so shall the Son of Man be three days and three nights in the heart of the earth." How could Jesus have been in the grave three days and three nights if He died on Friday and was resurrected on Sunday, since they buried Him on Friday afternoon and He rose on Sunday predawn? This is clearly not three days and three nights. It is two full nights, one full day, and part of two days. Jesus also said, "The Son of Man will rise again after three days" and "He will be raised again on the third day."

It comes down to a matter of the Jewish reckoning of time: *The Babylonian Talmud* (Jewish commentaries) says, "The portion of a day is as a whole of it." *The Jerusalem Talmud* declares, "We have a teaching, 'A day and a night are an *Onah* and the portion of an *Onah* is as the whole of it.'" What does this mean? An *Onah* is "a period of time."

The Jewish day starts at 6:00 P.M. It is based on Jewish beliefs that in the week of Creation, the first day began with a darkness that was turned into light, and thereafter each 24-hour period is identified as "the evening and the morning"—in that order.

Therefore, Jesus died on Friday at 3:00 P.M. but before 6:00 P.M.; Friday they considered "one day and one night." Any time after 6:00 P.M. on Friday to Saturday at 6:00 P.M. until Sunday when Jesus resurrected would be "one day and one night." From the Jewish point of view, this is "three days and three nights," from Friday afternoon until Sunday morning (Josh McDowell, *The Resurrection Factor,* Here's Life Publishers, Inc., pages 121–123).

Jesus Appeared Unto Many Different People and Many Different Groups After He Was Resurrected

1. Mary Magdalene

2. The women at the tomb

3. The disciples

4. The two travelers on the road to Emmaus

5. 500 witnesses

6. Jesus' brother James

Substantiation and Historical Evidence That Jesus Resurrected from the Grave

If all the evidence is weighed carefully and fairly, it is indeed justifiable, according to the canons of historical research, to conclude that the tomb in which Jesus was buried was actually empty on the morning of the first Easter. And no shred of evidence has yet been discovered in literary sources, epigraphy, or archaeology that would disprove this statement. (Paul Maier, Historian)

Many try to refute that Christ rose from the grave. Here is the evidence that He did indeed rise from the grave:

Seven Historical Facts to the Resurrection of Jesus Christ

1. The breaking of the Roman seal.

2. Both Jews and Romans admitted that the tomb was empty.

3. The two-ton stone was removed and carried a distance away from the sepulcher while the Roman guard stood watch.

4. The Roman military unit sent to watch the tomb fled and had to explain why they deserted their post or else they would face punishment.

5. The Jewish authorities had to bribe the Roman guards to lie about what actually happened.

6. The grave clothes were still in the tomb but no corpse.

7. Jesus appeared unto many and to over 500 witnesses at one time.

8. Broken Roman seal: If a person was caught breaking a Roman seal, it was execution by crucifixion, upside down on a cross.

9. The Jewish authorities bribed the tomb detail to tell a lie because they knew the tomb was empty.

10. Large stone rolled away: The Gospel writers mentioned the removal of the stone. It was rolled up an incline and carried a distance away. In Chapter 20 of the Gospel of John, the apostle used the Greek verb *airo* to describe the stone being carried away: According to the Arndt and Gingrish Lexicon, the word *airo* means: *"To pick something up and carry it off or away."* The women and disciples were witnesses to this fact. The Bible is not just the Word of God but it is also a historical book filled with witness accounts of Jesus, His miracles, His resurrection, and His appearances to many.

11. The disciples were afraid and hid. They did not go near the tomb. Only John and Peter went to the gravesite after Mary Magdalene told them that the body was gone.

12. Historical writings gathered from Jewish and Roman sources and traditions that range from the Jewish historian Josephus to a compilation of fifth-century writings called *The Toledoth Jeshua* acknowledge an empty tomb.

Theories to Explain Away the Resurrection

1. The Unknown Tomb Theory: That the executioners cast the body into an unknown gravesite.

2. The Wrong Tomb Theory: The disciples mistook another tomb, which was empty, to be where Jesus was buried.

1. The Legend Theory: The accounts of Christ's resurrection did not crop up until years later, some say not until the Dark Ages.

2. The Spiritual Resurrection Theory: The argument is that Christ's resurrection was merely a spiritual resurrection, not bodily. His body decayed in the tomb.

3. The Hallucination Theory: This theory says that Jesus' post-resurrection appearances were hallucinatory hoaxes. Those witnesses

who testified who saw Jesus were said to have visions or dreams of His resurrection.

4. Resuscitation or Swoon Theory: Jesus only fainted on the cross and was buried alive. When He came to, He rolled away the stone and freed Himself.

5. The Passover Plot: Jesus planned the resurrection by plotting to have the disciples drug Him (the wine-vinegar on the sponge) while on the cross and that the disciples come in the night to take Him away. The Roman soldier thrusting the spear into His side subverted the plot, but the disciples came and stole the body.

All of these theories are proved to be false. The Jewish authorities knew where the body was buried. The Romans knew where His body was and placed sentries at the tomb. Joseph of Arimathea asked Pilate for Jesus' body so he could place it in his newly carved sepulcher.

The Bible is a historic book with witness verifications. Jesus was seen in a physical body by many individuals and by 500 witnesses at once. If Jesus had passed out on the cross and revived in the tomb, He would have had great difficulty in shedding off the grave clothes. He would have been too weak to roll away a two-ton stone. More than likely, there would not have been sufficient oxygen to stay alive. They would have found His body in the tomb.

The crucifixion detail made sure He was dead by thrusting a spear through His side to confirm His death while the other executioners witnessed the ordeal. There was a Roman seal on the two-ton stone and guards set at the entrance. He would have had to fight them off.

None of these theories with all the known facts and witnesses can effectively be proven.

Six Important Security Precautions Taken to Make Sure Jesus Remained Dead and in the Tomb

(Josh McDowell, *The Resurrection Factor*, p. 61)

1. Christ was put to death by crucifixion.

2. The body of Christ was buried in a solid rock tomb.

3. Christ's body was wrapped with 100 pounds of spices according to precise Jewish burial law and customs.

4. The stone rolled in front of the tomb entrance weighed approximately two tons.

5. A Roman security guard was positioned to protect and guard the tomb.

6. The tomb was sealed shut with the official authority and signet of Rome.

Theories of the Resurrected Saints

And the graves were opened, and many bodies of the saints which slept, arose. And came out of the graves after His resurrection, and went into the holy city, and appeared unto many. (Matthew 27:52–53 New Standard Version)

The resurrected saints came back to life right after the first earthquake when Jesus died on the cross. They remained at their gravesites and did not go into the holy city (Jerusalem) and the surrounding areas until Jesus arose from the grave after the second earthquake on the third day. Many were alarmed and frightened, as you would reason they would be.

Resurrected Saint's Theories

1. The resurrected **saints of old** came back to life after being resurrected again to this earth as a testimony to the resurrection of Jesus Christ: Moses, Joseph, and King David; the prophets: Isaiah, Jeremiah, Daniel, and Habakkuk; the patriarchs: Abraham, Isaac, Enoch, and Noah; in addition to many other saints of old.

2. The resurrected saints of old came back to life along with those who had recently died.

3. The resurrected saints were those who had died recently.

4. The resurrected saints were apparitions.

5. People saw visions and hallucinations of their resurrected loved ones, friends, and saints.

6. The resurrected saints had a spiritual body but were not of flesh.

7. The resurrected saints were allegorical.

8. The resurrected saints had a resurrected body like Jesus.

Jesus told the disciples that He was of flesh and bone. "No spirit hath flesh and bones as you see I have." To prove it, He ate food when He appeared to the disciples in the upper room and again on the shores of the Sea of Galilee.

Were the Disciples in the Upper Room on the Day of Pentecost?

The answer is no. *Tradition* says that on the Day of Pentecost the disciples, the women, and other followers, a total of 120 in all, were in the Upper Room when they received the baptism of the Holy Spirit. This is recorded in Acts 1:13–14. The disciples, the women, Mary the mother of Jesus, and their brethren remained in the Upper Room between the Day of Ascension and the Day of Pentecost (Acts 1:12–14). In Luke 24:52–53 and Acts3:1, it says the disciples met every day at the Temple where they worshipped God at around 9:00 A.M. Acts 2:1–2 KJV says, "And when the day of Pentecost was fully come, they were all with one accord in *one place.*" The Greek word *oikos* used in Acts 1:13–14 means "house." It refers to any type of building or structure. The term "Upper Room" itself actually means a dining room. Rabbinical teachers refer to the Temple as "The House." The Greek word used, *HaBayit,* means "The House." On the Day of Pentecost, all of Israel was commanded to be at the Temple for the Day of Shavuot, as stated in Deuteronomy 16:16: "All men of Israel to present themselves before the Lord at the Temple on the Day of Shavuot." The disciples, the women, Mary the mother of Jesus, and 120 in all were in one accord in one house on the Temple Mount, more than likely at Solomon's porch, sometimes referred to as the Colonnade (Acts 5:12). The outpouring of the Holy Spirit took place at the Temple. The Upper Room could not have held three thousand people who came to see what was going on when they heard the roaring wind.

Purgatory: Is There Such a Place?

In 1160 and 1180, the Catholic Church gave rise to the idea of purgatory as a place, using the scripture 1 Corinthians 3:15. "This passage is using an illustration of things going through fire—as a description of believers' works being judged. If our works are of good quality 'gold, silver, costly stones,' they will pass through the fire unharmed, and we will be rewarded for them. If our works are of poor quality 'wood, hay, and straw,' they will be consumed by the fire, and there will be no reward. The passage does not say that *believers* pass through the fire, but rather that a believer's *works* pass through the fire. 1 Corinthians 3:15 refers to the believer 'escaping through the flames,' not 'being cleansed by the flames.'"

According to Catholic Church doctrine, purgatory is an *intermediate state* after physical death in which those destined for heaven "undergo purification, so as to achieve the holiness necessary to enter the joy of heaven." Only those who die in the state of grace, but have not in life reached a sufficient level of holiness, can be in purgatory, and therefore no one in purgatory will remain forever in that state or go to hell. The concept of purgatory as an existing place comes from medieval writings and points of view.

Is the doctrine of purgatory in agreement with the Bible?

Jesus died to pay the penalty for all of our sins (Romans 5:8). Isaiah 53:5 declares, "But He was pierced for our transgressions, He was crushed for our iniquities; the punishment that brought us peace was upon Him, and by His wounds we are healed." To say that we must atone for our sins by cleansing in purgatory is to deny the sufficiency of the atoning sacrifice of Jesus.

The very idea of purgatory and the doctrines that are often attached to it (prayer for the dead, indulgences, meritorious works on behalf of the dead, etc.) all fail to recognize that Jesus' death was sufficient to pay the penalty for *all* of our sins. Jesus, who was God incarnate (John 1:1, 14), paid an infinite price for our sin. Jesus died for our sins (1 Corinthians 15:3). Jesus is the atoning sacrifice for our sins (1 John 2:2). If we must in any sense pay for, atone for, or suffer because of our sins, that indicates Jesus' death was not a perfect, complete, and sufficient sacrifice.

For believers, after death is to be "away from the body and at home with the Lord" (2 Corinthians 5:6–8; Philippians 1:23). Notice that this does not say "away from the body, in purgatory with the cleansing fire." No, because of the perfection, completion, and sufficiency of Jesus' sacrifice, we are immediately in the Lord's presence after death, fully cleansed, free from sin, glorified, perfected, and ultimately sanctified.

Hell, Hades, Sheol

The following I thought might be interesting in terms of describing hell and some of its chambers, levels, or geographical areas. The three geographical areas of hell are Hades, Sheol, and Tarsus. The New Testament has three Greek words for hell: "Hades," "Gehenna," and "Tartaroo."

These levels of hell are thought by some theologians to be designed according to your sins. Those who have committed sins but not atrocities are assigned in Sheol. Those who have committed acts of violence and horrendous sins are cast in Hades where there are everlasting fires. Tarsus is the place where the fallen angels are chained and imprisoned until the Day of Judgment. The biblical account of judgment is that only when one's name is not found in the Book of Life is that person judged for his works or deeds. The Book of Deeds contains a record of the works one did during his life.

In the Old Testament, the word for hell is Sheol in Hebrew. It was the world of the dead (Psalm 16:10, 49:15; Hosea 13:14) or the abode of the dead. People that reside in this area are sinners who have not done terrible deeds but have never accepted the Lord. In other words, they are people who were basically moral but had never accepted Christ as their Savior.

The word Hades is used for the place of the departed spirits of the lost and is found in Matthew 11:23, 16:18; Luke 10:15, 16:23; Acts 2:27, 31; and Revelation 1:18, 6:8, 20:13, 20:14.

Gehenna is the place or state of the lost or condemned and is found in Matthew 5:22, 29–30, 10:28, 18:9, 23:15, 23:33; Mark 9:43, 45, 47; Luke 12:5; and James 3:6. Gehenna is the word Jesus sometimes used sometimes to describe hell. It was a pit or valley in Jerusalem where trash and even bodies were burned. The fires there were continuous. When referring to hell, Jesus would use Gehenna as an example because the populace was familiar with it and it gave a good description of hell.

Tartaros is the subterranean abyss of Greek mythology where demigods were punished. The apocryphal book of Enoch mentions it as the place where fallen angels are confined. It is found only once in the Bible, and only in its verbal form. Peter appropriated the word to describe God's incarceration of fallen angels to a netherworld dungeon until the day of final judgment (2 Peter 2:4).

God loves every person. He has done everything to spare each person from the judgment of hell. Jesus went to the cross to suffer and die, once and for all, for every person, to pay the penalty of God's judgment on sin. The proof that His work was effective was His resurrection from the dead. The Bible teaches that an individual goes to hell because he has rejected God's love, the Savior, and His work on the cross.

"I said therefore to you, that you shall die in your sins; for unless you believe that I am He, you shall die in your sins" (John 8:24).

Since we are all sinners (Romans 3:23, 6:23), Jesus Christ is our only hope. Every person in hell is there because of his own choice. He has rejected God's grace and the gift of His Son.

No one ever goes to hell that has not had a fair chance. God knows each heart and every circumstance. He is smarter, more loving, and more merciful than we are. C.S. Lewis wrote as clearly as anyone on the matter of hell and judgment. He wrote in *The Problem of Pain*, "The doors of hell are locked on the inside." We are rebels. It is precisely because a person will not lay down his arms and end his rebellion against God that he goes to hell. Jesus will pronounce the judgment of the Lake of Fire, but it is the individual who has condemned himself. Jesus, in a real sense, honors each person's rebellion and God "loses" because He has made the provision of salvation available to everyone.

Scriptures Referring to Hell Taught by Jesus

"But I say to you that everyone who is angry with his brother shall be guilty before the court; and whoever says to his brother, 'You good-for-nothing,' shall

be guilty before the supreme court; and whoever says, 'You fool,' shall be guilty enough to go into the fiery hell" (Sermon on the Mount, Matthew 5:22).

"If your right eye makes you stumble, tear it out and throw it from you; for it is better for you to lose one of the parts of your body, than for your whole body to be thrown into hell. If your right hand makes you stumble, cut it off and throw it from you; for it is better for you to lose one of the parts of your body, than for your whole body to go into hell" (Sermon on the Mount, Matthew 5:29–30).

"Enter through the narrow gate; for the gate is wide and the way is broad that leads to destruction, and there are many who enter through it. For the gate is small and the way is narrow that leads to life, and there are few who find it" (Sermon on the Mount, Matthew 7:13–14).

"Not everyone who says to Me, 'Lord, Lord,' will enter the kingdom of heaven, but he who does the will of My Father who is in heaven will enter. Many will say to Me on that day, 'Lord, Lord, did we not prophesy in Your name, and in Your name cast out demons, and in Your name perform many miracles?' And then I will declare to them, 'I never knew you; depart from Me, you who practice lawlessness'" (Sermon on the Mount, Matthew 7:21–23).

Now when Jesus heard this, He marveled and said to those who were following, "Truly I say to you, I have not found such great faith with anyone in Israel. I say to you that many will come from east and west, and recline at the table with Abraham, Isaac and Jacob in the kingdom of heaven; but the sons of the kingdom will be cast out into the outer darkness; in that place there will be weeping and gnashing of teeth" (Encounter with the Roman Centurion, Matthew 8:10–12).

"Do not fear those who kill the body but are unable to kill the soul; but rather fear Him who is able to destroy both soul and body in hell" (Warnings of Persecution, Matthew 10:28).

"But he said, 'No; for while you are gathering up the tares, you may uproot the wheat with them. Allow both to grow together until the harvest; and in the time of the harvest I will say to the reapers, "First gather up the tares and bind them in bundles to burn them up; but gather the wheat into my barn"'" (Tares Among Wheat, Matthew 13:29–30).

"So it will be at the end of the age; the angels will come forth and take out the wicked from among the righteous, and will throw them into the furnace of fire; in that place there will be weeping and gnashing of teeth" (Instruction on the Kingdom of Heaven, Matthew 13:49–50).

"If your hand or your foot causes you to stumble, cut it off and throw it from you; it is better for you to enter life crippled or lame, than to have two hands or two feet and be cast into the eternal fire. If your eye causes you to stumble, pluck it out and throw it from you. It is better for you to enter life with one eye, than to have two eyes and be cast into the fiery hell" (Warning of Impediments to the Kingdom of God, Matthew 18:8–9).

"But when the king came in to look over the dinner guests, he saw a man there who was not dressed in wedding clothes, and he said to him, 'Friend, how did you come in here without wedding clothes?' And the man was speechless. Then the king said to the servants, 'Bind him hand and foot, and throw him into the outer darkness; in that place there will be weeping and gnashing of teeth.' For many are called, but few are chosen" (Inadequate Preparation for the Kingdom of God, Matthew 22:11–14).

"But woe to you, scribes and Pharisees, hypocrites, because you shut off the kingdom of heaven from people; for you do not enter in yourselves, nor do you allow those who are entering to go in. ... Fill up, then, the measure of the guilt of your fathers. You serpents, you brood of vipers, how will you escape the sentence of hell?" (Condemnation of the Religious, Matthew 23:13, 32–33).

"The master of that slave will come on a day when he does not expect him and at an hour which he does not know, and will cut him in pieces and assign him a place with the hypocrites; in that place there will be weeping and gnashing of teeth" (Christ's Return and Judgment, Matthew 24:50–51).

"For to everyone who has, more shall be given, and he will have an abundance; but from the one who does not have, even what he does have shall be taken away. Throw out the worthless slave into the outer darkness; in that place there will be weeping and gnashing of teeth" (Christ's Return and Judgment, Matthew 25:29–30).

"The King will answer and say to them, 'Truly I say to you, to the extent that you did it to one of these brothers of Mine, even the least of them, you did it to

Me.' Then He will also say to those on His left, 'Depart from Me, accursed ones, into the eternal fire which has been prepared for the devil and his angels; for I was hungry, and you gave Me nothing to eat; I was thirsty, and you gave Me nothing to drink; I was a stranger, and you did not invite Me in; naked, and you did not clothe Me; sick, and in prison, and you did not visit Me.' Then they themselves also will answer, 'Lord, when did we see You hungry, or thirsty, or a stranger, or naked, or sick, or in prison, and did not take care of You?' Then He will answer them, 'Truly I say to you, to the extent that you did not do it to one of the least of these, you did not do it to Me.' These will go away into eternal punishment, but the righteous into eternal life" (Christ's Return and Judgment, Matthew 25:40–46).

Was Joseph, Mary's Husband, Still Alive When Jesus Died on the Cross?

There are some writings and books that say Joseph died when Jesus was about 14 and another says that Joseph died at the ripe old age of 110. Here is one account from the Urantia Book:

All did go well until that fateful day of Tuesday, September 25 [A.D. 8] when a runner from Sepphoris brought to this Nazareth home the tragic news that Joseph had been severely injured by the falling of a derrick while at work on the governor's residence. The messenger from Sepphoris had stopped at the shop on the way to Joseph's home, informing Jesus of his father's accident, and they went together to the house to break the sad news to Mary. Jesus desired to go immediately to his father, but Mary would hear to nothing but that she must hasten to her husband's side. She directed that James, then ten years of age, should accompany her to Sepphoris while Jesus remained home with the younger children until she should return, as she did not know how seriously Joseph's injuries were. However, Joseph died of his injuries before Mary arrived. They brought Joseph to Nazareth, and on the following day, they laid him to rest with his fathers. (The Urantia Book)

Apocryphal writings. Protevangelium of James and History of Joseph the Carpenter claim that Joseph lived to age 111. Other writings say that Joseph lived to be 110, that he was already of old age when he was involved with Mary. They also say that he was a widower at the time he was engaged to Mary, and he had other children from his previous marriage. Other apocryphal writings include the Gospel of James, Pseudo-Matthew, Gospel of the Nativity of the Virgin Mary, Story of Joseph the Carpenter, and Life of the Virgin and Death of Joseph. These writings are unreliable and not a good source. I believe St. Catherine Emmerich also writes about Joseph.

More than likely, Joseph was *not* alive during Jesus' ministry and crucifixion.

For one: Joseph is not mentioned as being present at the wedding at Cana. Of course, this could be that it was not important to have mentioned him.

Two: Joseph is not mentioned at the crucifixion where he would have, under Jewish custom, been expected to take charge of the body of Jesus. Joseph of Arimathea took charge of the body.

Three: It seems that Joseph would have been with his wife Mary during the crucifixion as a support to her as well as being there for Jesus. John 19:25–27 references those were present at the crucifixion: Mary the mother of Jesus, Mary's sister, Mary the mother of Cleophas, Mary Magdalene, and the disciple John.

As John stood nearby, Jesus said to His mother, "Woman, behold thy son!" Then He said to the disciple John, "Behold thy mother!" The scripture passage continues on to say, "From that hour, that disciple took her unto his own home." This would not have been the case if Joseph were still alive, as Mary would have been expected to remain with her husband, attending to household and wifely duties.

It was Jewish custom that the firstborn son was to take on the responsibility of providing for his mother if she were a widow. If he could not to be around, the son would make sure that his mother would be taken care of. More than likely, this is why Jesus asked John the disciple to take care of His mother Mary.

The question may be asked, "Why not one of Jesus half-brothers?" The reason, more than likely, was that none of them believed Jesus to be the

Messiah, although James did become a believer after the resurrection. Jesus had taught John the ways of the Lord and of spiritual things and of things that were to come, so He wanted Mary to be under John's influence and mentoring. In addition, Jesus knew John would live the longest of all the disciples and that he would not be martyred.

Another aspect is that Mary and Jesus' siblings followed Him around during His ministry, illustrating that possibly Joseph was not around, as it was Jewish custom for the women to stay at home. It is presumed by scholars that Mary was a widow at this point, and since Jesus was the firstborn, He was taking care of her. Some scholars think that perhaps Jesus lived at home with Mary until He began His ministry at the age of 30. She traveled with Him because He was taking care of her even then.

It is also asked in Mark 6:13, "Is this not the carpenter, *the son of Mary,* brother of James, and Joses, and of Juda and Simon? And are not his sisters here with us?" They called Jesus the son of Mary, not the son of Joseph of Heli (as Joseph was known). If Joseph were alive at this time, they would have more than likely referred to Jesus as the son of Joseph of Heli.

NOTES

Claiming Sanctuary: There was an ancient custom of "claiming sanctuary" by grabbing the horns of the altar to escape punishment, persecution, or execution.

Silver Cord: In Ecclesiastes 12:6–7, it speaks of the silver cord. It says, "Let not the silver cord be broken." People who have had near-death experiences have said that they have seen this silver cord between the shoulder blades. It is about one inch in diameter and seems to glow. If you go beyond the reach of the silver cord, you can no longer come back to your body. It is the link between your spirit and your body.

Desert Horned Viper: A viper native to the regions of the Holy Land. It has horns on the top of its head and looks very demonic, sometimes referred to as "the fiery serpent."

The Whole Land Turned to Darkness: This could have been a total eclipse, but total eclipses do not last very long. In Matthew 27:45, it says the whole land was dark. *"Now from the sixth hour there was darkness over all the land unto the ninth hour."* What kind of phenomenon was taking place? It says nothing about a storm or dark clouds. In some writings it says the moon was like blood.

Dark Cavern under the Cross: Many people reading this chapter wonder what is going on here. Some are confused. What does it mean? It is a metaphorical representation of Christ's blood falling onto the Mercy Seat of the Ark of the Covenant. In the days when animal blood sacrifices were carried out for the atonement of sins, the high priest would enter into the Holy of Holies.

No one was allowed into the Holy of Holies except the high priest. When he entered the Holy of Holies, he sported bells on the hem of his sartorial garments. A rope was tied around his ankle, which led out from the Holy of Holies to where the other priests stood. If the high priest did not follow the ceremonial procedures or performed it incorrectly, he would perish right on the spot in the Holy of Holies. If the priests in the adjoining room could not hear the bells jingling, they assumed the high priest to be dead.

They would pull the body out by the rope. This had happened before. No one was to go beyond the veil. Why was God so inflexible, exacting, and seemingly severe in demanding absolute perfection in performing this ceremonial procedure? Because He is a holy God, He requires respect, obedience, and devotion. He means to be taken seriously. That is why the sacrificial lamb and other animal offerings had to be perfect with no blemishes. God is holy and demands a high regard, veneration, and honor for His person and deity.

The high priest took the hyssop dipped in blood and sprinkled it over the Ark of the Covenant and on the Mercy Seat for our sins. When God received the sacrifice, He descended onto the Mercy Seat. High priests who witnessed the ordeal said that between the wings of the cherubim there was a blue-arc of flame; it became very bright like molten fire.

The idea for this allegorical imagery came from an amateur archaeologist, Ron Wyatt. He found the Ark of the Covenant in a cavern or chamber at the end of a maze of tunnels near or under the Temple Mount, along with the other vessels and artifacts from Solomon's Temple. The story is amazing in that this cavern was about 20 feet directly beneath the alleged site of the crucifixion of the Christ. A large crack or crevice caused by the earthquake extended downward from the where the cross had been placed in a carved-out square hole. On the Mercy Seat of the Ark of the Covenant, Ron found a dark substance sprinkled all over the Ark. He scraped off a bit of the dark material and took it to be analyzed. When the technologists evaluated the substance, they found it to be blood, but not like normal human blood. As soon as they put a saline solution on it, the blood came back to life. The experts said this was impossible.

They further concluded that the blood was missing the father's chromosomes. The DNA contained only 23 chromosomes, all from the mother, and lacked the 23 chromosomes from the father. There are normally 46 chromosomes per person. It was also missing the Y chromosome from the father. This is not possible. They said the blood had to come from an extraterrestrial being.

The entrance to the cavern where the Ark of the Covenant rests was covered with a metal plate and buried under twenty feet of dirt by the Israelite authorities. They do not want the location discovered for fear that it might incite a holy war. They will not unearth it until the right time.

Whether Ron Wyatt's story is true, I do not know, but it makes a great representation of Christ's blood falling on the Mercy Seat for the reparation of our sins. Sacrifice is no longer needed for the atonement of our iniquities because Christ died on the cross for our sins. His blood fell on the Mercy Seat to compensate for man's sins, as Jesus is now our high priest. He is the sacrificial lamb.

(Ron Wyatt's Archaeological Research website: wyattmuseum.com/discovering/ark-of-the-covenant, Ark of the Covenant, March 28, 1999.)

Falling Asleep on Watch: If a soldier fell asleep while on night watch or guard duty, he was punished by death. The soldier would be stripped of his garments and the garments thrown into a pile. The soldier would be burned alive by his own garments. If it were not apparent which soldier fell asleep, then lots were drawn for one to be punished for dereliction of duty for the whole unit. The entire tomb watch would not have fallen asleep while safeguarding the sepulcher.

Hell or Hades: The scenes in hell I wrote very illustratively so that no one would want to go to hell, but all would accept Jesus as their Lord and Savior. God does not want any man to go to hell. He never created it for man. It was created for Satan and the fallen angels and demons. A person sends himself or herself to hell. Some have said, "I don't believe in hell, because how can a loving God be so cruel?" God is not merciless. That is why He "sent His only begotten Son, so that whoever may believe on Him should not perish, but have everlasting life" (John 3:16). That is why Jesus, being the Son of God, died on the cross and resurrected again so that a person does not have to go to hell. God made a way for you.

Jesus Descends into Hell (Hades): It is somewhat controversial that Jesus descended into hell or Hades, but in Ephesians 4:8–10 and Acts 2:31 it says He descended into hell and was not left there to decay. 1 Peter 3:19 says he went into the lower parts of the earth to preach to those in prison, Abraham's bosom, or some call it paradise. Some translations say He went into the lower chambers of earth or lower regions of the earth. Those who died before Noah and before the crucifixion went to Abraham's bosom until Jesus' resurrection. Jesus told them of His death on the cross and the plan of salvation. Other scriptures point to His descending into Hades or hell: Psalm 16:10; Romans 10:6–7; 1 Peter 4:6; and Revelation 1:17.

On the Road to Emmaus: There is some evidence that Cleophas, sometimes named Cephas, may have been in fact Peter, who also went by the Aramaic name of Cephas. There was one who was called Cleophas who was the husband of one of the women, so there is some controversy as to who it may have been. Some scholars, theologians, and commentators believe the other person who walked with Cleophas may have been Luke. I tend to think it may have been, as he was with the disciples, and he wrote detailed accounts of their comings and goings.

Jesus Walking on the Water: I wrote this in because it represents baptism, being immersed into water to represent death and rising up out of the water to represent resurrection. Another reason I wrote this section is that movies always depict a mild storm, a slight rain, and minor waves, but in reality, it was a full raging storm. Fierce storms hit the Sea of Galilee with hurricane-force winds, the waves reaching as high as twenty feet. The Sea of Galilee can be very treacherous in a storm. The earthquake that hit when Jesus died on the cross and again when He was resurrected from the dead changed the typography of the area and the lake shores. Geologists say that the lake used to be much larger during the time of Jesus. They say now that the sea loses a couple of inches of water every year.

Herod Eaten by Worms: Josephus, the Jewish/Roman scholar and historian, gives the account of Herod being eaten by worms. It speaks of it as well in the Bible.

On the Day of Ascension: *"Five hundred witnesses at one time"* (1 Corinthians 15:6). Paul states that there were five hundred witnesses at one time, but some of the gospels state that it was only the eleven disciples. I wrote in five hundred people at the ascension because of what Paul stated.

Orion Constellation—Heaven: Some Christian astronomers and others believe that behind the Orion constellation lies heaven, that Orion is the gateway or portal to eternity and beyond the cosmos. In Psalm 48:1–2, David refers to heaven as residing on the "sides of the north." Isaiah 14:13,

Psalm 75:6, and Job 26:7 refer to Zion (heaven) in the north." Astronomers say that the North Star never moves, which is in the Orion constellation, and that there is a void or empty place in this northern region of our universe. There are no stars in that region. There is something akin to a black hole in the middle of the Orion constellation.

Throne of God: Many think that God sits on a White Throne, but this is not the case. He will reside on a White Throne on Judgment Day when He judges all humankind, Lucifer, and the fallen angels. For now, He sits on a blue-sapphire throne, which represents multi-facets of wisdom; found in Ezekiel's description of God and His Throne Room.

BIBLIOGRAPHY

Visions of St. Catherine Emerick used by Mel Gibson for *The Passion of the Christ*

The Mystical City of God by Maria de Agreda used by Mel Gibson for *The Passion of the Christ*

The Archko Volumes: The Sanhedrin's report concerning the resurrection of Jesus, Chapter 7

The Resurrection Factor, Josh McDowell

The Book of Nicodemus

The Hole in the North by Dennis C. Miller and Louis Watrous

Heaven and the Afterlife by James Garlow and Keith Wall

90 Minutes in Heaven by Don Piper

23 Minutes in Hell by Bill Wiese

To Hell and Back by Maurice S. Rawlings, M.D.

Dante's Inferno

A Divine Revelation of Hell, Heaven by Mary Baxter

20th Century Miracle by Thomas Welch

The Book of Enoch (described in the Bible)

The Lost Gospel of Peter

The Kregel Pictorial Guide to the Temple by Robert Backhouse

Shlomo's Passover Adventure, Temple Institute

Letters of Pontius Pilate, Letters of Herod to Pilate

The Christ Commission by Og Mandino

Matthew, Mark, Luke, John, Ezekiel, Daniel, The Revelation, Book of Acts, 1st Peter, 2nd Peter, 1st Corinthians, Genesis from the Holy Bible (various translations), other parts of the New Testament, various translations

Pulpit Commentary: Epistles of Peter, John, Jude and The Revelation, WM.B. Eerdmans Publishing Co., 1950

The Pulpit Commentary: Acts and Romans, WM. B Eerdmans Publishing Co.

Just Give Me Jesus, Anne Graham Lotz, page 262, Chapter 12

Hall of Hewn Stone, Temple Institute

Hall of Hewn Stone, Wikipedia

Ryle's Expository Thoughts on the Gospels: Luke, Zondervan Publishing House

The Acts of the Apostles: Expositions and Homiletics

The Acts of the Apostles, Vol. II by A.C. Hervey

Commentary on the Revelation

Recommended Reading?

This is only some of the resource material I reviewed and researched, but these were the most significant. I think you'll find them fascinating.

The Mystical City of God by Maria de Agreda was the other book that Benedict Fitzgerald and Mel Gibson used for *The Passion of the Christ.*

The Archko Volumes talks about Caiaphas and his report to the Sanhedrin concerning the resurrection of Jesus, Chapter 7.

The Resurrection Factor by Josh McDowell is a really good read! I highly recommend the book. In it, he describes the events of the resurrection and how they might have taken place. The four gospels seem to contradict themselves, but Josh McDowell brings all the events into perspective and in chronological order.

The Book of Nicodemus in its second part speaks of the resurrection, of Christ's descent into hell, and His preaching to the saints and of bringing them out of hell. It speaks of two men, Charinus and Lenthius, who were killed and resurrected. In my screenplay, *Resurrection After the Passion,* I wrote a subplot linear story revolving around these men, which made an interesting story, especially of them being brought before the Sanhedrin, Caiaphas, and Annas to testify about being resurrected along with Jesus. Everyone knew them, including Caiaphas, Annas, and the Sanhedrin.

Books on Heaven:

The Hole in the North—Is This the Entrance to Heaven? By Dennis C. Miller and Louis Watrous

Heaven and the Afterlife by James Garlow and Keith Wall

90 Minutes in Heaven by Don Piper

Books on Hell:

23 Minutes in Hell by Bill Wiese Dante's Inferno

A Divine Revelation of Hell, Heaven by Mary Baxter

20th Century Miracle by Thomas Welch

To Hell and Back by Maurice S. Rawlings M.D.

Books about Angels and Demons:

The Book of Enoch (described in the Bible) is fascinating. It gives accounts of the fallen angels along with their names, the fall of Lucifer, and how the angel and demonic hierarchy work. It also talks of Enoch going into heaven.

The Lost Gospel of Peter is interesting and gives an account of the resurrection.

The Book of Nicodemus describes the crucifixion along with Jesus descending into hell and I believe the resurrection.

The following books describe how the Temple works and the many aspects of the Temple involving the sacrifices and temple operations.

The Kregel Pictorial Guide to the Temple by Robert Backhouse

Shlomo's Passover Adventure, Temple Institute

Other reference material:

Letters of Pontius Pilate, Letters of Herod to Pilate.

Matthew, Mark, Luke, John, Ezekiel, Daniel, The Revelation, Book of Acts, 1st Peter, 2nd Peter, 1st Corinthians, Genesis from the Holy Bible (various translations), other parts of the New Testament, various translations,

Pulpit Commentary: Epistles of Peter, John, Jude and The Revelation, WM.B. Eerdmans Publishing Co., 1950

The Pulpit Commentary: Acts and Romans, WM. B Eerdmans Publishing Co.

Ryle's Expository Thoughts on the Gospels: Luke, Zondervan Publishing House

The Acts of the Apostles: Expositions and Homiletics

The Acts of the Apostles Vol. II by A.C. Hervey

Commentary on the Revelation

PLAN OF SALVATION

The plan of salvation is for all. No one is exempt. The reason for this book and the upcoming feature film is so that all may come to the Lord. That is why Jesus died on the cross and was resurrected back to life, so that we may come to Him. John 3:16: "For God so loved the world, that He gave His only begotten Son, that whosoever believeth in Him should not perish, but have everlasting life."

If you would like to accept Jesus Christ into your life for the forgiveness of your sins, simply pray this prayer:

Dear Jesus, I repent and ask you to forgive me of all my sins. Please come into my heart and become the Lord and Savior of my life.

There is only one way to heaven and eternal life, and that is through Jesus Christ. "No one comes to the Father but through Me," said Jesus. You can live a moral life and never ask Jesus to come into your heart, but that does not mean that you are saved or that you are going to heaven. You can ask Jesus to come into your heart and continue living an immoral life of sin with a willful heart *not* to change. That again does not mean that you are saved.

Salvation is a two-part process: asking Jesus to *forgive* you of your sins, and to *repent*, which means to turn away from your sins. You can ask Jesus to forgive you of your iniquities (sin) and still sin. To willfully sin and not care whether you are sinning, does not constitute forgiveness. It simply means that you do not care and are unrepentant. To ask Jesus to forgive you of your sins and to repent means that you will strive to live a righteous life. It is another thing for a person to ask Jesus to forgive them of their sins and yet still struggle with a sin. This is different in that you do not *want* to sin, but keep finding yourself doing so. Ask God to help you conquer that sin, which may take time. It is not always an overnight success.

Set yourself apart from the world. Be sanctified (holy, consecrated, and dedicated) and be filled with the baptism of the Holy Spirit. Start reading your Bible—obtain one if you do not have one—and begin a prayer life.

Go to a church that speaks the truth and the gospel. There, you will find like-minded believers who will stand with you and pray for you. They will encourage you and you will learn the ways of God.

Finally, living a sanctified life after you have become a Christian does not mean you are legalistic. Being a Christian is living the life of Christ who set for us examples of how to live a moral life. It is by no means a boring life, and it is not religion where there are religious (man-made rules) to follow. You are simply a follower of Christ.

I give You praise, honor, and glory, my Heavenly Father.

Milton Keynes UK
Ingram Content Group UK Ltd.
UKHW011313210224
438230UK00001B/235